D0004849

Crafting
As a Business

Crafting
As a Business

Wendy W. Rosen

Edited by Amy M. Feinstein   Art & Design by Kris McCurry

Distributed by Chilton Book Company

Crafting As a Business
Copyright © 1994 by The Rosen Group, Inc.
All rights reserved. No part of this book may
be reproduced or transmitted in any form
or by any means, electronic or mechanical,
including photocopying, recording, or by an
additional storage or retrieval system, without
written permission of The Rosen Group, Inc.
For information, contact: The Rosen Group,
Inc., 3000 Chestnut Ave., Suite 300,
Baltimore, MD 21211. (410)889-2933.

First printing 1994
ISBN 0-8019-8632-X
Written by Wendy W. Rosen

Editor & Features Writer: Amy M. Feinstein

Art & Design: Kris McCurry

Copy Editors: Carol Sorgen, Laura W. Rosen,
and Sharon Perfetti

Contributing Writers: Kurt G. Calia,
Candace Forsyth, Charles Geser, Rita Linder,
Thomas Mann, Sharon Perfetti, Laura W.
Rosen, Wayne Stahnke, and Gail Sustare

About the Cover: Cover Design by Kris
McCurry, The Rosen Group, Inc., Baltimore,
MD, Art Direction by Adam Shanosky,
Shanosky & Associates, Baltimore, MD,
Photography by Raymond Lee, Baltimore,
MD

The Rosen Group, Inc., has taken every
precaution to check the accuracy of the
information provided herein, and does not
assume responsibility in case of unforseen
error. Any business venture undertaken as a
result of information found in *Crafting As a
Business* is the responsibility of the parties
involved.

To Mom, who introduced me to my first art fair experience.
Without her energy and adventuresome spirit none of this would be possible.

And for all of the "artrepreneurs" who inspire me
to do what I do.

TABLE OF CONTENTS

■ EDITOR'S NOTE ■

The author, Wendy W. Rosen, created the national Buyers Markets of American Crafts, which has grown to include 1,200 craft artist exhibitors at its Philadelphia location, and over 1,000 in Boston, however, it was not always this way. Her company, The Rosen Group, like many craftspeople, had a humble beginning–it was born at a craft show. This seems only fitting when you consider Wendy's contribution to American crafts. Wendy, founder and president of The Rosen Group in Baltimore, Maryland, developed the idea for her business from the inspiration she received at a retail craft show. From that time on, she has dedicated her professional life to improving the way crafts are sold and marketed, both in the United States and abroad.

Wendy began her career in advertising sales. After the birth of her first child, Wendy was reluctant to return to that line of work. One day she decided to take her mind off her job worries by visiting a local retail craft show. After making a purchase, Wendy engaged in conversation with a craftsman. Wendy mentioned that she was looking for a new line of work that would still allow her to make use of her background and experience. "Do you know who needs advertising and marketing help more than anyone in the world?" the craftsman asked her, but did not wait for a response: "I do. I can't market myself properly. I can't get into the right shows. I don't even know the right shows to get into. I don't know how to approach galleries. I need to meet my buyers."

"The idea came to me suddenly," Wendy recalls. "I then attended other local craft shows where I talked with enough exhibitors to figure out where I should begin." After much research, Wendy developed an understanding of the unique needs of craftspeople. This helped Wendy define her mission—to provide a network where artists could meet retailers who are searching for new and exciting craftwork.

Wendy fully committed herself to her new venture, and worked daily to bridge the gap between crafts and business. "What craftspeople needed," she says, "was support from the kind of infrastructure other industries had already developed—trade shows, publications, associations—but adjusted to the needs and values of the craft artist." In 1980, Wendy created The Rosen Group with the idea that it would function like a trade association for American crafts. Over the years, The Rosen Group has grown to include a publishing division, *NICHE* magazine–a leading periodical for craft retailers–and an international operations division. The Rosen Group is headquartered in the historic Mill Centre, a restored 19th century factory that Wendy helped renovate and develop into a thriving arts center.

In addition to The Rosen Group, Wendy founded the American Craft Retailers Association (ACRA). She also serves on the board of the Craft Emergency Relief Fund (CERF), and holds a Certified Exposition Management designation in the International Association of Exposition Managers. Wendy has been the keynote speaker at the National Craft Convention, and has spoken on "The Business of Art and the Art of Business" before an audience of Russian artists and business leaders in Moscow.

Wendy believes that art and business are compatible, and that they will move closer together in the coming years. "Artists don't have to starve," Wendy says. "They can provide a comfortable life for their families, and flourish as artists as well."

By providing a forum for artists to wholesale their work, Wendy has pushed the marriage of art and business one step further. She allows artists to gain tenure in her shows, which are held annually in Boston and Philadelphia. By guaranteeing tenure, Wendy makes it possible for artists to plan ahead, since they don't have to wait to find out if they've been chosen for a particular show that year.

As she looks to the future of American crafts, Wendy is enthusiastic: "The United States has never before been an international leader for visual impact and design. The world has always looked to Europe for that. Now is the time when we will create a distinctively American style. A style that is recognized and appreciated everywhere because it expresses our national traits of energy, high spirits, enthusiasm, and humor."

Amy Feinstein

To my readers:

I discovered quite a while ago that what I love best about this business is that I am constantly surrounded by dreamers. The people I meet are not just dreaming—they are actively pursuing ways to make those dreams come true. My greatest thrills don't come from my own daily business decisions—they come from my interaction with artists on the phone, or on the Compuserve computer information system.

It is my hope that, with this book, I can help you find your path to creating your own craft business, or shape an existing one. The information provided in <u>Crafting As a Business</u> is not meant to be a cover-to-cover read like a novel, but rather a manual designed as a support system for those everyday business questions and problems. <u>Crafting As a Business</u> is written in a format that provides you with instant access and options for every craft business situation that might otherwise frustrate the emerging "artrepreneur."

For decades, craftspeople have offered each other advice during rainy weekends when craft shows are slow. With this book we provide a network of mentors—stories from those who have walked in your shoes. <u>Crafting As a Business</u> is not only a path, but a paved road. Please don't hesitate to pass along to us your own suggestions, or lessons you have learned that would improve the information <u>Crafting As a Business</u> provides; we love hearing from craftspeople at various stages in their careers.

Included in these pages are many incredible mentors—people who inspire us with their accumulated knowledge, and the beauty of their work. One day, I hope you too will take the responsibility to be a mentor to a craftsperson just starting out. If you accept this challenge, I am sure you will find it among the most rewarding endeavors you have ever undertaken. The craft community is one of the fastest growing sectors of the American economy. As a community, we need your involvement, your designs, and your ideas. General Patton once said, "Lead, follow, or get the heck out of the way." Craftspeople are natural leaders; they are business CEOs, CFOs, mayors, and senators—but most of all, they are the foundation for who we are, and who we can be—self-reliant, enterprising, and caring.

GOOD LUCK!

Wendy

3

Getting Started

"There's no use trying," she said: "one can't believe impossible things."
"I daresay you haven't had much practice," said the Queen.
"When I was your age, I always did it for half-an-hour a day.
Why, sometimes I've believed as many as six
impossible things before breakfast."
—Lewis Carroll

The idea occurs to everyone from time to time. As much as you would like to restrain those feelings, it has become obvious that the only way you will find peace of mind is to actually take the plunge, to find out if what you create can help you earn a living.

Your family and friends have given you support, but now it's time to see if the rest of the world agrees. After all, by purchasing your work, someone has paid you the ultimate compliment.

Along the path to building your own craft business lay many more pitfalls than triumphs. Starting a business takes persistence and resilience if you are going to succeed. One important thing to remember as you meet obstacles on your way: Everyone starts his or her craft business the same way—with a simple idea. Once you have that idea, your next job is to find a mentor—someone who is familiar within the area of craft you are about to enter.

You will also need a group of other craftspeople in your region who can provide emotional support when you are ready to quit, as well as assist you in the area of networking and troubleshooting.

Statistics indicate that 93% of all business start-ups fail within the first three years. But 90% of businesses that open within a community of start-ups succeed!

Find that community or network through your local guild, arts center, a local shop or gallery owner, or wherever small businesses are found in your area. More than start-up money, you need start-up encouragement. When searching for that mentor, choose someone whom you not only respect, but someone whom you also trust to give you a straight answer, even when it hurts.

History has shown us that whenever the economy takes a turn for the worse, that people looking for jobs often begin by starting a business at home. This is not surprising since you can start a home-based business with as little as a few hundred dollars, which you might be able to borrow from your family, your friends, or your credit cards.

If money worries have been holding you back, throw that excuse away! You are now one step further in realizing your dream.

Tabra Tunoa: Small Town Girl Finds Success with Jewelry

Rags to riches is a perfect title for Tabra Tunoa's story. The daughter of farmers in Stillwater, Oklahoma, Tabra always dreamed of a different life. After her four-year marriage ended, Tabra and her young son moved to Texas where she earned her teaching degree, and then moved to Spain where she taught English. While in Barcelona, Tabra began taking jewelry classes at night, sparking an interest—and a career—that has lasted more than two decades.

Those classes made Tabra realize that she enjoyed making jewelry much more than she enjoyed teaching. In 1972, with $500 borrowed from her father to start her craft business, Tabra returned with her son to the United States and moved to Berkeley, California. "It was the first time in my life that I felt like my son and I fit in," Tabra recalls. "There were all different kinds of cultures in Berkeley. One of my close friends was an American Indian with long black braids. My boyfriend was Japanese."

Tabra found a job at a jewelry factory by day, and was creating her own pieces by night. Soon she was selling her work from a table display on Telegraph Avenue. Tabra found, though, that selling on the streets could be difficult. Artists had to sleep at their spaces to hold them before the big Christmas season. Tabra remembers the rip-offs, the cold winters, and the fumes from passing cars. "But I loved it," she says. "The most successful I ever felt was when I made $100 in sales in one day! Eventually, that was my average." Seeking refuge from the cold, Tabra exhibited at several retail shows, and only sold on Telegraph Avenue during the holiday season. Wholesale shows

THE CONTEMPORARY CRAFT MOVEMENT

The contemporary craft movement began with the post-World War II baby boomers. The rebellion that started the movement was led by the largest demographic group in history, those who were teenagers in the turbulent sixties. These artisans strung beads, tie-dyed shirts, and "crafted" a future that in no way resembled the past of their war-era parents. To them, craftmaking was symbolic of peace, tolerance, and a new sense of freedom. Today, craftmaking is still a revolution, as many art forms are.

Craftmaking represents your effort to do things differently, from how you create an object to the way you live your life. Craftwork still represents the conscience of our nation, to question ideas we take for granted, and expand our sense of values concerning our world, and our future.

Contemporary craft collectors purchase artwork for many reasons. Some collectors are interested only in the aesthetics or beauty of an object, while others are intrigued by the way a design breaks from tradition, balance or symmetry. Some collectors enjoy the ideals or lifestyle a piece may suggest.

The craft lifestyle is one that is full of creativity and freedom of expression. As an artist, you will probably leave behind steady nine-to-five work days for a business that indeed offers more flexibility, but can consume every part of your personal life, including evenings and weekends. While it is not an easy life, it can be a fulfilling one, offering more control over your destiny, and freedom from the traditional workplace.

In the last decade, the craft community has grown from a diverse group of individuals, to a well-organized, fully-networked community that functions professionally in its own unique business environment. The structure that is created for the craft industry has provided a way for

---

were Tabra's next—and more successful—venture, allowing her to stop retailing entirely.

In the mid-seventies, Tabra bought a secondhand punch press for $300, and hired several people to work out of her home. With her new workforce, Tabra decided to "go for it." Tabra amassed an annual sales volume of $450,000. By 1991, Tabra's company employed 70 people, grossed $5,000,000, and was listed in Inc. Magazine as one of the 500 fastest growing, privately held companies in the United States. Among her many celebrity collectors are Whitney Houston, Carly Simon, Dolly Parton, Priscilla Presley, and Isabelle Allende.

Tabra has not forgotten what it was like to struggle back on Telegraph Avenue. Most of her workforce today is made up of refugees from countries such as Laos, Vietnam, and Cambodia. "Many have gone through a great deal of pain," she explains. "I want to give them an opportunity to work in a safe place, where they are respected for their contributions." Tabra offers her employees profit sharing plans, as well as classes in English on company time for all who are interested. The aversion she had to "bosses" in the past was wiped away when she realized she could be her own kind of boss.

Tabra asserts that she is an artist first, and a businesswoman second. She has, happily, reached a level of success where she can turn over many of the required daily chores to others, leaving herself more time to do what she loves, to create.

craftspeople to communicate through magazines, newspapers, guilds, and trade shows. But at the same time, the industry provides the necessary freedom required for the creation of art.

THE CRAFT COMMUNITY

Will you fit into the craft community? You can find the answer to this question within yourself. Are you friendly, and outgoing? Are you independent? Are you a risk-taker? Are you honest and direct? These are some of the qualities found in successful craftspeople. The craft community consists of thousands of entrepreneurs, but what differentiates these people from other business people is their strong motivation to succeed at work they love. For a craftsperson, success often means being true to one's own artistic and ethical vision.

Compared to other "industries" the craft community is quite unique. Rarely do you hear of theft of craftwork or of an artist's design, and when you do, craftspeople tend to quickly and internally resolve any problems that arise. Craftspeople are a generous, kind, and supportive group of people who do their best to take care of their own. How does this nurturing environment exist in the business world? It's hard to say, but it does exist, and it's part of what makes the craftwork itself very special.

Aid to Artisans

Founded in 1976, Aid to Artisans, or ATA, is a nonprofit organization dedicated to providing craftspeople in underdeveloped countries with economic opportunities. ATA members include design and business consultants, a board of directors, and many volunteers who work tirelessly to help establish handicraft businesses so that craftspeople in developing countries can enter the world market.

The goal of ATA is to help local artisans get their products to market. Assistance is provided at every level: product development, production, market research, and sales. ATA counts American Express, Esprit International, Citibank, and Xerox among its corporate supporters; many successful craft artists in the United States also support ATA. For more information, write: Aid to Artisans, 80 Mountain Spring Road, Farmington, CT 06032, or call (203)677-1649.

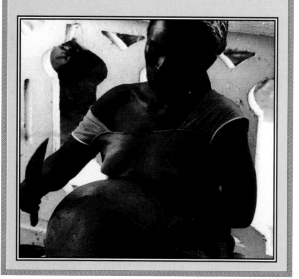

Ron Larsen: From Mathematics to a Full-Time Member of the Craft Community

Ron Larsen's interest in ceramics developed while he was in graduate school—studying math! After earning his doctorate in math, Ron began teaching at Yale University, and taking pottery classes on the side through an adult education program.

A few years later, Ron was teaching at Wesleyan University. While there, he joined a craft co-op that enabled him to learn more about pottery, while having unlimited use of studios and facilities. After five years, the climate in the math department was changing. Jobs in mathematics were scarce, and many colleges and uni-

▪ THE HISTORY OF CRAFT ▪

Second only to agriculture, craft production has always been the foundation of economic growth for every culture. Many primitive societies prospered by making and trading goods with other communities. In today's sophisticated cultures, craft objects are no longer used as trading currency, but instead represent our free-spirited, independent past, a time when technology and big business weren't in control of our lives.

Crafts are spiritual—they reflect our ideas, our values, our feelings, as well as the ever-changing trends. Crafts are works of art, prized collectibles that add beauty, function, and even humor to our lives. Craftwork is a unique form of art that we can all appreciate, regardless of our age, financial status, or level of education.

The first arts and crafts school, Rookwood Pottery was founded in 1880 in Cincinnati, Ohio. Following close behind was the New York School of Ceramics in Alfred in 1900. In approximately the same time period, Berea College and Arrowmont were founded in the southern United States. Many of the institutions from this time period are still around today.

Craft guilds in the United States were born in the early 1900's. The Southern Highlands Handicraft Guild, one of the oldest, was founded in 1930. Today the SHHG has 675 members, and operates the largest retail craft gallery in the nation at the foot of the Blue Ridge Parkway in Asheville, North Carolina. Each year 345,000 tourists visit the gallery, spending six million dollars on crafts that range from simple inexpensive wooden mountain toys to expensive sculptural blown glass and pottery. Above the retail store visitors can also view special exhibits in the guild's own gallery.

Today, most regions of the country, as well as many individual states, have guilds that run galleries, sponsor special fairs, and provide important services to their member artists. Some guilds require prospective members to apply with their work, while others have less restrictive policies. Generally, even the most restrictive guild will have special opportunities for non-members or for out-of-state artists.

---

versities were encountering financial problems. At the same time, Ron's wife decided to return to work, which allowed him to leave the world of academia and become a full-time potter. After writing several math texts and teaching for fifteen years, "the novelty had worn off," Ron recalls. "I had contributed all that I could to mathematics."

So Ron built a kiln and a studio in the back of his house, and founded Crary Mills Pottery. He found the switch from math professor to potter refreshing. "No one was ever looking over my shoulder to tell me to grade these papers, or go teach that class. "[The pottery] was my responsibility, and I knew it had to get done." Ron credits the smooth transition between careers to the experience he had had teaching, and the discipline it had developed in him.

Soon after this transition, Ron co-founded The Dinosaur Potter's Club, an organization dedicated to the encouragement and recognition of the individual studio potter making functional pottery by traditional hand methods. Ron says that pottery satisfies him, not only physically and intellectually, but also, finally, financially as well.

Ron Larsen in his teaching days.

■ THE GROWING ECONOMY OF CRAFT ■

The amazing growth of interest in American crafts has frequently been referred to as a "movement." It has now become clear though that American crafts is not just a movement, but much, much more.

The label "movement" today seems to be quite an understatement and suggests that crafts are a fad, that a time will come when the "hype" will die down, and craftwork will become relegated to flea markets and garage sales. Nothing could be further from the truth. As long as the demands of a rapidly growing industry are met, success is a given in the industry of American crafts. Yes, crafts is an industry, and became recognized as such when the American economy began receiving an annual boost of two billion dollars from crafts.

But why is the industry of American crafts thriving when so many big businesses are down-sizing? The answer lies within each and every person who offers a product that is sold through a personal relationship with the purchaser. This method of doing business is reminiscent of days past when personal service was the order of the day. Times have changed, but today, that same one-to-one approach is giving you, the craft entrepreneur, the competitive edge over the large manufacturers.

Why are big businesses shrinking? While small, independent craft businesses personally see their product through from start to finish, concentrating on just one medium, big businesses produce huge volumes of products through a complicated, lengthy, and expensive process. This process includes market research, product development, automated systems design, national advertising, legal fees, package design, and sales and distribution. The product that was initially inexpensive to produce now becomes an expensive proposition to get out of the factory and into the hands of the consumer. The large

---

The U.S. economy gets an annual boost of two billion dollars from craft sales.

---

manufacturer can easily fall victim to the "domino theory" when any part of the process fails.

Today's craftspeople have more flexibility, less capital investment, and the ability to oversee and plan all phases of production and marketing of their products. This gives artists the opportunity to change the design, production schedule, and marketing strategy in a flash, nipping potential problems in the bud.

Buyers from galleries and small shops often prefer buying from craftspeople directly, not only because they offer unique designs and quality work, but also because of the personal relationship established with the artist. When a buyer needs a problem solved, a product shipped, a custom-made item created, or any other personal service, he or she can speak directly to the craftsperson, rather than to someone who had no hand in the creation of the product. Small store owners often get pushed aside by large manufacturers looking for that big order.

Overlooking the needs of that small retail business is a big mistake. If you, as a craftsperson, are confident of your product's value and marketability, and provide top-notch customer service to independent galleries and shop owners, you are well on your way to success in the crafts industry. It all boils down to one simple reason why crafts are now preferred by wholesale buyers. That reason is YOU!

STATISTICS

- Craft booth space has gone from 1600 to 6000 booths in trade shows since 1980.
- 40,000 U.S. retailers buy American crafts.
- The craft industry contributes 2 billion dollars in sales toward the American economy.
- Craft artist exhibitors at the Philadelphia Buyers Market of American Crafts wrote 18 million dollars in sales in 1993.
- On average, buyers attending the Boston Buyers Market spent $10,000 at the 1992 show.
- 67% of all craft gallery sales are for items costing $50 or more.
- Approximately 10,000 craft artists nationwide sell contemporary crafts to galleries within the United States.
- 3,000 American craft retailers polled in NICHE magazine indicated that they made a combined $644 million annually in sales.

Bill & Marcia Finks–Adversity Sparks a Venture into Craft

After twenty-one years as a salesman, Bill Finks was thrown into the unemployment lines in Flint, Michigan, along with hundreds of recently laid-off General Motors factory workers. Marcia had just finished college, and found herself in a similar predicament. After nearly six hours standing in the unemployment line, Bill and Marcia both decided something had to change. They knew what they didn't want to do–conventional nine-to-five jobs–but they couldn't decide what they did want to do.

Bill had been creating twig furniture to supplement their income while Marcia was in school, so they came up with the idea of turning their love of folk crafts into a business. The Finks developed their own brand of folk art using metal, wire, and paint to create three-dimensional sculpture and wall art. A lack of funds was the first problem that arose. Bill and Marcia had enough money to either buy materials, or to pay the entry fees to exhibit at craft shows, but they couldn't afford both. Bill and Marcia decided that their money would best be spent paying the shows' entrance fees, so finding materials on their own was their only alternative. They ripped ceiling beams from old barn roofs, and picked metal scraps out of a nearby junkyard. Armed with photos of their work, Bill and Marcia visited a local folk-art museum, and returned with what they considered to be a large order. "That order gave us the confidence to continue," Marcia says. "But that confidence was short-lived. Our next couple of shows were bombs."

Bill and Marcia decided to scrape together enough money to participate in their first wholesale show in Niagara Falls. "It was four hundred dollars to get in, plus travel expenses," Marcia recalls. "Bill slept in this 1970s dilapidated van so that we could afford to enter the show. After the show ended, he called to tell me how we did. We made $200! That's all! I started to cry, convinced we were never going to make it. Our only goal was to pay the bills, not get rich, just to pay the bills."

But Bill's enthusiasm and never-look-back attitude kept them going. "He never takes two steps forward, and one step back," Marcia says. "He only takes two steps forward, and then two more." Two months later, Bill and Marcia found quick success. An article in the local paper featuring their work ignited interest in them that has just kept increasing. A scout with a national magazine saw the article, and got them more publicity. Marcia believes that networking has been the key to their success. Her suggestion to artists just starting out is to "meet as many people as possible."

The Finks' company, Primitive Twig, has been moving and shaking ever since. Among those who collect Bill and Marcia's Americana and Southwestern-influenced work are Charlie Watts of the Rolling Stones, and actor Richard Thomas. For wholesale shows, Bill and Marcia have found a good match with the Buyers Market of American Crafts Philadelphia and Boston shows, in which they have been participating since 1991. In terms of galleries, the Finks' consider themselves fortunate to be represented by many folk galleries throughout the United States.

Your Business &
Your Customer

*I'm working so hard on my time management
that I don't get anything done.*
—Anonymous

▪ THE BUSINESS PLAN ▪

A well thought out business plan is a detailed road map to success. If you can create a solid plan that maps out your goals, and gives an accurate portrait of your current status, you then have the foundation on which to build your business. The key to your plan is to remember that it is a tool to be used in everyday business decisions. It will also help others (bankers, lawyers, and accountants) understand your business down to the most specific detail. The plan is not to create yet more paperwork, but rather to produce a guide that will help you with long-term planning and daily business dilemmas. Now, before you dismiss this step as bureaucratic and unnecessary, realize that the time you invest implementing the plan is less costly than the money you will lose jumping into a business with your eyes closed!

What will you find in a business plan? Your basic business plan encompasses seven areas: **product development, marketing, sales, operations, personnel, finance, and management**. **Product development** implies that you are working regularly to refine what you make to meet your customer's needs and desires. **Marketing** is the way in which you inform your customers about what you create, how, and why. **Sales**, in a craft business, means talking to your customers, and getting them to buy from you. **Operations** has to do with the day-to-day workings of your particular business. If you are a weaver, for example, you would include in your daily schedule: Weaving five blankets, working on new designs, doing paperwork, and taking orders. **Personnel** concerns managing the people whom you employ. Money matters are handled under the heading of **finance**. In this area, you will measure your desired results against your actual financial status, and use that comparison to identify your priorities. Lastly, **management** means making sure that the other six areas are covered, and that they work well together so that you can achieve your business goals.

After you have defined what each category means to you, list for all seven items:

- The desired outcome for each area.
- The materials and resources that are needed to achieve your goal in each area.
- The steps you have to take to make your goals a reality.
- How you will judge the outcome of each category.

Answering these questions will help you make the "big picture" clearer, and determine realistically how much capital is needed.

Now you can get down to the business of actually writing your plan. The first page of your plan is the **title page**. Your title page should identify the name of the business, the title of the plan (Bob's Ceramics Studio Plan), and the date. You may also want to consider putting on the title page a brief disclaimer regarding confidentiality. This will protect you if your idea is stolen after someone has read the plan (with or without your knowledge). Again, this is not a necessity, but considering how little time it will take to write the disclaimer, isn't it worth saving yourself trouble in the long run?

The next part of the plan is the **entrepreneur's summary** (yes, you are an entrepreneur). Having previously defined your own seven steps, you have all the materials you need to write your summary. The summary must include a definition of your purpose or mission, your short- and long-term goals, and the steps that you intend to take to achieve them. Attention to detail at this point is crucial; remember, this is not only a guide to use yourself, but also possibly the means by which you receive or don't receive loans or grants!

The table of contents will help others find the information that they need. Create your table of contents using Roman numerals for the headings and capital letters for the additional information needed under each heading. Your first heading should be entitled **the business.** The heading **the business** is Roman numeral I, to be followed by sub-headings that start with the letter "A." Under this topic, you will first list the **status** of the business (whether it is a start-up, an expansion, or an existing business belonging to someone else that you want to be a part of). The second sub-heading will be **background**, which should include a brief listing of the product (the medium) and types of products that you will offer your customers. If you make functional pottery, for example, list that. Your third sub-heading will be **competition**. This category will explain why people will want to buy your pottery over the next guy's, or in other words, what makes your work special (this is not the time to be modest). The last subheading in the first section is **goals**: short- and long-term.

Your next heading will be **products offered.** In this section you will have the opportunity to describe your work in detail, but beware—just because you know the vocabulary of your medium, doesn't mean that the average person will understand, let's say the language of glass-blowing. In other words, use laymen's terms whenever possible. Your first sub-heading will be the **specific products** or lines that you sell, or wish to sell. For example, if you do one-of-a-kind and production pieces, list both, and describe both in detail. Your next sub-heading should be **added value**. Added value indicates the characteristics that make your work special to your customers, i.e., a certificate comes with each piece, detailing the story, or cultural background of the piece, or that you donate a percentage of each sale to a non-profit group.

Following **products offered** is **market description**. In this section you will need to describe what kind of demand there is for what you produce. You want to

Rick Faulkner: Candle Maker Looks at the Business of Craft

Rick Faulkner started Barrick Candles, and began making and selling candles because he needed a summer job during high school. Before Rick decided to make candles his living, he had his mind set on going to business school, earning an M.B.A., and finding a job in the corporate world. Although Rick's candle business had originally been born as a means to make some extra spending money when Rick was in his teens, he had always been interested in accounting. "More than anything, I wanted to learn about business," Rick says. But after receiving his degree from Cornell University, Rick found his way back to Barrick Candles, this time, though, with new insight.

Rick admits that in those early years, he never put a formal business plan on paper. "I think I always had a business plan in my mind," he says. "Having gone to business school, I had learned to look at the big picture, so I think I always looked at my business from a business plan perspective." Rick believes that there are many things that people don't consider before they start their own business. "Doing a business plan is a great idea for people who don't have a lot of business experience," Rick suggests. "It can be a very valuable exercise."

When asked what he learned in business school, Rick recalls his most important lesson. "Keep overhead low," he advises. "Overhead kills more small businesses than anything else. Overhead is any expense that you commit to that won't go away easily, like a lease."

Rick believes that his education, while not necessary for his candle company, has come in handy, because it taught him how to think, and how to prioritize. A business background also helped Rick judge what will have an impact on his business, and what won't.

convince the reader that you know your market, and that client base is something you have thought about. Your first sub-heading under **market description** will be the **industry**. In this category, you will discuss major trends in your medium (and in American crafts), and any uncontrolled variables (government regulations, or the economy, etc.) that may affect your chosen field. Your next sub-heading should be called **customer**. Now is the time to define your target audience (see "Who is Your Customer?"). Explain who your customers are, what need your product meets in their lives, where they live, and their buying habits (do they buy your work as a gift for others, or do they collect it themselves?). Also, is your customer a seasonal customer, or does your product sell steadily year-round? Explain the size of your market. If your target market is women between the ages of 18 and 34 who buy your product as a wedding gift, is this group growing, and do you have the materials to keep up with that growth? You will want to tell the reader all that you know about the relationship between your customer and your product. Finally, talk about your **location**. Demographically, are you located in a city that will be amenable to your stylish urban designs, or are you in a rural setting where country-styled items are the fashion?

Approach to selling is your next heading. Here is your opportunity to discuss your **philosophy** about sales and business. Will most of your sales be to retailers, and if so, how will you approach them? Do you believe that you can never provide too much customer service? Say that! Also discuss your returns policy, payment due dates, and thoughts about shipping and receiving. Talk about your marketing plans and practical advertising strategies that will attract more people in your target group. Make sure to mention any opportunities where you can promote your work at a reasonable cost.

Describing how you make what you make comes next under the heading of **production process**. The first sub-heading should be **production**, or the way you produce a piece of your work. What equipment is required in each step of the process, and how much time goes into each piece? Next you will discuss **operations**, such as quality control, inventory control, and the vendors from whom you buy your materials. It is important to stress that for every material needed, you know of a back-up vendor who can deliver the same materials at approximately the same price if your chosen supplier is unavailable.

Who will be working for you, and what their qualifications are should be answered in **management and personnel**. The saying "the chain is only as strong as its weakest link" should come to mind here. List any partners or major participants and their business or artistic credentials. What part will these people play in your business, and what skills do they possess that will be an asset to you? What part will you take in daily operations? Will you be on-site or in the studio, while others cover paperwork and financial matters? If you have not hired anyone, what skills are required, and what tasks will each individual need to perform? List only your absolute needs, and the reasonable salary that you will need to pay each person. If you will be the sole employee, that's fine too, but indicate what you intend to pay yourself.

Perhaps the most important section, if the goal of your business plan is to receive financing, is **financial data**. In the first sub-heading, the **financial proposal**, you need to indicate what you will do with the funds you want to borrow. Also, you must detail the equity or start-up funds you plan to contribute to the business. Your next category is a **balance sheet** if you have one, or if not, a chart documenting overhead and income. Finally, you will want to provide any personal or business tax returns from the past three years. Getting all of these pieces together can be taxing (no pun intended), but banks and other financial resources take these matters quite seriously.

Summary and conclusions wraps up the previous sections. Here you must restate your objective, and indicate what you envision for your business further down the road. Follow this section with the last heading, **supporting documents**. Include credit reports, credit references, letters of recommendation, or account statements. Any document that will prove you are a good risk belongs in this section.

When you have completed your plan, make copies (remember that neatness counts), and put them in attractive binders that you can purchase at any office supply or stationery store. Keep this plan in a safe place, where it will not be damaged or thrown away in the daily shuffle.

OUTLINE FOR YOUR BUSINESS PLAN'S TABLE OF CONTENTS

■ WHO IS YOUR CUSTOMER? ■

Merchants have always known that their customers have special interests, needs, and attitudes that are different from those of the store owner across town. Your customers also have a special "profile" not only of likes and dislikes, but also of how they live, what they wear, what music they listen to, what food they eat, and how they pay for purchases. The information you collect can be used to create a profile of your target customer, helping you to find even more customers who are interested in your work.

A retail craft fair is the best place to identify those people who fit your customer profile. Buy a small notebook where you can jot down brief descriptions and observations about your customers. Pay attention to details. How is their hair styled? Is it natural, or is it stiff, with not a hair out of place? What kind of clothes are they wearing? Are they alone, or do they have small children? How did they pay for their purchase? Do they live in the city, or the suburbs? All of these items will be put together to tell you if your customer is traditional or contemporary, very concerned with their appearance and what surrounds them, or more laid back. These questions can help you to create your customer profile. Through your customer profile, you can find ways to target special interest groups and attract new customers.

The demographic information that you gather in your notebook can now be used to point you in the right direction for mailing lists. It is possible to purchase a list (check your local library for *Standard Rate and Data Mailing Lists*) of people who fulfill the following criteria, for example: females between 35 and 49, who spend over $1,000 a month on a credit card, and who live in the city of Philadelphia. Demographics can also assist you in analyzing trends. If you know that your best customer is a woman between the ages of 35 and 49, you can figure out how her life will change in the next ten years (i.e., the kids will be grown or in college), and how your new products can fit into her changing lifestyle.

Your customer profile should become a tool that you use daily. Take advantage of your creativity and imagination to bring your customer to life. Try this visualization exercise to flesh out the details about your customer so that you will have a clear image of who he or she is.

Your imagination is a powerful tool that can help you a great deal in the identification of your customer. Another helpful technique is to create a collage that identifies your customer. After using the creative visualization process, buy a magazine that you think your customer might read. Cut out photos that remind you of your customer, such as furniture, pets, children, cars, a decorated room, and clothing. Glue these pictures to a piece of posterboard and display the collage in your studio. Let your observations guide you to understand your customer better.

Expanding your customer profile can benefit you in many ways. If you find that many of your customers share a particular interest apart from your work, you can target those interests. Courtney Miller of Courtney Designs, for example, found that many of her customers loved animals. With that information, she came upon the Devon Horse Show in Devon, Pennsylvania, although not a craft or jewelry show, it's a great place for Courtney to sell her work. This show paired her jewelry with a group of horse enthusiasts. The result was success.

Tune in to Your Customers

Find a quiet, dimly lit area with an armless, comfortable chair. Ask a friend to be your partner for this experience.

Have your partner quietly recite the following information, leaving you time between each instruction to experience and visualize in your imagination. Listen to your partner say:

- *Close your eyes, and let all thoughts leave your mind.*
- *Start to relax, first with your eyes.*
- *Relax your nose, your mouth, and your entire face.*
- *Relax your shoulders, your upper arms, your wrists, and your fingers.*
- *Relax your breathing, and your stomach muscles.*
- *Relax your legs, your ankles, and finally, your toes.*

Your partner should read to you the following passage, pausing for 30 seconds between sentences so you can respond based on what you see in your imagination. Now, imagine you are at a

Courtney Miller and Lee Peterson: Nature-Inspired Jewelry Expands Price Points for Wider Appeal

Courtney Miller and Lee Peterson of Courtney Design have made some unusual choices in order to locate their customers. In addition to exhibiting at wholesale

gift shows, Courtney Design participates in many charitable organization retail craft fairs, the Devon Horse Show near Philadelphia, and the Jazz and Heritage Festival in New Orleans. "Our customers are mostly

craft fair. A customer approaches your booth. Imagine him or her in detail, the hair, the eyes, the age, the jewelry and the clothing. Is your customer alone, or with someone? What does the customer say? Now imagine the customer purchasing one of your pieces. You wrap the piece, and the customer leaves the show. Follow your customer as he or she drives home. What color, make, and model is the car? Imagine the car arriving at the customer's home. Where is the house? What kind of house is it? How is it decorated? The customer takes the package into the house and carefully unwraps it. Where is the piece placed? Thank your customer for allowing you to enter this private space. Leave the house. Open your eyes.

During the next ten minutes, tell your partner about your customer. Write down everything that was said during the creative visualization experience, and during the discussion that followed. Keep these notes in your notebook, as well as in your workspace, perhaps near the phone.

what I call the rich and rustic—old money," Courtney says. "These are people who don't have to be wearing what was on the pages of Vogue last month; they are confident in what they like, and how they look."

Many of Courtney's pieces feature animals, including insects and sea creatures. Courtney's animal designs appeal to a wide range of customers. At a retail show that accompanied the American Society of Zoologists convention, many of the people interested in her work were research assistants and students who didn't have much money. When Courtney realized that the price of her jewelry was too high for many of these young people, she created a dangle earring collection featuring

small animals, shrimp, and other crustaceans. Her new, reasonably priced collection was an immediate hit!

The Jazz and Heritage Festival in New Orleans puts Courtney Design in touch with yet another customer. "The festival is always held just before Mother's Day, so many young people accidentally discover me, and find something that they just must have for Mom," Courtney says. "They might not buy that item for themselves, but Mother's Day gives them a reason to make the purchase."

Courtney Design's customers are both young and old, but they all share a fondness for the whimsical. "People who take themselves too seriously usually don't like my work," Courtney confides. But if one looks at how successful Courtney Design has become, there must be many people out there with a good sense of humor.

INTERPRETING TRENDS TO BUILD YOUR BUSINESS

Donna Milstein, owner of Hanson Galleries in Houston and past president of the American Craft Retailers Association (ACRA), embraces a concept that many people in the crafts community resist—watching and capitalizing on trends. With a wealth of experience in retailing, including fourteen years in the buying offices of Federated Department Stores, and another fifteen years as co-owner of Hanson Galleries, Donna has developed a keen eye for buying and merchandising, and she leaves "no stone unturned" when it comes to finding ways to improve her retail business.

Donna offers artists and buyers the following framework for identifying trends, showing how they can be translated and applied to one's business. "Not to be confused with fads which have no staying power," Donna explains, "Trends are often predictable and cyclical throughout the years."

Donna Milstein's steps for capitalizing on trends:

- **Recognize**
A trend might be something predictable, like environmentalism. Trends influence society, while fads do not.

- **Interpret**
Take in all the stimuli around you, and then determine what's appropriate to your business. Example: What does the warming of the color palette mean to me?

- **Timing** (and creating an effective time frame)
Ask yourself: When is the best time for me to jump in? Be careful not to move too far ahead of your customers tastes.

"Studying newspapers, television, and magazines gives you first-hand information about trends," Donna says. "You can pick up a copy of *Metropolitan Home* and quickly learn that terra cotta, granite, and polished aluminum are hot commodities for homes in the '90s." Donna points to another example—the recent return to the '60s fashion movement, with tights, mini skirts, Pucci prints, oversized jewelry, and wide headbands, now filling women's clothing and accessory departments. "While the '80s were known as the service decade, the '90s are a decade for value," says Donna, who believes that retailers of added-value merchandise such as American crafts should promote that facet of their businesses.

"Objects depicting dolphins and other endangered species are faring well," Donna observes. Donna has also discovered her customers' enthusiasm for mixed media handcrafts, such as ceramic vessels with polished steel decoration, and raku pottery combined with pine needles and feathers. Another trend that Donna spotted early and turned into a hot seller is kaleidoscopes. "Kaleidoscopes started as a trend, maybe," she recalls, "but now scopes are a solid merchandising classification within [our] business. We've been selling them for fourteen years, with gains in dollar volume each year."

Trends in your medium will follow the same cyclical pattern they do elsewhere: They have a beginning, a flourish, and an eventual decline.

Donna has often seen trends originate on either coast before slowly migrating to her region (Texas) of the country. In her enthusiasm, she has sometimes presented an idea too early to her customers. Donna remembers, for example, a striking display of married metal jewelry in her gallery several years ago and receiving an under-whelming response. She has since brought the work back and it is now enthusiastically hailed by her customers. "I often hear retailers say, 'I tried that in my store and it didn't work,'" Donna says, adding, "What they don't realize is that just because a product or category didn't work three years ago doesn't mean it won't work today." So she advises retailers to be inspired by trends coming out of California, New York, or even Europe, but to carefully consider what's happening in their area before taking a big plunge.

Changes in our nation's economy, and shifting standards of living in American lifestyle such as the rise in single parent households, are all social trends that can greatly affect your business. "What often happens during a stagnant economy, though, is that people make fewer purchases but they buy better goods," Donna says. "While it is wise for artists to offer items at the low end, they should not eliminate the bigger, more luxurious pieces that help retailers make a dramatic statement with the work."

So, while your instincts may tell you to create only pieces that will sell fast and furiously, don't forget that extra sizzle is always needed to enhance the image of your work.

Courtesy of NICHE magazine and Donna Milstein.

Donna Milstein: Experienced Craft Buyer is Motivated By Color and Trends

Donna Milstein has been co-owner of two mall gallery locations in Houston, Texas for the last fifteen years. Before opening the first of two Hanson Galleries, Donna was a fashion buyer for such department stores as Bloomingdale's and Foley's. In her capacity as a fashion buyer, Donna learned the importance of trends, and how they affect what people will wear, and what they will want to buy.

In crafts, Donna finds that the change in color palettes is very important. "Subscribing to a service like the Color Institute can be very expensive for an artist just starting out," Donna says. "Instead, browse through as many magazines as possible, especially for fashion and current events. Then ask yourself: 'How does this affect me?'"

Donna suggests that the environmental movement will continue to have a significant influence on trends, especially in the art world. "You see so many more earth tones now than you have in a long time," Donna says. She believes that the greening of America will continue to promote natural fibers, and updated shades of greens, browns, and blues will be popular. Influenced by her eye for trends, Donna keeps abreast of what's happening among consumers. "I like to see artists doing new and different things all the time," Donna says. "That keeps things interesting."

10 Ways to Spot Trends

1. Read a consumer magazine.
2. Visit a museum.
3. Read the fashion section of a big city newspaper, like *The New York Times*.
4. See a recently released movie.
5. Browse *The New York Times* bestseller book list.
6. Visit a big trade show.
7. Read a trade magazine like *NICHE* or *The Crafts Report*.
8. Check your local library for new books on trends.
9. Read a current issue of *American Demographics*.
10. Talk to kids! They know everything!

Trend Resources

Available At Your Local Bookstore

Megatrends For Women, Patricia Aburdene and John Naisbitt

Megatrends 2000, Patricia Aburdene and John Naisbitt

The Popcorn Report, Faith Popcorn

John Naisbitt's Trend Letter
1101 30th Street, NW
Washington, DC 20007

FINANCIAL WORKSHEET: START-UP COSTS

Estimated Monthly Expenses

Your Base Salary: _____

Other Salaries or Wages: _____

Rent or Mortgage: _____

Advertising: _____

Shipping Expenses: _____

Supplies: _____

Telephone: _____

Utilities: _____

Insurance: _____

Payroll Tax: _____

Business Tax: _____

Professional Services: _____

PR and Marketing: _____

Miscellaneous (List)_____: _____

Total: $_____

Start-Up Expenses *(Most of these are one-time costs only!)*

Equipment: _____

Supplies: _____

Start-Up Advertising/Promotion: _____

Business Cards: _____

Stationery: _____

Miscellaneous (List)_____: _____

Total: $_____

Total Cash Needed For Start-Up: $_____

RETAIL CLIENT INFORMATION SHEET

Name: _____ Date: _____

Address: _____ Referred by: _____

City: _____ State: _____ Zip code: _____

Phone: Work ( ) _____ Home ( ) _____ Birth date: _____

Biographical Information:

Single ❑   Married ❑   Divorced ❑

Spouse's Name: _____ Birth date: _____

Children (name & age): _____ _____

Pets (what type): _____

Occupation: _____

Highest level of education completed: _____

Household income: _____

How is their home decorated? _____

Preferences:

Colors: _____ Craft Medium: _____

Style: _____ Size: _____

A preference for Functional or Decorative crafts: _____

Notes: _____

Last contact date: _____ Last mailing date: _____

Additional information and observations:

_____

_____

_____

What have they purchased:

Date	Item	Source: show, phone, etc.	Cost

Product Development

3

*I trust a good deal to common fame, as we all must.
If a man has good corn, or wood, or boards, or pigs,
to sell, or can make better chairs or knives, crucibles
or church organs, than anybody else, you will find a
broad hard-beaten road to his house,
though it be in the woods.*
—Emerson

▪ PRODUCT DEVELOPMENT ▪

Barry Leader: Developing Products for Hard Times

When Barry Leader, of Raintree Carvings, realized there were many people who wanted hand-carved items who couldn't afford them, he decided to develop a line to meet the needs of these potential customers. He created what he calls his recession items to fill that gap.

Barry created picture frames and bird houses that could be sold at lower prices than many of his other items. "If it hadn't been for the economy, the spark might not have appeared for these pieces," Barry says. His recession birdhouses can still be used outdoors, and feature his trademark bright, exciting colors.

Arts for the Birds is the name of Barry's retail shop where he test-markets new products to gauge customer reaction. After an item has done well at his shop, it debuts at a wholesale show. "Good gallery sales are usually an indicator that a piece will do well at the shows," Barry advises. His advice to other craftspeople who are developing new products is to know the cost of your materials: "You have to do research on what's out there. You have to know what similar items are selling for." Barry has learned that by saving money in production, an artist can come up with a more competitive selling price, thus becoming a leader in the craft market.

From the dawn of the industrial age to the present, our world has continued to be more complicated by the manufacturing process. Henry Ford probably spent less time developing the first Model T than the five-and-a-half years and 350 steps it takes to develop a new car today! If you ever, as a single producing craftsperson, thought you were at a disadvantage compared to large manufacturers—you are **wrong**!

Today's producing craft artist has an infinite number of advantages over any domestic or foreign competitors! Just be sure to follow the rules of the game.

1. Make something that appeals to a small but accessible group of people. Manufacturers can only afford to go after the masses—remember, they have to sell volume.

2. Include as a part of your work an item(s) that requires hand fabrication—something that can't be stamped out, quickly molded, or printed to achieve the same look or effect.

3. Promote your product's uniqueness and the skill, time, and effort that goes into each piece.

4. Use materials that aren't commonly used by manufacturers. Use materials that you can get only in limited quantities—just make sure there's enough for your needs!

Manufacturers can't easily find a large source for bubinga wood, ancient glass from the Red Sea, or rare sweet grass!

5. Design for a neglected part of the marketplace. Quilter Ellen Kochansky decided long ago that there were enough quilts on the market retailing for $2,500 and up. She also knew that there was no shortage of quilts priced at $400 or less. Ellen found her niche right in between those two price points, selling her contemporary quilts to customers who fit into an upper middle income category.

Design is a strategic activity. Whether you intend to design for a unique fit in the marketplace or not—your success or failure will depend on finding the right niche.

The Relationship Between You and Your Work

Your product line has a natural relationship to your innate love of making things. It doesn't have to be as forced as saying, "I will make this, or that." Your line will most likely begin with one or two great ideas and grow into a group of items that complement those first ideas. Your sensibility as an artist will inform the way in which you design and develop a product. Your interest in archaeology, for example, might lead you to create vessels based on ancient designs, or to borrow imagery from social and cultural traditions.

The way to create a product line is to examine and consider the designs you are currently making, then assess how they will sell in the marketplace. Along the way you will make numerous adjustments.

Product design must become part of your entire business experience every day. It is not something you can put out of your mind. You will always be testing a new product or idea and soliciting feedback from buyers, gallery owners, friends, and fellow artists. As you work each day, new product ideas or changes in current products will occur to you. Keep a notebook nearby to write down these ideas—most small business owners even keep a notebook by the bed, for those a.m. ideas. On your business calendar there should be time scheduled for production, selling, and product design.

Tip: Most successful artists increase their product line by 30% each year!

Whenever you design new work for your line, you must consider what items to drop out of production, or at least which to drop off your price list and brochure.

The first step is a leap—a creative leap. If you have trouble getting started, go to the library or to a book store and buy a copy of *A Whack on the Side of the Head* by Roger von Oech. This inspirational book will tell you how to get those creative juices flowing.

Product Value

Your product must compete with others in the marketplace. The fact that your product is handmade is an important element that adds value—but only if it is properly communicated to the customer. Once you have created a product, you must find as many ways to "add value" as possible.

Every product has two basic elements:
1. Features
2. Benefits

Features are the tangible, "descriptive" parts of your

product. For example, a birdhouse's features are: the type of wood, the finish, the hole, the perch, the hanging mechanics. The aesthetic part of your work is also a

Sandra Magsamen: Artist Creates New Product Lines to Suit a Variety of Customers

Sandra Magsamen has come a long way in a short time. In the last year Sandra has taken her business from a part-time venture to that of a full-time adventure. What started with ceramic tiles and accessories has grown to include her designs on t-shirts and greeting cards.

Sandra's newest line features tiles with fruits, vegetables, and herbs. "The inspiration for this line came from the garden I planted with my daughter, Hannah," says Sandra. "All of my work comes from things in my everyday life." Table Tiles, Sandra's company, has several other lines of ceramic tiles including her black and ivory collection, and her original line, which have whimsical verses or titles. Sandra believes that the image and the sayings strike a chord with her customers.

Sandra's advice to the novice craftsperson is to think about the things that are influential in your life, and include them in your work. "Many of my best ideas come from my daughter," she says. "Kids can come up with the greatest ideas, and the most original perspectives."

feature. **Benefits** are the reasons why the customer buys a birdhouse. To draw birds into the yard. To decorate a patio. To feed hungry birds in the winter.

Increase your product's value through creative graphics and advertising copy on your hang tags, pamphlet of instructions, gift cards, adoption certificates (remember Cabbage Patch dolls), club memberships (join the Smith Paperweight Society) and more. Your creativity doesn't end with making a product—continue to add value and improve profits with the way you express features and benefits!

Psychological Factors of Product Value

What are the psychological factors that contribute to the value of a product? Here are some suggestions to help you demystify this subject!

1. Expectation. The customer's general impression of what your product is worth are based on his or her previous experiences and education. Many customers have never before considered buying a handcrafted object. It is your job to educate each customer about your product's features and benefits. There is still another reason why people buy crafts—because they respect your lifestyle and values. They are curious, and maybe a bit envious about how you decided to leave a traditional lifestyle and create your own business!

2. Customer need. Does the customer want or need what you are selling? Remember the laws of supply and demand. Craft is best sold in an environment where it is considered unique.

3. Image. Your customer has a never-ending need to increase the value of his or her self-image. Your product can help by making your customer: an environmental activist, an art collector, a good parent, or an animal advocate.

What Adds Value?

Adding value means positioning your product apart from others, especially from manufactured products and imports. By following these tips, you will be able to achieve more value and showcase your product in a special light.

1. Sign your piece. Everyone knows that a signed piece is special!

2. Add features. The more uses you can package in one item, the more reasons a customer has to buy.

3. Add benefits. Use your hang tags, information pamphlets, packaging, etc. to add more reasons to buy—no item is self-explanatory.

Bradley Cross: Hang Tags Help Artist Convey Product Value to His Customers

Bradley Cross of Harmony Hollow Bell Works crafts in bronze, copper, brass, aluminum, and steel to create bells and chimes for outdoor use. Bradley places hang tags on all of his items to inform customers about his products.

The bronze bells created by Bradley have a hang tag that states the bells have a 250-year guarantee. "This lets my customers know that these bells aren't fragile, that they are meant to be used outdoors, and enjoyed for a lifetime," Bradley explains. This guarantee sets Harmony Hollow apart from other artists in the minds of potential cus-

tomers. "To get a customer base, you have to differentiate yourself from someone else by doing something special," Bradley said.

Harmony Hollow started creating bells, then chimes, and has grown to reflect Bradley's interest in nature and the outdoors. His newest line provides everything for the garden, from sculptural garden stakes to bird feeders.

4. Write a creative statement or message. Your creative image is expressed in the written message to your customers. Tell a story, write a poem, or deliver a personal wish to your customers.

5. Educate. Tell your customers how your product protects the environment, contributes to the well-being of the community, or helps their families. Tell them how to properly care for and clean the product or how to display it best.

6. Inform. Most customers don't know what is actually involved in blowing glass, making a ceramic teapot, or knitting a sweater—tell them (or show them in photos) how difficult it is and how long you studied before you were making products of high quality.

7. Create a work of beauty. Understated, but of overpowering value!

8. Display your product to its best advantage. What lighting is best? Should it be in direct sun, or shade? Can you put it outdoors?

9. Be the first. Go ahead and brag! If you don't, who will?

10. Be the best. If someone has said it—pass it on! Use quotes from newspaper articles that have been written about you. Ask gallery owners, museum directors, educators, civic leaders and celebrities for their testimonials.

11. Talk about historical or cultural significance. Tell the story of why and how your work was created.

12. Number or limit production of an item. A customer wants to know that they have something that won't be found in everyone else's home.

13. Promote geographic or regional significance. Visitors, tourists, and even local residents like to support their own hometown success stories.

14. Tell your story. Let people know about your accomplishments, your education, your awards.

15. Discuss how the piece was made. Most people don't have any idea why your work is different from other artists' work or even from a factory-made piece. Tell them what goes into your items.

16. Relate the history of the process or materials. How was the same object made a thousand years ago? Where did the materials come from? Tell the story.

17. Make your work unique. Why is your work unusual? What makes it stand out from the crowd?

18. Warranties, guarantees and service! Stand behind your products. Satisfied customers will return.

The Committee Approach to Product Design

The most common method of product design in the industrial world today is the committee approach. The *styling* department sends its design ideas to the *engineering* department, then to the *sales* department, then on to the *marketing* department, and so on and so on. Problems arise in this process when no arm of this huge octopus has the authority to solve problems until the process has gone too far and it's too late.

Today, many large manufacturers have discovered that smaller teams that work together are a better way to produce a new product. Fortunately, you don't have any of these problems—but you do have another—being objective as you play the role of each imaginary department. Ask yourself these questions:

  1. Does it work?
  2. Will it sell?
  3. Is it profitable?

The Tasks of Product Design

Determine the character of the product. Decide on the style and production method. Analyze the function of the product. Does it hold water? Is it well balanced for handling? Will it pack up, UPS, or gift wrap easily? In what type of environment will it go? Are there additional uses for the product? What assembly processes must be employed? Identify any special skills that must be learned by you or your assistants. Identify sub-assemblies and ways to simplify the process.

When and how will quality control happen before items are shipped to customers? Organize an inventory strategy for parts and supplies, and calculate how many finished products you will keep on hand. How will scraps be recycled or used for other purposes. Many successful craftspeople will tell you that at one time or another they've developed a new product from odds, ends, and leftovers!

EVALUATING A NEW PRODUCT

Use this form to judge the potential of success for new products.
It is important that the product is judged in comparison to your other products.

	BELOW AVERAGE	AVERAGE	ABOVE AVERAGE
Appearance			
Appropriateness for market			
Availability of materials			
Cost of materials			
Design			
Hours of labor			
Price			
Profitability			
Technique			
Timelessness			
Uniqueness			
Usefulness			

THE CREATIVE CURVE

It is crucial to your business to always have new products. Most craft artists plan to introduce a new piece, or a new line at key times throughout the year. It is extremely important that you plan creative time in your studio so that your ideas are always in the works. Product development isn't a twice a year obligation, rather it is an important part of a craft business. How do you know when its time to introduce something new? By charting your sales!

This chart illustrates a new ceramic product. The product is charted from the month that it was introduced, its rise, its stabilization, and its eventual decline. Notice the change in sales after changes or improvements were made to the piece. At the point where a product has hit its peak, and begins its decline, it is time to introduce a new product, or make the necessary changes that will once again make the sales improve.

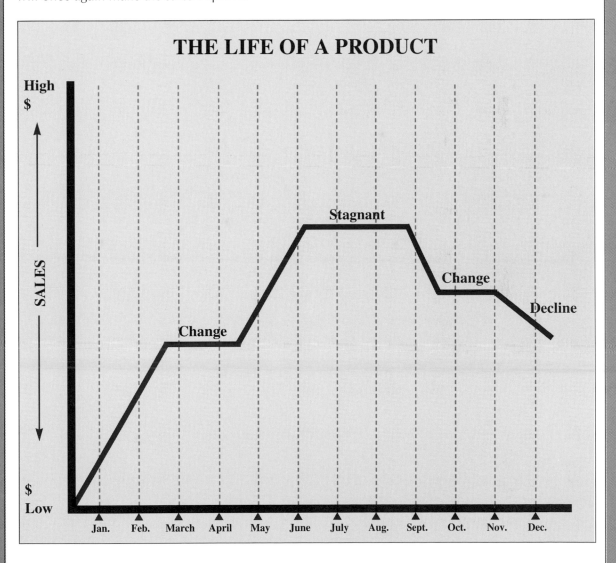

Pricing

Life is painting a picture, not doing a sum.
—Oliver Wendell Holmes, Jr.

Correct pricing of a product separates the amateur from the professional craftsperson. As an amateur, you may only hope to make enough to replenish materials and cover costs. At the point at which you want to enter the professional crafts marketplace, you can seriously undercut competition by pricing too low, making life difficult for those around you at retail shows, AND "shooting yourself in the foot" at the same time by just breaking even.

While you may sell out early in the day, you will soon discover that being out of product may mean being out of business because you haven't made enough to cover your costs and pay yourself as well.

Pricing your work is basically simple, but it is unrealistic to apply a rigid formula since few craftspeople work a traditional forty-hour week. A craft lifestyle reflects and accommodates the artist's urge to meet the creative challenges found in designing and making objects rich in form and/or function, **as well as** the need to earn enough money to maintain at least a reasonable standard of living.

Roughly expressed, the formula goes like this:

Production Costs + Overhead Costs + Selling Costs + Profit = Wholesale Price

The Law of Supply and Demand

The marketplace is a strategic balance of product availability and market demand. To price any product you must have a clear understanding of the supply and demand of items similar to your own in the marketplace.

Manufacturers often prefer **high supply** in a market of low demand which, in turn, creates an environment for heavy discounting. On the other hand, craftspeople work in the exact opposite manner providing high demand and **low supply**. For decades, craftspeople have controlled supply and demand for their work by limiting the number of stores they sell to in a given region. This practice of **exclusivity** serves as one type of control over market saturation and discounting.

Production Costs

Before you set a wholesale price on your product, you will have to compute the labor and materials costs to produce one item, or one unit, **efficiently**. To produce an item efficiently, it may be necessary to produce many pieces or copies at once. It may also be necessary to buy supplies in large quantities to keep material costs in line with your pricing structure.

Using the simple formula above, it is easy to see why assistants are an important part of any production craft business. An assistant can keep you productive in the design process, and help you to produce the work—if not

Sonia Rhea: "Pricing is the Basis of Your Business"

Sonia Rhea, half of Schmidt/Rhea Glass, feels that even if your work is excellent, poor pricing can mean the difference between failure and success. "It doesn't matter, sometimes, how great you are—if you price your product too low, your business will slowly collapse, and you will have produced all of that work without any profit to show for it," Sonia says.

Overhead, Sonia believes, is the item that most people forget to calculate when pricing. "Overhead can be travel expenses, salaries for assistants, your phone bill, or repairs to equipment," Sonia points out.

Pricing your product too high can be just as bad as underpricing. Sonia suggests testing your prices at retail shows. "Retail shows can be great opportunities to check the price of a piece, and work out the bugs [on that piece] at the same time," she advises. Gallery owners, Sonia recommends, can also provide good advice on the pricing of your work. "We see many people who have been in business as long as we have, who haven't gotten pricing problems solved," Sonia says. "They aren't as successful as they could be, and they always wonder why."

in a time efficient manner—certainly in a cost efficient manner. Also, you are free to spend time on other impor-

	Time	Labor Cost/Hr.	Materials Cost	Total Cost
Labor (Yours, $15/hr.)	:30	$7.50	$1.25	$8.75
Labor (Assistant, $8/hr.)	:45	$6.00	$1.25	$7.25

tant areas of the business—shows, marketing, and promotions and training of additional assistants.

Overhead Costs

Overhead costs are defined as all the costs of products and services required to operate your business and studio, such as your rent and your phone bill. These are known as **fixed costs**, meaning that they are the same from month to month, whether you make ten items or 100 items.

Any cost that isn't easily figured into the activities of production or sales is considered an overhead cost. For craftspeople, overhead costs are the first place to look for budget cuts. Keeping overhead down, and production and sales up, is the key to adding to your own income.

Selling Costs

Selling costs—or the cost of sale—is the most important and most misunderstood element in pricing: It can be the deciding factor in determining whether "you make it or break it" as a professional craftsperson.

Keep in mind that time spent selling your product is **time spent away from production and the creation of new designs**. You must account for the time you spend packing and unpacking your work for shows, or the expense of business cards or brochures handed out to customers. Forget these selling costs and you will watch your profits erode! As one artist says, "You don't see it until you're not making it!"

The cost of sale is higher in retail sales since the expense and effort involved in selling the crafts product falls directly on you or on the retailer. This also explains why most stores **keystone**, or double, the wholesale price to arrive at the retail price. You may even find stores that mark up craft items more than 200% to cover the cost of a great location or the expense of a glossy Christmas catalog that includes your work!

Profit

Most entrepreneurs think of profit as all the money that's left over after expenses, but many make the mistake of confusing profit with "bonus" or "salary." Profit is neither. Profit is the "cushion" that provides you with **growth**

Thomas Mann:
Adding Apprentices into His Pricing Formula

Thomas Mann, of Thomas Mann Design, believes that apprentices are the key ingredient in his personal pricing equation. Thomas employs nearly thirty people in his two New Orleans shops. Of these thirty people, fourteen of them work directly under Thomas, executing his designs. "In my company we have three levels of apprenticeship: trainee, apprentice, and artisan," Thomas explains. "Only 20% of people who begin as trainees end up as artisans."

Thomas believes that without his apprentices, he could not produce his jewelry at its current price. "My principal concept is to provide jewelry with a high degree of aesthetic content at an affordable price," he says. "The only way I can make a reasonable income is based on quantity." So, to produce his designs in a high quantity, apprentices are crucial.

"Apprenticeships are beneficial," Thomas says, and he speaks from experience. Thomas was an apprentice himself, in Allentown, Pennsylvania.

"But only for a short time," he laughs. "I'm a quick study."

cash and keeps the bill collectors away when things are tight. Profit is not an option; it is a necessary part of your operating expenses, and it must not be compromised for any reason.

Use Thomas Mann's pricing form to work out the various expenses that comprise your wholesale price.

Wholesale Price

Too often, after you add up all the costs of production, overhead, selling, and profit, you discover that a pair of ceramic earrings will price out at the unreasonable amount of $40 wholesale!

Here's where your creativity is put to its best use in business. Go over all the numbers and seek ways to reduce costs. Overhead is where you can usually find the best possibilities for budget cuts. Sometimes an additional assistant can bring down the cost of production. Perhaps a new tool might cut production time for each piece. You might also choose to work an additional five hours a week, thus reducing your hourly rate. After you are satisfied with your adjustments, it's time to bring the marketplace into the equation.

Wholesale Price vs. Market Price

How does your wholesale price measure up in the marketplace? There's really only one way to find out—visit a craft retailer. Select a retail store that best suits your product. Remember that stores in the midwest may not be able to get the same price as a store in a popular resort area.

Talk to a few retailers. Don't ask questions that require only a "yes" or "no" answer. "Do you like my work?" is not appropriate for this exercise. Here is a short list of the type of questions you might ask if you are researching functional glass:

- **What type of customer buys glass in your store?**
- **What price points of paperweights do you carry?**
- **What price point in lamps sells best?**
- **What kind of information does your customer want with his or her purchase?**

The answers to these questions will help you determine if a particular gallery is the right forum for your work. Whenever possible, visit the shop or gallery for a first hand impression. This is often the best way to determine if your product fits the style and the price point that the gallery has been successful in presenting to its customers.

Clarksville Pottery: Gallery Owner and Artist Offer Advice on Relationships with Retailers

Syd and Arnie Popinsky, owners of Clarksville Pottery, provide new artists with an education upon visiting their shop. Arnie, and the apprentices in the shop, create approximately 25% of the ceramics sold at Clarksville Pottery, so when Arnie gives advice, it's from personal experience as an artist and a retailer.

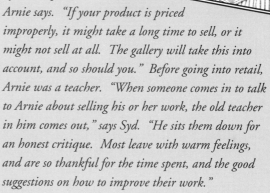

"My first recommendation is to visit the gallery or shop, to see if what you make fits—in style, and price,"
Arnie says. "If your product is priced improperly, it might take a long time to sell, or it might not sell at all. The gallery will take this into account, and so should you." Before going into retail, Arnie was a teacher. "When someone comes in to talk to Arnie about selling his or her work, the old teacher in him comes out," says Syd. "He sits them down for an honest critique. Most leave with warm feelings, and are so thankful for the time spent, and the good suggestions on how to improve their work."

Another thing the Popinskys look for is whether a craftsperson is ready to do business with them. "So many people who come in here don't have a price list or invoices, or anything," Arnie observes. "An accurate price list is important when you are selling to galleries." Arnie's advice has helped many artists refine their work. "So many of the people I 'counsel' are back within a year or two with work that can be sold with us, or with another gallery," Arnie says. "That's what makes it worthwhile."

OVERHEAD COSTS FORM

NOTE: Insert costs that <u>do not</u> pertain directly to production selling. For the % of total, do this calculation last, as a percentage of the total overhead costs.

ITEM	BUDGET ESTIMATE	ACTUAL	% TOTAL	MONTHLY EXPENSE
Rent/Mortgage				
Real Estate Taxes				
Utilities				
Telephone				
Property Insurance				
Fire/Casualty Insurance				
Equipment (All)				
Health Insurance				
Stationery/ Office Supplies				
Packaging				
Maintenance/ Cleaning				
Freight				
Payroll Taxes				
Payroll (Non-production)				
Loss due to breakage, theft				
Bad Debts				
Professional Fees				
Entertainment				
Publications/ Memberships				
TOTAL				

SELLING COSTS FORM

NOTE: Insert costs that pertain <u>directly</u> to production selling. Add your own labor involved in the activity of selling. Think about the amount of work you cannot produce when you are selling instead of creating! (This will be calculated later.)

ITEM	BUDGET ESTIMATE	ACTUAL	% TOTAL	MONTHLY EXPENSE
Advertising				
Show Fees				
Samples				
Commissions				
Photography				
Printing (brochures, cards)				
Sales Labor (yours and others)				
Travel				
Meals/ Entertainment				
Credit Card Processing Equip.				
Credit Card Process Bank Fees				
Postage (brochures, invites)				
TOTAL				

Crafting As a Business

A FORMULA FOR PRICING

COSTS TO CONSIDER IN ANY INDIVIDUAL PIECE:

- Labor & Materials
- Overhead
- Profit

LABOR & MATERIALS

A. Labor/Yours and Others
1. Training time for helpers
2. Fair wages for semi-skilled or skilled labor
3. What you must pay yourself to keep from getting another job!

B. Materials
1. Metals, stones, etc.
2. Supplies (saw blades, drills, etc.)
3. Shipping of same

OVERHEAD

A. Studio Costs
1. Rent/mortgage (interest on financing)
2. Insurance
3. Utilities
4. Maintenance

B. Marketing
1. Entry fees, booth fees, agent commissions
2. Travel expenses
3. Labor/yours and others
4. Cost of displays
5. Photography
6. Printing/mailing
7. Phone/utilities

PROFIT

1. To create a business cushion
2. To create a self-serving business grant (who needs the NEA, anyway?)
3. To give, a way to help others (tax deductible)
4. To finance your kids' education
5. To have fun (retirement, we all do it, then we die)

GUIDELINES

1. Labor/materials should not exceed 1/6 of Retail Price or 1/3 of Wholesale*
2. Wholesale is 3x materials/labor*
3. 1/3 of wholesale is for studio, overhead, and marketing*
4. 1/3 of wholesale is profit*

REMEMBER: There is always something to be said for CASH FLOW!

Compliments of Thomas Mann Reproduced from © *Design for Survival*

*Tom is a jeweler working in New Orleans, LA. Materials and geographic variances
may be different for each artist's work.*

Networking

5

Nothing is more dangerous than an idea,
when it's the only one we have.
—Emile Auguste Chartier

■ NETWORKING: ■
HOW CAN IT BENEFIT YOU?

Working alone may sound like a great option, but it can be to your disadvantage. It is far better to build a network of other craft artists, gallery or retail shop owners, and professional support, such as lawyers and accountants, than to attempt to go it alone. Family members and friends may provide you with excellent emotional support, but other people who have started and run small businesses (experts) are the kind of practical network necessary to survive in this competitive market. Forming a craftsperson roundtable is one idea that can be put to good use. Seek out people from your area, either through classes, or at local shows. Arrange to meet on a regular basis to discuss ideas, business, or marketing techniques.

In this type of forum, you can learn about mistakes others have made before you make them yourself! This is also a great way to learn about new retail opportunities.

Another idea to help you create a support network: **community studios**. All over the country, studio complexes are being formed informally by artists who find a great location that is too large for themselves alone, so they sublet space to others. Other community studios are formal organizations, with selection processes, artist managers, and educational programs. Many of these studios also have shared equipment like kilns and glory holes.

Sergio Lub: Craft Co-op Strengthens All Participants

Sergio Lub developed a co-op called On-Approval, to share with others what he had learned about the business of craft. Sergio has found that On-Approval provides a network of artists from different media to share marketing expenses, and to provide support.

On-Approval began with eight artists, one from each craft medium, who worked together to build their businesses. One of the ideas they employed was co-op advertising—sharing the cost of a single ad that promoted them all. Another idea was a way of referring "approved" buyers to other co-op members. Today, the co-op is now primarily a roundtable, where the artists get together several times a year to share experiences and questions. Their discussions encompass such issues as workmen's compensation, successful trade shows, product packaging, and new exporting regulations, to name just a few.

"One of my rules is to only do business with people you like," Sergio says. His co-op provides him with built-in support that helps him stand out among other craft artists. Sergio strongly believes that trust is an important factor when doing business, and co-ops, or roundtables, forge friendships and build business contacts.

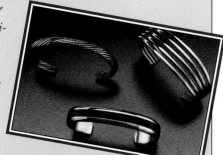

The Mill Centre: A Model Community for Artisans

The Mill Centre is an artist's community, located in a restored 19th-century textile mill in Baltimore, MD. Available in the Mill Centre are offices, artist and photography studios and galleries, offered to artists at affordable rates.

"Places like this are hard to find," says a sculptor, who speaks from experience. "It's a whole combination of things that makes it such a good place to work." Some of the "extras" offered at the Mill Centre include receptionist services, photocopying privileges, on-site management, gallery space, loading docks, and much more. Cathy Hart, a potter at the Mill Centre, believes that the camaraderie makes her more creative. "There are tremendous benefits to having other artists around," Cathy says. "When I worked at my home by myself, I often got into ruts, and my work became stagnant, here, all of the creative energy keeps you going." Cathy also feels that such events like the **Arts Weekend** would not be possible if she were the only artist in a building. "There is definitely power in numbers," Cathy says. "Twice a year we have an open house, for which we all send invitations, and invite the public to see what we do, and hopefully, we attract new customers. Alone, none of us could attract this much attention."

The Mill Centre is home to more than 50 artists. For more information on the Mill Centre, please call: (410) 366-MILL.

photo by Aaron M. Levin

Craft Guilds

A **guild** is defined as an association of persons of the same trade or similar pursuits, formed to protect mutual interests and to maintain standards. In crafts, a guild refers to artists who create in the same media, or in the same geographical area. Most craft guilds require their members to pay annual dues in exchange for services available to them. Some of these services can include publications or newsletters, craft and business workshops, show promotions, local craft fairs and invitations to participate in various exhibits.

See our "Guilds & Associations" listing in the Resources section

The Craft Emergency Relief Fund: There When Artists Need Assistance

The Craft Emergency Relief Fund, or CERF, is a good name to know when disaster strikes. "CERF is a non-profit foundation which provides immediate support to professional craftspeople suffering career-threatening emergencies such as fire, theft, illness, or natural disaster," explains Lois Ahrens, director of CERF. CERF is able to provide "loans" with no payback date to craftspeople who derive most of their income from selling their work. "It's more like a family fund than a loan," Lois believes.

In addition to loans averaging one thousand dollars, CERF is able to donate services ranging from a one-year subscription to The Crafts Report to waived booth fees at shows. "Many promoters are willing to waive their fees," says Lois. Many suppliers are also affiliated with CERF, so when an artist is eligible for a loan, he or she can also receive discounts on supplies.

In the last year, CERF has given assistance to craftspeople who have been financially wiped out by hurricanes, earthquakes, mudslides, and fire, injured in falls, or taken ill with cancer. "We won't give help to people who have financially over-extended themselves, or who have created a new line that hasn't sold," Lois says. "But we try to help those who have had disasters that were beyond their control." For more information on CERF, call: (413) 586-5898, or write: CERF, 245 Main St., #203, Northampton, MA 01060.

James and Deborah Greene: Affiliation With Organizations Proves Profitable

Life Celebrations, James and Deborah Greene's wearable fiber company, began by chance. But it has been the support of groups like the Kentucky Art and Craft Foundation that has kept their business growing.

James has always been a painter. "I thought of myself as a serious artist," says James. "Not someone who painted material for clothing." After much urging from Deborah, James agreed to paint some fabric for a dress Deborah wanted to make for the grand opening of the Radisson Hotel in Lexington, KY. James and Deborah attended the gala, and were met with many admiring gazes. Finally, a woman approached them, said she was the hotel developer's wife, and explained that she wanted to buy the dress, right then. "And that's how Life Celebrations was born," says James with a chuckle.

From that point on, James and Deborah have been going non-stop. But James believes, without the support of local groups, they might have stalled out long ago. The couple's hard work and excellent craftsmanship caught the eye of The Kentucky Art and Craft Foundation, which has since been one of Life Celebration's biggest fans. "A few years ago, the Kentucky Art and Craft Foundation made a video about local artists that included us," James explains. "That video was seen by many people, and it really gave our business a push, and added credibility."

Since then, Life Celebrations has been involved with many groups which support all kinds of Kentucky crafts, from the Governor's Derby Breakfast to the Louisville Craftsman's Guild. James encourages artists to stick with their craft, as long as it is something that they love. "Do what you like, and do what you feel first," James believes. "The love must be there, because there are times when you are working too hard, and the love will keep you going."

FINDING ■ THE RIGHT ■ PROFESSIONAL

How do you know when you need an accountant or a lawyer? How do you know when you have chosen the right professional to suit your business needs? Many business people seek an accountant or a lawyer from a big firm with a name people recognize. This isn't always the right professional for you, and you might be paying a lot more money for things that you can do yourself.

The right professional is someone who understands your business, your industry, your financial situation, and most important, speaks your language. This is also someone who will let you know when you can do something yourself to save money. For example, you can save money by picking up documents yourself from your lawyer or accountant's office instead of having the documents messengered to you. Also, you can participate by doing some background research, instead of having your lawyer's staff do it themselves.

To find the right accountant or lawyer, ask around within your industry. People love to make suggestions about the professional they have chosen. If the same names come up again and again, you're on to something! Make an appointment to meet with anyone you are interested in doing business with. Remember, you are hiring this person, and you would never hire anyone without an interview, would you? Ask questions about the clients he or she represents. See how knowledgeable the professional is about your industry, and specifically, how interested he or she is to learn more about it! If you are then satisfied, invite him or her to visit the studio to see you in action.

Here are some of the ways that an accountant and a lawyer can assist in building your business:

ACCOUNTANT

- Keeping you up-to-date on tax laws, and how they affect you
- Assisting you in setting up an efficient record-keeping system
- Advising you on the feasibility of business growth
- Explaining the necessary paperwork you will need as an employer
- Providing technical support in all financial matters
- Preparing tax returns

LAWYER

- Helping you to avoid any liability problems
- Counseling you on trademarks, patents, and copyrights of products
- Conducting trademark, patent, and copyright searches for your business name, product, and product lines
- Filing any documents relating to incorporation
- Advising you about contracts and business concerns

SIX STEPS TO CHOOSING A LAWYER AND AN ACCOUNTANT

by Rita A. Linder, Esquire, and Charles H. Geser, C.P.A.

1. Make certain your prospective professional concentrates on small businesses. Many lawyers and accountants who deal primarily with large corporations or work in large firms do not have any idea about a small business owner's problems.

2. Check out referrals from current clients. Ask if they are satisfied with the overall service and how the professional contributes to the profitability of the business. Bear in mind that attorneys and accountants are ethically prohibited from disclosing names of clients without their consent.

3. Ask exactly who within the firm will be functioning as your advisor. You could be referred to a well known professional who then assigns your work to a novice associate.

4. Does your prospective professional keep abreast of legal and tax law changes? Ask about new or pending issues that might affect your business. Is there a newsletter detailing this information? Does your lawyer or accountant attend continuing education seminars?

5. Know in advance what, how, and when you will be billed for professional services. Are fee schedules negotiable? Is interest charged on past-due accounts?

6. As far as choosing a CPA versus a non-certified accountant, much depends on your needs and your state's and bank's requirements. All attorneys must be licensed by the state in which they practice, and many belong to specialized professional organizations. There are advanced professional degrees in both law and accounting. Once you have confirmed these credentials, select the individual with whom you feel the most comfortable.

Rita Linder is a partner in the law firm of Abramoff, Neuberger and Linder in Baltimore, MD. Charles Geser is a partner in the accounting firm of Milstein and Geser in Towson, MD. Both Rita and Chuck speak at craft workshops and seminars across the country.

Printed with the permission of IB: Independent Business Magazine.

EIGHT QUESTIONS TO ASK YOURSELF ABOUT YOUR PROFESSIONAL

1. Does your professional explain all costs to you before they are incurred?

2. Is your professional easy to reach, or do you feel sometimes that you are getting the run-around?

3. When speaking with your professional, do you sense that he or she values your business?

4. Is work completed within a reasonable amount of time (and is it right the first time)?

5. Does your professional know about your line of business, or is he or she willing to learn?

6. Has your professional made you aware of how new tax laws or legislation might affect your business in the future?

7. Does your professional make recommendations on how to save money on legal or accounting fees?

8. Do you believe that your professional is an asset to your business?

PATENTS & COPYRIGHTS: ▪ USES IN CRAFT ▪

By Kurt G. Calia, Esquire

WHAT IS A PATENT?

A patent is an exclusive right to prevent others from making, using, or selling your invention without your express permission. Patents are a form of limited monopoly granted to encourage the research and development of useful inventions. The life of a U.S. utility patent is seventeen years from the date it is granted. Patents in the United States exist under federal law only.

Federal statutes only allow for patents on certain types of inventive creations. The basic categories for patentable subject matter are:

1) Processes: electrical, chemical, or mechanical procedures, such as a method of smelting iron, or a chemical reaction which yields a new material.

2) Machines: ranging from complex machinery, such as microprocessors, to simple machines, like a pulley.

3) Articles of Manufacture: objects used to create other things, like hand tools.

4) Compositions of Matter: things such as a new chemical compound, or a metal alloy.

5) Any New and Useful Improvement to Any of the Above.

Patents generally do not extend to forms of creative expression or designs, like sculpture. If, however, a design is a part of any of the above, then a patent may be granted on the design.

Any invention which fits into one of the above categories can be considered for a patent as long as it meets three more requirements. First, the invention must have a useful purpose. In legal terms, this is called the **utility requirement**. Second, the invention must be new. If the invention is known, or used by others in the United States, or if it is patented elsewhere before the date of invention, then it is unpatentable. In addition, certain activities can negate the ability to obtain patent protection. If the invention is patented or described in a printed publication, or in public use or on sale in the U.S. more than one year before the date of filing, it is unpatentable. Finally, the creation must not be something that is obvious to a person of ordinary skill in the particular art of that invention. This requirement is known as **nonobviousness**.

As a craft artist, the patent you should be most aware of is a **design patent**. Design patents are awarded to new ornamental designs for articles of manufacture. A design may consist of surface ornamentation, shape, or a combination of both. For this patent, you still must fulfill the utility and novelty requirements and it must be nonobvious, but much more leeway is provided. For example, you cannot patent an ordinary chair, but you could patent a chair with unusual carvings and features. It is in your best interest to consult an attorney if a design patent is what you seek.

WHAT IS THE BENEFIT OF A PATENT?

In simple terms, a patent is actually a right to prohibit or exclude others from making, using, or selling the patented invention. Patent law also provides guidelines for filing lawsuits against anyone who infringes upon a patent right. Damages can be recovered by the inventor from the date of infringement only if the product is properly marked with the U.S. patent number. The patentee may also be able to obtain an injunction to prevent the infringer from making, using, or selling the invention.

WHAT IS A COPYRIGHT?

A copyright is a legal right to exclusive publication, production, sale, or distribution of a tangible creative expression. Like patents, copyrights are covered by federal law, and may also obtain international protection. Copyright protection of crafts may be easier to attain than patent protection, because the patent requirements may be more difficult to satisfy. Copyrights protect creative expression in many forms—literature, paintings, sculptural works, films, music, etc. Copyright protection can extend to such commercial products as catalogs, advertising materials, decorative designs or products, fabric designs and patterns, and even computer programs. Copyright protection is also available for compilations, or works derived from one or more existing works (called **derivative works**). An example of a **derivative work** is a movie based upon a novel.

All works must be in a **fixed medium of expression** to obtain a copyright. For example, one cannot copyright mental plans for a ceramic vase, but the vase itself may be copyrightable. In addition, the work cannot be so elementary that it lacks **sufficient creativity** to obtain a copyright. An artist, for example, cannot copyright the shape of a circle, yet an artist can incorporate a circle into a work that can be copyrighted. Most crafts will be in a **fixed medium of expression**, and of **sufficient creativity** to obtain a copyright.

WHAT IS THE BENEFIT OF A COPYRIGHT?

Copyrights give the owner several exclusive rights: The right to reproduce a work by making copies; the right to make **derivative works** based on the original work; the right to sell the work; the right to perform the work; the right to display the work; and the right to allow others to do so. If another person performs one of these tasks without the permission of the copyright holder, then that person may be liable for copyright infringement. Infringement may occur if the copyright owner is able to demonstrate that the infringer had access to the copyrighted work, and that the two works are substantially similar. Unlike patent law, however, if someone independently creates the same work, that person will not be liable for infringement. Copyright protects artists against unlawful copying or "knock offs" of their work. The available remedies include an injunction against further copying, an injunction compelling destruction of the infringing works, and monetary damages.

Photographing copyrighted works is a form of reproduction. This is one of the exclusive rights covered by the copyright. Unauthorized publication of photographs of copyrighted work may be infringement. For example, a craft retailer might purchase a work with the intent to sell it in his or her shop. The retailer might then photograph the work to use in advertising. Without the artist's permission, however, the act of photographing and publishing the photograph of the copyrighted work is infringement.

HOW CAN A CRAFTSPERSON APPLY FOR A COPYRIGHT?

An artist can apply for a copyright without the services of an attorney quite easily. Copyright protection begins as soon as the work is created in a fixed form. To obtain statutory damages for infringement, you must provide notice that the work is protected. To gain access to federal courts you must receive proper copyright registration. To let the public know that a work is protected, the piece should simply carry a copyright notice comprised of the symbol ©, the word "copyright," or the abbreviation "Copr.," together with the name of the copyright holder, and the year the product or work was first created.

The registration process has two parts: Making a deposit, and filling out a copyright application. The deposit and application requirements may be fulfilled by sending the Library of Congress two copies (photographs should do) of the work, a completed application, and a nominal fee. It is preferable to do so within three months of the creation of the work to preserve the right to statutory damages and attorney fees, should they be necessary. To receive information on copyright forms, call the **copyright hotline at (202) 287-9100, and request form VA for visual arts**.

HOW LONG DOES A COPYRIGHT LAST?

The general rule for duration of copyright protection for a work created on, or after January 1, 1978, is the author or artist's lifetime plus 50 years after his or her death. The copyright statute does provide for specific exemptions to infringement. A **fair use** defense to infringement exists for certain educational and religious uses. Also, some libraries and archives may be permitted to make single copies of a work under special circumstances.

FOR MOST CRAFTSPEOPLE, WHICH IS BETTER, A PATENT, OR A COPYRIGHT?

For crafts, copyright protection may be preferable to patent protection because a copyright is generally less costly to obtain. Also, since most crafts are more a form of creative expression than articles of manufacture (depending on the type of craft), copyright protection is more suitable. However, the protection afforded by patents and copyrights differs. Patents allow the patentee to keep others from making, using, or selling the invention. Copyrights only permit the owner to prevent others from copying their works.

Artisans deciding whether to pursue copyright or patent protection should consider what type of protection applies to their work. Also, one should consider what type of protection is desired, the duration of protection desired, the geographical scope needed, as well as the monetary investment required. Competent legal advice may be useful (although not required to obtain a patent or a copyright) because patent and copyright are rapidly changing areas of law, especially regarding new technology.

Kurt Calia is an associate at the law firm of Howson and Howson in Spring House, PA, specializing in intellectual property law.

HOW LONG WILL IT LAST?

WHAT TYPES OF CREATIONS ARE COVERED?

WHAT ARE THE REQUIREMENTS?

WHAT ARE THE BENEFITS?

DO YOU NEED A LAWYER?

U.S. PATENTS & COPYRIGHTS MADE EASY

PATENTS	COPYRIGHTS
17 years for utility patents. 14 years for design patents.	Lifetime plus 50 years (many exceptions).
Processes, machines, articles of manufacture, & compositions of matter.	Creative expression, such as: literature, paintings, sculpture, crafts, film, music, etc.
Must fit one of the four categories as listed above. Also, must be "useful" and "nonobvious."	Fixed medium of expression, sufficient creativity.
Protects against unauthorized production, use, or sale; infringers can be sued for monetary damages and/or sales can be halted.	Protects against unlawful copying of work; can get an injunction against infringer to prevent further copying, and have copied works destroyed; can sue infringer for monetary damages.
Is often helpful, strongly recommended, but not necessary.	Not necessary.

CHOOSING A COMPUTER SYSTEM
▪ FOR YOUR BUSINESS ▪

By Wayne Stahnke

The selection of your business computer system can be quite confusing. With a little bit of research and guidance, you will be able to make the decision that is right for your company. Remember, your decision could affect your business for years to come.

Your electronic office will be divided into two areas: **hardware** and **software**. The **hardware** consists of a printer, monitor, and accessories (i.e., mouse, scanner, modem, and network). The **software** are the programs (i.e., word processing, spreadsheet, database records management) which operate on the hardware you have chosen, and make the system work for you. If you have inadequate hardware, your software may not perform properly, if at all. It is advisable to choose your software package first, and then buy hardware that will allow the software to perform optimally.

Computer hardware is a very competitive business, and prices will vary between dealers. If you are new to computers, make sure that you buy your equipment from a dealer who can offer you service and support. Any experienced user can tell you just how valuable good technical support can be.

Selecting Software

There are literally hundreds of software programs available to help you run your business. They range in price from under $100 for a general program, to as high as $10,000 for a highly specialized package.

Usually, the less expensive programs are generalized for a wider range of users. Programs that are written for a specific group are usually more expensive, but have many features that the general programs lack.

As a craftsperson, you have needs that the majority of business programs do not address. Probably the single most important need is **production management**. **General business programs** usually create invoices, sales commissions, reports, and accounts receivable. To fully manage the production end of your business, you need much more. Information about product sales, who your best customers are, and buying trends by geographical area, will help you to make better, and more informed, business decisions. Without information on future orders, you may find yourself short of materials required for production, and end up paying overnight shipping fees to get materials fast!

Good production management software will also keep you informed of your future workload, so that you can plan ahead. Other important functions should include a U.P.S. shipping manager, to calculate your freight charges and make shipping labels. Also important is a report generator to send letters to your customers, handle consignment orders, and alert you when a customer must be called.

The selection of software is one of the most important choices that you can make in your business. Buy with growth and flexibility in mind. Make sure that you research ahead of time the limitations of the software. Software support is another important factor. Ask for a list of users whom you may call to get their opinions about the software, and the technical support. Find out what the support is limited to, for how long, and how much does additional support cost after the initial time period is up. Advances in software design are continuously being made. The software that you select should be flexible enough to take advantage of current technology. Ask when the program was last updated, and when the next update is planned. Also, make sure that you can return the software within a short period of time if it won't fit your needs. Most reputable software companies include this policy as part of their guarantee.

If you need assistance in choosing a computer program, there are a number of places that you can start looking.

• **Trade shows:** Software companies that make programs for your industry usually have a booth to demonstrate their software.

• **Industry publications:** Many software companies advertise their products in publications that their users read.

• **Other artists:** Ask around at your next show, or make a few phone calls. You might get as many suggestions as people you talk to!

Then, make a choice and get started. The longer you wait to get into business computing, the longer it will take to make a profit on your investment. You'll never know how you managed without your new computer!

Wayne Stahnke is an independent software developer, specializing in database solutions for the craft and gift industry. His business, called "Office Mate," is located in Irvine, CA.

The CompuServe Crafts Forum: A Network for Craftspeople to Share Ideas

CompuServe, an on-line computer network, offers the craftsperson access to a global community of artisans with its Crafts Forum. On Crafts Forum, artists can share ideas ranging from craft techniques to strategies for improving their craft businesses. As a participant on the network, you have the opportunity to "pick the brains" of other artists who share many of the same questions and concerns you have.

CompuServe's Crafts Forum is divided into a variety of areas of interest, including glass, ceramics, knitting, quilting, and weaving, to name a few. Within each category there are three main functions: the message board; the libraries, where text and graphics files are stored; and the conference rooms, where actual meetings take place.

Perhaps of greatest interest to craftspeople is the Crafts Forum's collection of shareware. Shareware is public domain software, and demonstrator versions of software that are of interest to the crafts community. For more information on CompuServe, call (800)848-8199, operator #304.

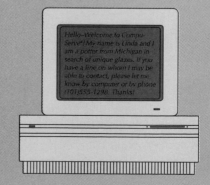

Hello-Welcome to CompuServe! My name is Linda and I am a potter from Michigan in search of unique glazes. If you have a line on whom I may be able to contact, please let me know by computer or by phone (101)555-1298. Thanks!

Your Image

It is better to be making the news than taking it;
to be an actor rather than a critic.
—Winston Churchill

■ YOUR IMAGE ■

The person most in control of creating a positive or negative image for your craft business is you! What differentiates you from everyone else is the way you present yourself to the craft-buying public. For this phase of your business, self-promotion and public relations are as important as your product.

Eye-catching designs and logos create interest, but it is the content, or the **whole package** that is going to make you stand out to a customer. Promoting yourself is an art that can take a number of forms, from printed materials to direct mail catalogs. Learning how to best present yourself in print to the public is the first step in making a name for yourself.

Ray Tracey: Successful PR Strategies Help Artist to Create an Image

Ray Tracey of Tracey, Ltd. came back to being a full-time craftsperson after a brief career as an actor in Hollywood. He had a feature role in the movie "Seems Like Old Times" with Chevy Chase and Goldie Hawn, and a lead in the movie "Joe Panther." During the Screen Actors Guild strike, Ray realized that being an actor did not provide the steady income that he needed to raise a family. Ray had been creating jewelry as a hobby for quite a while, and so he decided to start his own jewelry business.

"The thing I learned most from acting was how to create an image through marketing," Ray says. "As an actor, you need to promote yourself, or have an agent to do your advertising for you," says Ray. "The same holds true for any small business, especially crafts." Realizing that his strength did not lie in business and marketing, Ray hired Kristin Middleton to meet his business and public relations needs. "Hiring Kristin is probably the

smartest thing I've ever done [in business]," Ray believes. "You can never promote yourself as well as someone who believes in you can."

Ray's advice for those starting out is to realize your personal limitations. "Recognize what you do well, and seek someone out to do the other things," Ray says. He also believes in developing a good mailing list to let customers know where you will be and when. Tracey, Ltd. sends out postcards before every show to customers in the geographical region of the event. "It's amazing when people approach me at my booth holding my postcard," Ray exclaims. "It reminds me of how well a good list can work."

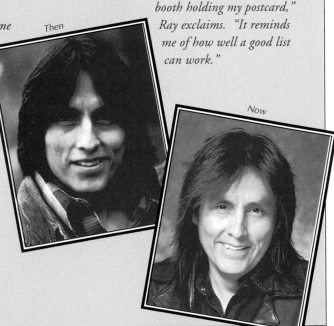

Then

Now

An example of a hang tag from Gango Gallery featuring the work of Sandra Magsamen.

SANDRA MAGSAMEN

An artist who explains her [...] as being "scenes from my [...] that's what you see," Sandr[...] Magsamen's storybook wo[...] full of color and life. Sandr[...] professional life is a challe[...] combination of her work a[...] as well as art therapy con[...] the elderly. Her work is exh[...] several galleries througho[...] United States.

Gango
GALLERY

GANGO GALLERY
205 S.W. FIRST
PORTLAND, OREGON 97204

Hang Tag

The message written on your hang tag is often the only information your customer will ever read about you. Let the paper, type style, and ink color make a statement about you and your work. Include a brief sentence or two, your photograph, and care and cleaning instructions for the piece.

Do not print your address or phone number on a hang tag. This would allow gallery customers to call you directly, circumventing the gallery entirely! Shop and gallery owners need to know that they won't be bypassed for the next sale.

The Benefit of Postcards

Postcards just may be the most important first investment for your business—they can serve as business cards or invitations to your studio, an exhibition, or an upcoming fair. They can also serve as great selling tools for retailers who might want to tell their customers about your work.

It is best to print postcards with little or nothing printed on the back—your local printer can personalize them a batch at a time as needed for special

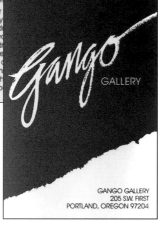

events throughout the year. Make sure you order enough for you and for your gallery accounts.

Don't think that you have to give the postcards to the galleries and shops—most retailers are quite willing to pay for the postcards to help offset your printing costs. Where else could they get a beautiful color mailer for a few cents a piece? Survey your retail accounts before placing an order with the printer—you may be pleasantly surprised with their enthusiasm.

◾ DESIGNING DYNAMIC ◾ PROMOTIONAL MATERIALS

When you contact buyers through the mail, you compete with all the other items they receive—mail that isn't as important as checks and bills! Many people review their mail while standing over the trash can—think about that while designing your promotional pieces. Each day your customers (retailers or consumers) receive brochures and price lists from large manufacturers as well as from small companies and individuals.

Your promotional materials must reflect your business—but they should also reflect **YOU!** Make sure your materials project your creativity, warmth, sincerity, and positive attitude. Highlight your individuality and design talents; use them as assets. Whether you will be designing your own brochure, stationery, business cards, hang tags or postcards, or hiring a graphic designer or ad agency, it's best to **ask yourself these questions first:**

1) Does your audience know who you are? Tell the reader something about yourself that is expressed through your work. Use graphics, type, and even paper and ink colors that reflect your design and artistic voice.

2) In what sequence would you like your reader to see your message? A good design leads your eye across a page in the exact sequence you intended. The reader's eye should naturally follow across the top, left to right, then diagonally across, down to the bottom left, then the bottom right of the page. Special folds, flaps, and splashes of color can do the trick for brochures and newsletters as well.

3) What do you want emphasized? Sure, everything is important, but some things are more important than others. Draw up an outline and assign values (A,B,C,D) to information, and then "weigh" them graphically from most to least important. Then use such devices as large type, bold type, and reverse

graphics. **Remember,** be concise and to the point. Many people are put off by too many words.

4) Who is your audience? Tailor each printed message to its specific target audience. Be aware of who you are contacting and what might excite or intimidate them. For instance, a slick, sophisticated, New York ad agency-looking brochure mailed to craft retailers may be well received by high-end galleries, yet ignored by mid-range stores because it "looks too expensive," or too much like that of a large manufacturer.

5) What is the action you desire? An order?—A phone call?—A visit to your booth? Good design will initiate the appropriate action—but be sure to say it CLEARLY!

6) Is this the right message at the right time? Who is getting your brochure? Buyers from summer tourist areas aren't likely to buy from you in August! Likewise, buyers in winter resort areas won't buy from you in March, and college and university retailers don't buy in June. Watch your calendar, and try to time your mailings for best impact.

7) Which style is best? All day long you see signs, posters, billboards, brochures, and stationery with exciting ideas which you could later use. Notice which of these pieces look best and why. You may be able to glean a few good ideas for your own ad campaign.

8) What is your budget? Don't overlook the value of a four-color brochure or color sheet. Four-color costs have been drastically reduced by companies that specialize in color sheets and postcards for product—some will even photograph the work for you. Check the phone book under **printers**, and shop around.

CREATING A BROCHURE
Your Checklist

Items for Inclusion	Omit	Needs To Be Done	Needs Updating	Completed
Cover Design				
Back Page				
Photos of Your Work				
Shows You Do				
Awards				
Artistic Philosophy				
Descriptive Copy				
Professional Artist Portrait				
Type Style				
Layout				
Color and Type of Paper				
Weight of Paper				
Name of Company				
Address/Phone Number				
Testimonials *(gallery and shop owners, or collectors are the best!)*				
Quantity				
Inserts *(biographical information, price lists, etc.)*				
Print Production Options				
Graphics				
Logo				

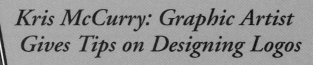

Kris McCurry: Graphic Artist
Gives Tips on Designing Logos

Kris McCurry, graphic artist, designs everything from logos to ads for craftspeople.

Kris believes that a good logo can be your passport to new business. "An eye-catching logo can make a great first impression, or it can create an immediate disinterest," Kris says. "Because of this, developing a strong logo is a key factor for any business."

When designing your logo, Kris makes these suggestions:

• Consult a graphic designer before sending your logo to the printer.
A designer can tell you what will and won't work visually. A designer can also help you stay within your budget when it comes time for printing. Sometimes a colorful logo can look nice, but cost a fortune to print.

Hint: Keep your logo to one or two colors at the most. This will save you money on printing costs.

• For what purposes will you use your logo (i.e. cards, stationery, signage)?
When logos are reproduced on business cards, they must be recognizable at a small size. A business card is 3 1/2" x 2", with generally less than 30% of that space allotted for a logo. If you plan to use a logo on a sign, remember that it must be recognizable at a glance. Too much wording is likely to be passed by.

• Will an icon (symbol) or a name convey a better understanding of the business?
If your business bears your name, unless you are world-famous, you should consider using a symbol to let the public know what it is you do. For example, if you are a fabric weaver, and your business name is Dorothy Smith, Handweaver, you could try a weaving icon:

• Does the style of the logo accurately represent your style?
The above sample indicates a classic style. Changing it slightly can create an entirely different interpretation:

Now the logo gives the impression of a looser, more whimsical style.

The bottom line is to develop a logo with as much thought and pride as you do your own product, because that is what it will represent.

YOUR PR AND MARKETING NEEDS

Type of Material	Not Needed	Needed	Needs Updating	Completed
Advertisements				
Brochures				
Business Cards				
Catalogs				
Envelopes				
Fliers				
Letterhead				
Logo				
Photos of Yourself				
Photos of Work				
Portfolio				
Postcards				
Press Packets				
Press Releases				
Resumes				
Slides/Transparencies				
Other _____				
_____				

THE ELEMENTS OF
A GOOD PRESS RELEASE

When creating your press release, remember that you have only a second or two to capture a busy reporter's attention. With this in mind, your words must be concise and articulate. That's right, you get to be an editor, too. And this time, YOU are creating the news, including selecting a headline, writing the body copy, and choosing corresponding photos. The following steps will help you to present interesting, newsworthy information to all of your media contacts.

THE HEADLINE

Every press release needs a headline. Your headline should summarize the entire release, but must also grab the reader's attention. Here are some headline examples for a jeweler who is promoting a new line of earrings, depicting endangered animals:

Jane Johnson Creates New Line of Jewelry   OK
Local Jeweler Promotes Endangered Species   Better

Notice how the second headline gives the media contact a better news angle. It is written as though the newspaper will take the release and run it verbatim, which is precisely what you want. The other difference is that the second headline ties the jeweler in with a national concern—that of promoting and protecting the world's endangered wildlife. Any other ties Jane has to wildlife protection organizations, like donating a small portion of her sales from a particular show, should be elaborated within the body of the release.

IN THE BEGINNING

The first paragraph of the press release should present the information by telling who, what, where, when, how, and why, in a brief and interesting way. Like the headline, the first paragraph of a release, known as the lead must be designed to capture the reader's attention, and to "explain" why this information is indeed worthy of attention.

THE END

Non-essential information belongs at the end of a press release. Imagine that your press release is an inverted pyramid, with the most important information on the top, and the least important information following. Editors generally cut from the bottom of an article if they don't have room for an entire piece. If an editor has space only for the first paragraph, has it been written so that it covers the basics?

After the last paragraph of the release, place three pound signs (###), or a dash thirty dash (-30-) to indicate the end of the information that needs to be typeset. After one of these symbols, you can write a brief note to the editor or contact concerning further instructions.

Reporters and editors like to receive information that is crafted to meet their needs. Calendar editors want brief notices on special events and exhibitions. Feature editors should receive a detailed press kit, including slides, transparencies, and black and white glossy photographs, because they often do full layouts. If you loan photography and want it returned in good condition, provide a stamped, self-addressed, padded envelope for its safe return. Be sure to put your name and address on slide mounts and on the backs of photos. Be aware that an editor putting together a four-color publication may tie up your photographs or slides for several weeks.

The Press Release Format

The essential element in a public relations campaign is the press release—typed, double-spaced paragraphs of copy, headed by:

Date (and usually city)
For Immediate Release
    OR: **For Release on** (date)
Contact: Jane Artist,
    (phone number and studio address,
        unless you are using letterhead.)

SAMPLE PRESS RELEASE

FOR IMMEDIATE RELEASE

Contact: Jane Armstrong
Phone (410)555-1437
Telefax (410)555-7171
2322 Green Road
Bethesda, MD 20742

Gets right to the point!

Jane Armstrong Offers "Transitional Vessels" to Interior Designers

July 20, 1993, Bethesda, MD—Jane Armstrong, a professional potter living and producing pottery in Bethesda, Maryland, announces the release of a new line of decorative pottery geared especially for interior designers. The new line is called "Transitional Vessels," and is already in demand by professional designers in the United States and abroad.

A special exhibition of Jane Armstrong's Transitional Vessels opens August 15 at Objects for the Home, a gallery of decorative accessories located at 6824 Riverside Avenue in Gaithersburg, Maryland. Marianne Martin, owner of Objects for the Home, is the host for this exhibition.

Credibility as a local news item

Ms. Armstrong conceived of her new body of work while talking with a friend, Mark Brody, a residential interior designer in Bethesda. "Many of Mark's clients love handcrafted vases, but the ones that are too strictly traditional or too contemporary are difficult to blend into his somewhat eclectic interiors," Ms. Armstrong says. Mr. Brody concurs: "The transitional series blends well with any number of different styles of home decor, including southwestern, country, contemporary, even traditional homes using a lot of antiques."

Tells how and why

The Transitional Vessels feature classic shapes and rich burnished glazes in colors that vary between russet and amber. They are a clear departure—both in form and in execution—from work typically produced by this accomplished American potter. Vessels in the new series range from $40 to $120 wholesale, with a minimum order of $200 required of qualified retailers.

Descriptive facts

Jane Armstrong has been a professional potter for twelve years, and her work is available throughout the United States. Ms. Armstrong graduated with honors from the University of Maryland, and also attended the Maryland Institute of Art, studying ceramics under the guidance of Dr. Stuart South. Ms. Armstrong has instructed students in the various principles of ceramics, including slab building and porcelain glazing techniques, at the Arrowmont School of Crafts in Tennessee in 1985 and 1986.

Brief background information

###

Note: A selection of 35mm slides and black and white glossy photographs of the artist and her work are available upon request—call: (410)555-1437.

Instructions to the editor

FINDING THE RIGHT PUBLICATION
■ FOR YOUR PRESS RELEASE ■

The most effective way to research a publication is to subscribe. That way, you will receive each issue and can scrutinize what kind of stories are published and who writes the various features. Most magazines post a publisher's statement on either the editorial page or the masthead (listing staff names, subscription information, and publisher's statement). The statement often describes the magazine's editorial style. Your local library stores copies of *Standard Rate and Data Service* (SRDS) and *Bacon's Publicity Checker*—comprehensive directories listing every PR resource imaginable, including date of inception, editorial slant, and the names of current editors. (SRDS is geared more towards advertising than Bacon's.)

The Public Relations Society of America (PRSA) has chapters in major cities throughout the United States. You do not have to be a professional publicist to attend their monthly luncheons and seminars. PRSA invites a wide variety of print and broadcast media people to speak at chapter meetings, providing a wealth of information for PR experts and novices alike.

Many professional craftspeople also send information to national magazines such as *Metropolitan Home, Elle Decor, Vogue,* and *Ladies' Home Journal. Omni,* the science magazine, featured the blown glass planets of Josh Simpson, a professional craftsman from Massachusetts, several years ago. The possibilities are endless for American craftspeople who want to harness the power of the press because:

- **You are admired for turning your craft into a real business.**

- **You are promoting products 'Made in America.'**

- **You provide a great diversion from mundane stories, and you probably have a product that photographs beautifully.**

Bacon's Publicity Checker

Call: (800)621-0561, or write:
Bacon's Information, Inc.
332 S. Michigan Ave.
Chicago, IL 60604

Standard Rate and Data Service

Call: (800)952-8159, or write:
SRDS, Inc.
3004 Glenview Rd.
Wilmette, IL 60091

Resource Suggestions

Create a list of important media contacts in your area. Make the list as diverse as possible, including many of the following:

Local newspaper
Home or lifestyle reporter; Fashion reporters if appropriate; Arts editor

Business publications
Is there someone who covers local entrepreneurs? There may be a column for awards and special accomplishments of local business people.

Special full-color magazines
Many cities have upscale magazines that often run sections promoting holiday gifts, with both ads and editorial—find out when you should submit slides and information to have your product considered.

Television and radio
You can improve your chances of getting television or radio coverage by participating in several charitable events throughout the year. If there are several worthy projects for you to choose from, ask the sponsoring organizations about their marketing programs and choose the one with the best reach.

■ PRESS KIT AS A MARKETING TOOL ■

By Candace Forsyth

Crafts are appealing to the public because they are more accessible than fine art. There is a bond between artist and collector. The more the purchaser knows about the craftsperson, the stronger that relationship becomes. This is the groundwork for building a following of clients who track a career, watch it progress, and buy along the way. The materials in a press kit are used to present your "journey" to the audience.

A basic press kit—usually housed in a double-pocket folder, plain, or with your company's name on it—is essential for craftspeople who are participating in retail or wholesale shows, and whose work is being carried in shops and galleries. The materials to be included are:

- **Resume**
- **Photocopies of other stories written about you**
- **Artist's statement**
- **Upcoming appearances list**
- **Color slides**
- **Brochure**
- **Color and black and white photographs**

The **resume** "rule of thumb" is to keep it short, but if more than one page is required, keep the most pertinent information up front, including recent exhibits, show honors, and education or training. The **artist's statement** expands on the craftperson's reason for creating his or her art; inspiration or history on how one arrived at this stage; and if the method used is unusual or distinct in any way, an explanation of the process. The description will help the salespeople at the retail outlet. The artist's statement can often explain why a piece is priced higher than similar looking objects, and it aids in educating the customer and shop or gallery owner as to the value of the work.

Along with **color slides** for show jury submission, it is important to have **photographs** of the work to be used for publishing purposes in magazines. Color photos can be made from slides. Black and white photos are unique

> *Marketing is the process of putting name, image, and product in front of the customer.*

and should be shot differently from color photos. Most galleries depend on newspaper coverage and advertising for their events and shows. Local papers prefer black and white, large format photographs. Artists should strive to have "8x10" black and white photos in their press kit, because when a gallery or shop sends out press material, the artists highlighted are often the ones who have provided photos. When prints are made of black and white and color photos, get extra sets to allow for overlapping shows.

Label with pertinent statistics: artist's name, address, title of the piece, dimensions, and medium. Titles for work can often enhance a piece with insights that were not immediately apparent to the audience, and that cause viewers to give more than a passing glance while they ponder the artist's reason for such an unusual name.

To facilitate the return of photos from the gallery or shop, enclose a self-addressed envelope and include or note the postage required. Be prepared to share your photographs with galleries and show operators, but don't squander your investment by sending a photo with every order. When recognition is received in the press, use the photo or article in your next display. You can laminate your write-ups in stand-up cardboard frames to set up in a booth at a show, as well as give your best retailers a copy to display near your work.

Marketing is the process of putting name, image and product in front of the customer. It is a continuously changing presentation to meet audience needs and keep pace with artistic growth. An updated press kit facilitates success in promotion and sales.

Candace Forsyth is a public relations consultant, currently living in Vermont.

■ GETTING ATTENTION FROM THE MEDIA ■

By Laura W. Rosen

Famous artists don't become famous solely because of their work—the truth is they use public relations to "work" at their image just as hard as they do to sell their work—and it pays off! Courting the press and generating local, regional, and national coverage is a considerable challenge for any artist. Once that task is accomplished, however, the published (or broadcast) message serves to win friends, influence enemies, and generate credibility in ways that advertising cannot. And, if the PR job has been done properly, the feature will put forth the information YOU want, the way you want it expressed.

When artists become adept at creating and implementing their own PR campaigns, every step of the process—including writing the releases, being interviewed, and forming relationships with press contacts—becomes second nature. In the scheme of things, being misquoted is not the worst thing that can happen to an artist. Being ignored by the press is worse.

While advertising is the paid marketing message, publicity is that which is unpaid and far more credible, and is earned by offering the **right message** to the **right person** at the **right time**.

Laura W. Rosen is the editor of NICHE magazine.

■ PRESS INFORMATION MANAGEMENT ■

The names of all your key PR contacts should be entered into a computer or stored in a manual card file. Once or twice a year, a form should accompany your PR mailing asking for updated information. Sending the right message to the right person takes time and energy, but is essential to a successful publicity campaign. Your mailings to press contacts needn't be limited strictly to press releases; send an occasional newsletter or promotional postcard to let editors and writers know what you're doing throughout the year. The press release, however, is the kind of "working news" your contacts are most likely to use.

FOLLOW-UP

After a release has been sent, don't hesitate to call the recipient and extend a personal invitation to the studio, or offer to send additional materials. It is best to wait about a week after you have mailed the information, so that it has been received and reviewed. Be considerate of the editor's hectic schedule, and offer to call back at a better time if he or she is too busy to talk.

Results from a PR campaign should be measured over the long-term. Sometimes an artist's efforts are rewarded a year or two later, when an editor finds exactly the right placement for the story. Always be helpful to the writer. Remember that writers work on tight deadlines, and may ask you to help them pull a feature together overnight. You may be asked to give a lengthy interview on a busy afternoon. Offer to provide photographs to illustrate the feature. Don't ever say you're too busy if a writer calls; you might not get a second chance.

WHEN THE PRESS CALLS

During the interview give candid, interesting information to the writer. While the writer is skilled at giving the information life on the printed page, it is your responsibility to provide interesting anecdotes and "quotable" quotes. If you are well prepared and knowledgeable, you will handle the interview like a pro. It is not rude to ask what will be covered ahead of time, so that you can gather information in any areas you may be weak. As a follow-up to the interview, offer to help the writer verify his facts and figures if there is a lot of detailed business information released. **Don't** ask to proof the article before it runs because that is an industry-wide "no-no." Feature writing is an art form, and the writer reserves the right to take your information and make it into a "good read."

Designing a PR Campaign

First things first: Research your market! Next:

A. Create a News Angle

You can write about your experiences building a business. American entrepreneurs are getting a lot of attention in the press today. Industry awards, special exhibitions and recognitions, and even your participation in wholesale shows can be worked into a very effective publicity program.

B. Set a Budget

Include: printing costs, mailing costs, freelance fee for a writer and/or a photographer.

C. Chart Realistic Deadlines

Example: To publicize a September exhibition, you should notify the trade press, and any monthly four-color magazines, 70-90 days prior to the desired issue of publication. Notify your local press 3-4 weeks prior to the show.

D. Write a Release

Make sure that you explain who, what, where, when, why, and how briefly at the beginning of the release, preferably in the first paragraph.

E. Send the Release

Mail your release in a letter-sized envelope to everyone you can possibly think of—even Aunt Gertrude in Siberia. Then select a smaller number of key writers for newspapers and trade magazines, and send them a complete press packet (a presentation folder with your release, color brochure, copies of past articles about yourself, business card, artist bio, etc.). Include a color slide and/or black and white glossy of your most recent work. Mention at the bottom of the release that they should call you for photos.

F. Watch For Results

*Subscribe to your key trade publications. That way, whether or not you find yourself mentioned in them, you can research the type of stories they do cover, and then tailor your next PR campaign accordingly. Pay close attention to **who writes what** so that your PR list can be kept up-to-date with people who will take an interest in your news.*

G. Send Thanks

It is customary to thank anyone who helps you get recognition of any kind. Send a short note of thanks, and maybe follow up with a phone call, especially if the coverage was particularly exciting!

*Contributor: Laura W. Rosen,
Editor, NICHE magazine*

Scheduling Publicity for an Event

60-90 days or more before the event:
First release / national media and four-color magazines

30-60 days before:
First release / local media

About 30 days before:
Phone calls to follow-up

14 days before:
Additional mailings and calls to local media

After the event / campaign:
Thank-you letters to those who provided coverage

PUBLICITY WORKSHEET

Use this model to help organize your ideas for an exciting PR campaign.

1) What are your reasons for publicizing yourself and your business?

   _____

2) List the strengths of your business. What sets you apart from others in the marketplace?

   _____

3) Think about what makes you newsworthy. Try to examine yourself as if you were a magazine editor. For example:

   What are your accomplishments in the industry?

   _____

   Have you ever invented an object or technique that is truly unique to that marketplace?

   _____

   Describe your role in shaping product style or color trends, or your relationships with independent retailers.

   _____

4) Be versatile with your articles. Fashion stories that may be of interest to *Jewelers' Circular-Keystone* and *Women's Wear Daily* would not be of interest to *Giftware News*. Try to identify the special interests of all those on your press list and, if at all possible, READ ONE OF THEIR ARTICLES TO GET A FEEL FOR WHAT THEY WILL AND WON'T WRITE!

   _____

5) Write a general press release. Always put a date, contact person, phone number, and a headline at the top of the page. The first paragraph of the press release should briefly tell who, what, where, when, why, and how.

   _____

6) For a complete presentation, use a special two-pocket presentation folder and insert the following materials:

   ❏ Press release
   ❏ Color brochure
   ❏ Copies of articles about yourself

   ❏ Slides of your latest works in plastic protectors w/typed descriptions
   ❏ Schedule of your events and exhibitions
   ❏ Self-addressed stamped envelope w/cardboard for slide return

7) Follow up. Write thank-you notes for any publicity received. Periodically evaluate and update the names and addresses of your contacts so that you will be using fresh information.

   _____

8) ENJOY THE REWARDS OF AN EFFECTIVE PUBLICITY CAMPAIGN!

■ THE VALUE OF NEWSLETTERS ■

A newsletter can be one of the most effective elements of your promotional materials. It can stimulate the interest of craft buyers, press contacts, and craft collectors. You can harness a lot of promotional "power" by generating newsletters that are:

Informative

Interesting

Inspirational

While many firms spend thousands of dollars on their company newsletters, many good newsletters are produced on a tight budget. If you have any talent at all for writing and basic layout principles, you can create a template on your personal computer into which you can pop in stories from time to time. Using a personal computer, you can create a "hot off the presses" image piece from start to finish, in as little as an hour's time. Or, do your own writing and have a freelance artist do the layout and add some interesting graphics.

A newsletter can be little more than an expanded letter, carrying a warm, personal message to your customers and business contacts. Begin by writing down everything that you want people to know about yourself and your product. Many of the very best newsletters take readers behind the scenes by sharing interesting details about the business that they otherwise would not have known.

Take into account the following items when preparing a budget for a newsletter:

Quantity needed

Mailing list, if necessary (unless you have a sufficient number of prospective readers)

Approximate printing costs

Approximate layout and design costs

Freelance writer's fee (if applicable)

Postage and processing costs*

This is to be factored in if you want to pay a firm to stuff the newsletters into envelopes, affix postage, and sort them for bulk mail distribution. If you plan to do that yourself, just use the approximate cost of postage instead. Remember, the post office can supply you with a booklet explaining all you need to know about each class of mail.

Artists who design their newsletters as a self-mailer save in a number of ways: They save paper and printing costs by not using envelopes and they save on the labor required to stuff the envelopes. Don't worry about the self-mailer looking too commercial or getting worn by the time it reaches the recipient—self-mailers generally hold up very well, especially if you ask the printer for paper that is heavier than average. Save newsletters that you

Jan Richardson: Artist Finds Newsletter to be a Valuable Resource

Jan Richardson of Windy Meadows Pottery believes that a newsletter is the best direct mail piece that a company can send. "I got involved with direct mail two days after I started the business," Jan says. "It is important to keep reminding people that you exist."

Windy Meadows Pottery puts its newsletter out three times a year. "Our newsletter is informal and friendly," Jan explains. "It is put together like a newspaper, with photos and three-column articles." Jan sends the newsletter to approximately 12,000 people on her mail-

ing list. "We keep people on our mailing list for three years," she says. "After three years, if we haven't heard from a customer, we send a postcard asking if they would like to remain on our list."

In addition to a newsletter, Jan also sends out mailers before shows: sales promotions, and postcards, to generate business. Her thinking is that you must keep in touch with customers to encourage business. "Creating a newsletter can be costly," Jan advises. "But it is the best way to keep your customer up-to-date on what you are doing."

receive from area retailers to your home and make notes about what you like and don't like. Take a blank sheet of paper and fold it various ways, trying to visualize how your articles will look when the recipient unfolds the piece.

Add sizzle to the information in your newsletter. Use it to tell retailers and collectors something you heard on the national news that morning. Include a picture of yourself at work in the studio. Ask for permission to reprint any valuable news clips to pass onto your buyers. When you learn about a buyer who devised a clever way to promote your work, ask the buyer if that idea can be passed on to other retailers. The buyer probably won't mind because most people like to be quoted in newsletters, and often enjoy sharing tips with other national retailers.

Once you have a number of topics to include in the newsletter, decide which stories will be long, and which stories will be short. Select your most important feature story for the cover with a corresponding photo or piece of artwork if available. Interesting quotes and positive comments about your work will also enliven the newsletter. As you add employees and craft apprentices, use their pictures and brief biographies in the newsletter, too.

Many of the retailers who will buy your work publish newsletters regularly for their customers, and run into the same dilemma each issue—what do I put in? Be prepared to provide these retailers with a few paragraphs explaining your work with several high-quality black and white photos of your latest design. If possible, include customer stories or comments.

Newsletters don't have to be intimidating. They are a tool that is accessible to everyone, and one that can be used to reach out to all of your customers and contacts.

■ CREATING A DATABASE ■

A database can be one of your most valuable assets as a craftsperson. The information gathered and stored will help you focus on your customer's needs, and provide focus groups to test new work. Your database will come in handy when you are introducing a new line, having an open house, or want to invite customers to your next show.

To create a database, start by keeping a guest book at your booth at every show. Ask anyone and everyone who makes a purchase for his or her address. These names and addresses can be kept on index cards, categorized by where they were obtained, but they are better kept on a computer, with any number of inexpensive record-keeping programs available at your local software outlet. With these programs you can easily create letters with name insertions, make mailing labels, and keep as much customer information as you can get on file.

Besides using this database to boost your own sales, you can sell, rent, or trade it with other artists, shop owners, and catalog publishers who sell American craft. Make sure to go through your list every six months or so to purge it of old addresses, wrong addresses, and of those people who haven't responded.

```
John Smith / Visions Gallery
123 Main Street
Coopersville, NM 89023
(101)555-1298
Carries jewelry, pottery and
glass. Pays on time.
```

Remember, databases are so valuable in today's market that many people are having their's copyrighted, so protect your list (and the time and effort that goes into creating it) by keeping it in a safe place. If the list is on your computer, make a back-up disk and store it in a safe place.

HINT: If you sell, rent, or trade your list, always "seed" it with a phony name or two at your address, or the address of a close friend. Use names that you will remember, like that of a favorite author, or that of a pet. This way, you can find out where your list has gone. If you get a catalog from a company to which you did not give permission in the name of "Scruffy Smith," then you know someone has "borrowed" your property.

Retail mail order is one of the fastest growing industries in the country—perhaps faster than the crafts industry! Almost 20% of everything sold this year will be sold by mail. We all know the stories about Banana Republic, Williams Sonoma, L.L. Bean, Sundance, Victoria's Secret, and even the Smithsonian! Direct mail has gone upscale with price points at an all-time high. Specialty items, like your hand-crafted product, are the best products for direct mail.

The safest way to get into mail-order selling is by cautiously starting with a small budget and working from there. Focus on a small portion of your business, perhaps just four products, instead of producing a twenty-page catalog. Advertise something unusual—but understandable. Every word counts, literally! At advertising rates of $40 per inch and higher in most magazines, you can't afford to risk more than your return.

There may be as many as 40,000 companies in the United States selling products by using various forms of mail order. One of the most common forms of mail order is called **"The Bounce Back."** A bounce back offer is the best and the most economical way to get the next order. Just place another order form or promotional flyer in the box with every order shipped, and with every sale made at retail fairs. The result is a no-risk, no-cost mail order offer!

Your lowest priced products, which can be described in less than ten to fifteen words, may sell very successfully by placing the sales message in the **classified ad sections** of consumer and business magazines. The cost for classified advertising will range from two cents per word to ten dollars per word in larger magazines.

Once a product is priced above $10 to $25, it is more difficult to sell in classified ads. More costly display ads become the medium for higher priced merchandise. If the message required to make the sale is lengthy in nature, the classified ads can be used to generate sales leads. The follow-up message sent through the mail does the actual selling job.

The object of the game is to keep detailed records on which publications and which ads perform the best. With this information on hand, you can easily select a good method of advertising for a specific product. (Be sure to consider the season and the reader's budget when deciding where and when to advertise.)

Once the ad proves to be successful with a small

profitable response, you're in good shape. That small ad response may build monthly and may be profitable for years to come. Remember, repeat advertising is essential. Few people respond the first time they see an ad.

ADVERTISING OPPORTUNITIES

Direct mail advertising is a specialty unto its own. Everyone selling by mail must learn how to create and write ad copy, or find someone who can. Because classified ads are abbreviated sales messages, you must learn how to describe your offer in the least number of words possible without losing the meaning. When larger ads are considered, you need to learn not only how to write an ad, but how to do simple ad layouts.

Column widths must also be considered when placing an ad. Magazine column widths are not all the same, so, as you plan to expand your advertising programs, you may find it necessary to accomodate these differences.

Your first benefit from advertising is the **names you collect.** This may be more important than the sale itself if the ad has a teaser for a catalog. Identify each name within your database as either an inquiry or a sale. You may find it valuable to also list the amount of the sale on your database as well.

MONITORING SALES

Using a good direct mail software program can help you evaluate progress as you grow. The computer, when used with a bounce back program, monitors the time elapsed from the shipment date of the package containing your message. If the bounce back offer is not returned within thirty days, a follow-up letter with another bounce back offer is sent. A second follow-up message can then be sent fifteen days later if there is still no response. This letter should be more direct: "We haven't heard from you!" Additional follow-ups have been found to be unproductive.

Information compiled from one or many offers is then used to qualify the buyers for future mailings. Some inquiry management systems use the telephone to qualify inquiries. Many find this method productive, though it is more costly than the direct mail method.

CODING RESPONSES

This method will help you organize your customer data

files for future use. Be sure to put a small code on every outgoing form or published advertisement, so that you can track its results. Most order forms carry a small code in the corner, identifying which magazine ran the ad. Classifieds are coded with a department number, or a box number at your address. Make sure to include source codes in your database.

SURPRISE THE CUSTOMER

A paying customer is a valuable one. Surprise your customer with a follow-up that begins: We hope that the (insert item here) you ordered was delivered in a timely manner. Please take a moment to let us know. (Two or three survey questions follow). Include a bounce back offer with the survey.

For additional information, write or call: **The Direct Marketing Association**, 6 East 43rd St. • New York, NY 10017 • (212)689-4977

NICHE Magazine: NICHE Awards Aid Artists in Gaining Exposure

The NICHE Awards competition was created in 1990 by the editors of NICHE, The Magazine for Progressive Retailers, to recognize individual artists, and to provide a new level of exposure for their work. "Receiving a NICHE Award adds credibility to a craftsperson's work," says Sharon Perfetti, assistant editor of NICHE magazine. "The finalists names are printed in our Winter issue, and the winners names appear in the Spring issue. Magazines like The Crafts Report and Ceramics Monthly also print portions of the list of winners."

Each year, the jury is comprised of leading professionals in the field of design, including specialty retailers, expert craftspeople, editors from various design, fashion, and gift publications, and art critics. The jury is different every year to provide each entrant a fair chance. Artists can apply in each medium in the categories of one-of-a-kind (which includes limited-editions) and production.

Winners receive a NICHE Award sculpture (designed by artist Stephen jon Clements), during the awards ceremony, promotional stickers to highlight their marketing efforts, and the opportunity to have their work displayed at the Philadelphia Buyers Market of American Crafts. "The winners are a combination of established craft artists and newcomers," Sharon says, adding: "One of our current winners just got started making jewelry a year ago." For more information on the NICHE Awards, call (800) NICHE-14.

AmericanStyle: Magazine Provides Direct Mail Opportunities to Craft Collectors

AmericanStyle, Contemporary Crafts for Living & Giving, launches its premiere issue in October, 1994. With a start-up circulation of 50,000, AmericanStyle combines informative articles geared toward the craft collector, with catalog-style pages providing an exciting direct mail opportunity for artists.

"The benefit is that craft consumers are brought directly to you, the artist, without the expense of adding another retail show, and without the time away from your studio," says Laura W. Rosen, editor-in-chief of AmericanStyle. In the catalog-style ads, artists list their name, address, and phone number, so the customers don't have to go through a fulfillment house; they contact the artist directly. Craft advertisers receive 20-30 copies of AmericanStyle to distribute at retail shows to their best customers, increasing circulation every time.

"AmericanStyle works for the craftsperson," Laura says. "It presents their work and other handcrafted gifts to a qualified audience of craft collectors." For more information on AmericanStyle, call: (800) 642-4314, or (410) 889-2933.

Retail Craft Fairs

*The idea does not belong to the soul;
it is the soul that belongs to the idea.*
—Charles Sanders Peirce

Each weekend, approximately 600 craft fairs take place across the United States. That's an estimated 30,000 fairs every year that offer the country's more than 10,000 full-time craftspeople the opportunity to make a living from their art.

APPLYING TO A CRAFT SHOW

Many of the most successful retail shows rely on an application process that includes the submission of 35mm slides. These slides are your portfolio when first starting your business. Good slides are your most important business tool. Whether you succeed or fail in this business will depend not only on the quality of your work—but also on the skill of the photographer shooting the slides! The investment you make in professional slides is not a luxury—but a necessity.

WHAT IS A GOOD SLIDE?

Jury slides may be different from the transparencies you would use in a brochure or a postcard. In a brochure you may wish to put several items in a single photograph, or show the product in its environment. **These photos are not jury slides!** The few seconds that a jury has to see your work must be used to your advantage. Use a professional commercial photographer with a portfolio that shows photographs that are similar to the slides needed. Do not, under any circumstances select the same photographer that did your sister's wedding! Show the photographer photos that would make good and bad slides. Point out the mistakes, so that they are not repeated.

The best shows in the country receive hundreds and sometimes thousands of applications for a single event. Regardless of the selection process, it's difficult for any artist to stand out in such a large crowd. The competition is the toughest where the rewards are the highest—some craft fairs can bring in as much as $25,000!

Rejection doesn't necessarily mean that your work is not up to the show's standards—instead, it often depends on many other factors, including who views your slides and what kind of equipment was used to view those slides. In a competitive jury system, slides that are seen first thing in the morning generally fare better than those viewed by tired jurors at the end of an eight-hour day! You can limit your risk by applying to shows that review your resume and other credentials as well as your slides.

Long's Park: A Craft Fair with National Attention

Among craft fairs, Long's Park stands out as one of the best and most professional in the country. Set in a Lancaster County, Pennsylvania park, the show is ranked in the top five of all retail fairs in the United States.

Craft artist Rick Faulkner of Barrick Design Candles started working with the Long's Park Art and Craft Festival with his father, Dick, a number of years ago. They had both been involved in starting and running other local shows, and had also been involved with the Pennsylvania Guild of Craftsmen. Rick had served on the committee for the annual state fair for a number of years, while Dick had been the president of the Lancaster County chapter of the Pennsylvania guild.

When the Faulkners got involved, Long's Park was being run by a non-profit group dedicated to providing music and entertainment in the park during the summer months. The organization was floundering, and needed to find a way to make money. The Faulkners were interested in lending a hand because they saw

many possible ways to turn the festival around. First, the level of quality needed to be improved—if you want to be the best, then you must attract the best.

Next, Rick put his marketing skills to work. "We set out to build the best show we could," says Rick. "We began advertising regionally rather than just locally—as far south as Washington, D.C." Direct mail turned out to be one of their more successful marketing techniques. "Your best customer is always someone who has previously bought from you, or from another craftsperson," Rick says.

The goal of the Long's Park Art and Craft Festival is to attract the best exhibitors in the country. "We instruct the jurors each year to keep in mind that we want to attract a wide range of customers—in terms of both price and product," says Rick. "It is very important to our customers that we show diversity." Instead of the normal craft show fare of hot dogs, hamburgers,

and pizza, Long's Park features food from local restaurants. "Our customers really appreciate the choices that this provides," Rick believes.

As a juried show, Long's Park is one of the most competitive in the country, with ten applicants for every space available. "Many talented, excellent artists don't get into the

show," says Rick. "We stress to everyone not to be discouraged—try again!"

To apply to exhibit in the show, you need five slides—four of work, one of your display—and a completed application. For more information about the festival, call: (717) 295-7001, or write: Long's Park Art and Craft Festival, P.O. Box 1553B, Lancaster, PA 17603.

WHAT YOU NEED TO KNOW
▪ ABOUT JURIED SHOWS ▪

There was a time when juried shows were thought of as the most equitable method for selecting participants for retail craft shows. For a juried show, five slides are shown to a group of peers or knowledgeable jurors who grade each artist's work. Applying artists may be required to pay a jury fee for the opportunity to have his or her slides shown to the panel, which may select only 10% or less of the artists to exhibit in the show. The other 90% of the artists paid a fee, but have only a slim chance of participating in the show. To many artists, this seems more like a lottery than a fair way to select the best work.

Some juried shows aren't really juried at all—often only one person is responsible for whether you are accepted or rejected.

Alan Revere: A Former Judge of Juried Shows Gives the Scoop

Alan Revere, founder of the Revere Academy of Jewelry Arts, author of *Professional Goldsmithing*, and a jeweler in his own right, has had a great deal of experience on both sides of the jurying process. Initially, Alan applied to these shows as an artist, but more recently, he has also been a juror for the ACE shows.

"For the ACE shows, a group of cross-media judges are gathered (meaning that jewelers jury jewelers)," says Alan. "Each applicant must submit five slides arranged in the order that the artist has requested, so the composition of all the slides together is very important. All of the applicants include a brief description on the slide holder, in case one of the jurors asks, but the information is not volunteered.

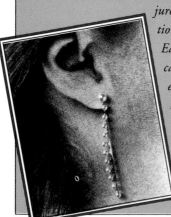

Each group is put into a cassette. The jury then sees each group of slides twice, the first time for five seconds (no notes are taken at this time, then there is a break, and the slides are then viewed again for another five seconds. For the second viewing, the juror gives a score of 1 to 5, 5 being the highest. The scores are then tallied, and the highest scores fill the slots for that medium."

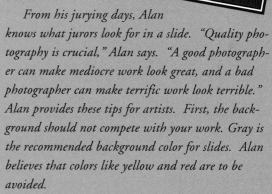

From his jurying days, Alan knows what jurors look for in a slide. "Quality photography is crucial," Alan says. "A good photographer can make mediocre work look great, and a bad photographer can make terrific work look terrible." Alan provides these tips for artists. First, the background should not compete with your work. Gray is the recommended background color for slides. Alan believes that colors like yellow and red are to be avoided.

Alan truly lives by the idea that we are all given two ears and one mouth for a reason. Listening to your customers is crucial to success in business. Doing what you love will also get you through some rough times. "Start out doing what you enjoy," he says, adding: "There will be plenty of time to make compromises later."

Knowing **who** will view your slides (a jury, a committee, or an individual) can be helpful in knowing which slides to submit. Some craftspeople will tell you that they spend more on their jury slides than on the entry fee for each show. Those same artists will tell you that it was worth it, because those great slides got them into the show.

RETHINKING THE JURY SYSTEM

Over the years, artists have discovered detours that abate the fairness of the jury system. For this reason, the jury system is no longer considered the best selection process by many. Some of the "tricks" used over the years have given certain artists an unfair advantage over others. Artists gain special advantage by sending more than one application to a show, or by asking jury members to "preview" their slides for an opinion before submitting an application. The juror can then easily recognize "previewed" slides and give a favorable rating. Although your anonymity can seem to provide a fair opportunity, the system does not prevent the jury from selecting someone who is copying or "knocking off" your style or design! Jurors may be fooled by someone impersonating your work!

NEW SELECTION SYSTEMS

The use of a combination of slides, accompanied by a written application, is now becoming a more popular method of selecting artists for shows. Some selection committees and show producers ask applicants to submit references—names of other artists who know them and know their work. Some of the best shows request your mailing list of customers in the geographic region where the show is to take place. The bottom line is that it is up to you to prove that you are a good "partner" for the show producer, and that is demonstrated through your work and your commitment to publicize the show, by inviting as many of your customers as possible.

JURY SLIDE RULES

- *In jury slides, a single item shot is generally considered most effective.*
- *A simple background of gradient gray is preferred.*
- *The entire outline of the form should be visible.*
- *There should be no shadows.*
- *Avoid any hot spots (light reflections).*
- *Use professional models if necessary (it's worth the extra cost).*
- *The color of your work in the slide should be as accurate and as bright as possible.*

SUBMITTING, ORGANIZING, & STORING YOUR SLIDES

- *Verify that you have all reproduction rights to the slides.*
- *Select 8 to 10 slides and have several sets made.*
- *Keep the slides in a protective sleeve to avoid scratches.*
- *Mark each slide with your name, address, and a brief description, including size. (12" teapot). Put an arrow pointing to the top of the slide.*

- *Always submit slides that have a family resemblance. A disjointed presentation leaves a juror feeling uncertain about where you're going with your work.*

PHOTOGRAPHIC TIPS

- *Use 35mm color film (slide film).*
- *Make sure the type of film will not distort color.*
- *Use a white, reflective tent around your piece to bounce light.*
- *Light the piece from all directions.*

- *Fill the slide with the object, leaving a small margin of space (1/8") around all sides.*
- *Avoid distracting props and backdrops.*
- *Never use wrinkled fabric as a background for your work.*

PHOTOGRAPHY AGREEMENT

Date _____

Company _____

Contact _____

Terms _____

Rate _____

I agree to perform photographic services for (insert your name or your company's name) at the rate indicated above, understanding that I am to provide:

- ❑ large format transparencies
- ❑ mounted 35 mm slides
- ❑ black & white prints
- ❑ color prints
- ❑ other (specify)

suitable for product advertising and promotion. I agree to release the original slides or transparencies indefinitely, and for use in the promotion of the product shown. The user agrees to print the photographer's name next to the photos whenever possible.

_____   _____

Photographer's Signature   Date

_____   _____

Artist's or Artist's Representative   Date
Signature

This agreement is meant to be used as a guideline, and may or may not be binding in a court of law.

■ FINDING RETAIL SHOWS ■
THAT MEET YOUR NEEDS

The first place to seek out craft fairs is in your own backyard. Check with the management of local malls and the area's Chamber of Commerce. Local craft retailers are also a good source of information. After exhausting local resources, many professional craftspeople discover that they must travel to larger, regional craft fairs where sales are better for quantity and quality of craftwork, and the customers are more educated and enthusiastic.

Finding the right show for your work isn't nearly as difficult as finding the right show for your wallet. The box on the right contains some suggestions on where to find show listings.

> **The Crafts Report** • (800)777-7098
>
> **AmericanStyle** • (800)642-4314
>
> **Fairs and Festivals:**
> **Northeast and Southeast**
> (413)545-2360
>
> **Sunshine Artist** • (407)332-4944
>
> For more show information,
> see our **Resource section**.

Ann Shamash: "Every Fair is a Learning Experience"

Ann Shamash, of Ann Shamash: Creative Clay Concepts, believes that you can't let retail fairs in one region dictate trends for the entire country. Through the summer months and the month of January, Ann is commited to production, meaning that she implements all of her ideas during these times. During the other times of the year, Ann attends various retail fairs to test-market her new ideas.

"During the year I'm constantly coming up with new ideas," says Ann. "After the ideas become product, they are tested at various locations." Ann's "test-sites" are Baltimore, MD, Washington, D.C., Long Island, NY, and Frederick, MD, for what Ann refers to as "suburban perspective." From these locations, Ann believes she can tell how a product will sell nationally.

To craft artists just starting out, Ann has a bit of advice. "If there is a show in your area that does not accept you, show up anyway on the day of the show," Ann says. "It is always possible that there will be cancellations, and the show promoter may be eager to fill the spot!"

■ THE PROS AND CONS OF CRAFT FAIRS ■

Craft fairs have both their advantages and their drawbacks for today's craft artist. It is important to weigh these factors before deciding what fairs you want to do, when to do them, and what distance is practical for you to travel. Cost is also an issue to consider when you sign up to do many retail shows.

Many artists, even those who sell the majority of their work wholesale, still do retail shows as a means to test-market new products. Unlike wholesale shows, retail fairs provide an opportunity for you to communicate with your end customer. By far the greatest advantage to selling retail is the money in hand the day of the show.

Retail fairs and festivals also have their downside,

however. Most important is the time away from your studio. You must also know the market of the location where the fair is to take place. In New York, one item may be a bestseller, while in Virginia, that same item won't sell at all. Be prepared for this by having the right products on hand, as well as the appropriate quantity of that product. Accurate inventory is also crucial to being successful in retail. If you have fairs scheduled two weekends in a row, will you be able to create enough of an unanticipated hot-selling item for the second weekend? The concept of tenure is missing from many retail fairs. In many of the best fairs, artists are required to apply each year, without the certainty of acceptance. The unpredictability can be devastating to your income when a show you've counted on turns you down. Rejection is tough on wallets and egos.

Look at the big picture when deciding to make the jump into a string of retail fairs. For the cost, keep in mind that many people attend these shows for recreation, and not with the intent to buy a particular item. But unlike wholesale shows, where every decision to buy is a business decision, people at craft fairs are more prone to the impulse purchase. Your selling skills must be top-notch!

Striking the right balance between wholesaling and retailing your work can be the ultimate formula for business success. In fact, balancing wholesale and retail can be a lot like walking a tightrope in a circus. Wholesale accounts don't appreciate the competition in their neighborhood, and for this reason, many artists select shows far away from their wholesale accounts. Because craft collectors travel, it is important to offer the same price from Maine to Florida, and from New York to San Francisco. The retail price of your work is at least twice your wholesale price.

Daniel Riccio: Using Scientific Methods in Market Research

Daniel Riccio came to be a craftsman via an unusual route—through the sciences. That is the field that Daniel was going to pursue before he entered the army. After fighting in Vietnam, Daniel decided that life shouldn't be spent doing what others want you to do. He decided that he would rather do something that he loves. "Life is too short," says Daniel. "You only get one chance." What Daniel decided to do was create collectible miniatures cast in bronze and silver.

While Daniel prefers wholesale shows, he exhibits at a few select retail fairs each year as research. "I use statistics to aid my market research," Daniel says. Daniel believes that it is most important to listen to what the customer has to say. "After a customer asks a question, or makes a suggestion, I always make a note for myself," he stresses. While there, Daniel asks the customer a few questions: "I

begin by asking the customer what he or she thinks is missing from a piece. Then I ask what he or she would like to see next time. I use these comments for future product development."
How you present yourself to customers ranks at the top of Daniel's list of important items.
"Customer relations are very important to me," Daniel says. "If people don't like you, they won't want to do business with you."

Crafting As a Business

QUESTIONS TO ASK
BEFORE APPLYING TO A SHOW

Ask these questions of the promoter or an exhibitor:

1. How are the selections made? Are they by invitation, jury, first come, first served?

2. Who will view the applications and the slides?

3. When will exhibitors be notified?

4. How many applications were received last year for this show?

5. When are selections made?

6. How many exhibitors from the previous year were permitted back?

7. How many new applicants were accepted for last year's fair?

8. Is there a tenure option, or an option to return to the show the following year?

9. What costs are involved beyond the space fee?

10. Is there a membership, parking, electrical, carpet rental, or program advertising fee?

11. Do you provide exhibitors with promotional tools, such as invitations or postcards?

12. What was last year's attendance?

    State fairs, expect attendance from 200,000 to 500,000

    Most craft fairs, expect 10,000 to 30,000

    (Numbers aren't as important as the trend up or down from the previous year!)

13. Do you fill spaces by category?

14. What is the style of the show (contemporary, country, traditional)?

15. What is the recommended price range of craftwork for this show?

16. How are space assignments made for corners, larger spaces, and front spaces?

17. Does the show allow demonstrations? Is there additional space allotted for demonstrations, or discounts for artists who demonstrate?

18. Will the show provide a list of exhibitor references?

19. How many years has the show been in this location?

20. If the show is outdoors, what is the policy for inclement weather?

21. Is there a minimum jury score requirement/cutoff to be accepted for the show?

WHAT TO PACK FOR A SHOW
Your Checklist

___Booth Display

___Extension Cords (30 ft. total)

___Chairs (2)

___Lighting

___Surge protector

___Small trash can

___Night cover (for security)

___Plastic display saddles

___Plate display stands

___Packing tape

___Duct tape

___Extra bulbs

___Glass cleaner

___Small tool box (hammer, screwdriver, needle-nose pliers, nails, tacks, touch-up paint, and brush)

___First aid kit

___Office supply kit (stapler, tape, scissors, staples, pen, pencil, safety pins)

___Charge card processing equipment

___Cash box

___Petty cash for change ($40 minimum)

___Small hand vacuum

___Receipt book

___Guest book for mailing list

___Business cards

___Price tags

___Hang tags

___Retail order forms/price lists

___Brochures

___Invitations to other shows or special exhibits of your work

___"Referral" sign, or cards of galleries that sell your work locally

___Steamer or iron

___Thermos or small cooler for drinks/snacks

___Miscellaneous _____

_____

F. B. Fogg: Advice From an Artist on Displays & Exhibits

F.B. Fogg creates works of art with paper she makes by hand. Her booth at craft fairs comes alive with her work. For artists struggling with the question, "how do I create a display?", F.B. gives the following advice:

A total package! The idea, creativity, technique—from concept and construction to display and packaging—it must bespeak the artist! That's what is unique about the art world that really **sells**! Never forget this commandment: "It's a total package."

Way back, more years than I care to remember, when I did "street" fairs, with a table and a screen—all of it was made of paper. The art work was the display; the display was the art work. The people would ask, "What material is this? How did you make it?" The conversation was begun, the interest was titillated, the sale was initiated.

The same creativity, flair, and care with which you make your product **must be put into your display!** Not only does that create interest, it leaves this impression—you are an artist full of great ideas—I want some of your world—I want what you are selling. The old adage of stop, look, and listen, is as valuable today as it was yesterday. If you can get the customer's attention in this competitive market, then you will survive.

In my booth, you will not see a chair for the artist, a book to read, or a corner in which to snooze. My booth is for buying! **My energy is for selling.** I don't drive all that way and pay all of those booth fees to sit and read, snooze, grumble, or close early. **I come to sell!**

So create an atmosphere, an ambiance of your product. Find the unique old ironing board, the crab trap, the column, the rice, the rickshaw. Invite the viewer into your world, and let them take home a piece of you. Remember, it is a total package!

TOP U.S. SHOWS & FESTIVALS

TOP WHOLESALE MARKETS
Philadelphia Buyers Market
Baltimore A.C.E. Show
Boston Buyers Market

TOP CONTEMPORARY RETAIL SHOWS
Ann Arbor Summer Art Fair
Coconut Grove Arts Festival
Baltimore A.C.E. Show
Long's Park

TOP TRADITIONAL CRAFT SHOWS
War Eagle Fair
Harvest Festival Fall Tour
Valley Forge (wholesale)
Beckman's (Chicago and Los Angeles, wholesale)

TOP FESTIVALS
Gilroy Garlic Festival
Jazz and Heritage Festival
Festival of the Masters at Disney Village Marketplace

TOP MUSEUM-QUALITY SHOWS
Smithsonian Craft Show
Philadelphia Museum of Art Craft Show
New Art Forms (Chicago)

TOP GIFT SHOWS
New York Gift Show
Atlanta Gift Show
San Francisco Gift Show

For more show listings, see the **Resources** section.

■ Q & A ABOUT CREDIT CARD ■ SYSTEMS WITH GUY McDONALD

Q: Will credit cards really add income to a craft business?

A: Yes. In the past three years, artists joining our group and setting up accounts for the first time have had an average increase of 38% of their gross. The lowest

increase was 25%. Credit cards are more important now than ever because of the incentives the card companies are offering, such as frequent flyer miles. It will not be as easy to convert card sales to checks or cash because the customer wants the perks offered by the card companies.

Q: How can a craftsperson get an account set up?

A: First they should try their local bank. You could get lucky, but most likely you will pay higher rates, and the equipment won't be designed especially for the craftsperson. Check with a craft guild, many times guilds have group plans available. Ask friends what group they are with, and ask if they are happy. Also, ask if they have been with that company for more than six months, because it some-

times takes that long for service and equipment problems to surface. Look for a company that specializes in equipment for your profession. Verify that the company understands your special needs, and that they have solutions to your problems. Find a company that sets you up as **part of a group** with the processing company for the bank. This will mean lower rates, better service, and more stability in your rate from year to year.

Q: Where can an artist find such a company?

A: Read craft magazine articles about credit cards. Also, my company, Arts and Crafts Business Solutions provides such a service solely to the arts industry.

Q: What do banks look for in a merchant?

A: Any company that is serious about offering you an account will look for stability in your

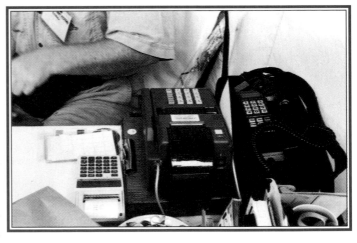

business. If you are opening an account for the first time, they will want to see your tax return from the previous year to establish that there is money coming in, and money going out. If you are changing accounts, they will only want to see your MasterCard or Visa statements from the current account. If you are dealing with a bank on your own, be prepared to have a bank officer visit your studio or house to verify that you are operating a business from that location. Also, be prepared for possible rejection because you don't have a storefront. Many banks won't deal with non-storefront merchants.

Q: What equipment is needed to process credit cards?
A: The banking industry is going to point-of-sale or P.O.S. equipment. P.O.S. for traveling artists doing a show means a cellular terminal, unless there will always be a phone jack in the booth. Some banks still allow keyed entry. This would involve an electronic credit card machine in your studio and a manual imprinter would be used at shows. You will pay a higher rate to do keyed entry, and most banks are eliminating keyed entry because of fraud risks.

Q: Is it better for an artist to put together their own cellular system, or to purchase one complete?
A: Buy one! If you put your own system together, you will most likely end up with obsolete equipment, because technology is changing so fast. You will want your equipment to accept debit cards as well as credit cards. Unless you are willing to spend six months to a year researching all of the factors involved in cellular credit card processing now, and just around the corner—buy one!

Q: How can an artist be sure if they are buying a good system and good service?
A: Ask for at least twenty references. All of the references should be from people in the craft community. Although the equipment doesn't know whether an artist or a cab driver is using it, when was the last time you saw a cab in a basement or a convention center? Certain equipment works much better indoors than others. If the phone is not an Audiovox, and you do indoor shows, don't buy it. Ask questions about service. Many companies offer a 24-hour, seven-day-a-week 800-service number for you to call. Ask the person at the service number if they have been trained in cellular and interfaces, and do they support the cellular side of your system, or only the credit card terminal.

For more information, contact: Arts and Crafts Business Solutions, Guy McDonald, (800)873-1192.

For more information on portable credit card processing systems, call or write the following companies:

ACBS Arts & Crafts Business Solutions
2804 Bishopgate Drive
Raleigh, NC 27613
(800)873-1192

U.S. Wireless Data, Inc.
4888 Pearl East Circle, Suite 110
Boulder, CO 80301
(303)440-5464

York Financial Services
696 San Ramon Valley Boulevard, #336
Danville, CA 94526
(510)820-3139

Trade Shows: Selling Wholesale

Art is long, life is short; judgment difficult,
opportunity transient.
—Goethe

Trade shows are big business—big business that creates still more business for those who take part. **The show's aim: To bring volume buyers and sellers together in an atmosphere designed to promote sales.** Unlike customers at retail fairs, trade show shoppers will buy several pieces of your work at once. As an exhibitor, you bring only samples to a trade show, and take orders for future delivery—allowing you to plan a production schedule, and spread business throughout the year. Buyers seek ideas, good service, and unique products; sellers seek sales and communication with their current and potential customers. What's more, trade shows and markets are a cost-efficient means to procure new accounts and to make customers for life.

Your first priority is to visit a show in which you would like to participate; then look, listen, and ask questions.

Asking questions is the key to success. Remember, there are no dumb questions! Talk to your neighbors about everything—pricing, displays, lighting, credit, and collections. Most professional craftspeople are as friendly as the people you have met on the retail show circuit, so take the first step and introduce yourself. Don't assume you can remember everything—buy a small notebook and divide it into sections:

1) **Business Practices**
2) **Exhibits & Display Design**
3) **Galleries & Craft Retailers**
4) **Selling Ideas**
5) **Contacts**
6) **Suppliers**
7) **Miscellaneous Notes**
8) **To Do**

Every chance you get, make notes about what you've learned. At the end of each day, write a note to yourself about overall impressions.

Arn Lowenthal: "Always Have Something New for the Buyers"

Arn Lowenthal is the business-minded half of Barbara Sexton's ceramic business. Having been an officer of a large industrial electronics firm on Wall Street, one day Arn found himself out of a job, and forced to drive a cab to make ends meet. At the same time, Arn was dating Barbara Sexton, who had a small ceramics business with accounts at two or three shops. They agreed that Arn would take responsibility for the business aspects, while Barbara would produce pottery. Arn and Barbara have been partners since 1977.

At each show in which Barbara's work is sold, Arn is there. "Selling has to be one of the most important skills I brought with me from my previous career," Arn says. "No matter how wonderful you think your product is, if you can't sell it, it doesn't amount to much." Listening to the public is also an important skill. "When you introduce your product to the market, you must be prepared to listen to the market rather than to yourself."

At wholesale shows, Arn feels that changing your booth from year to year keeps buyers interested. "Always have a new design waiting to come out," Arn says. "This is so that with each show there is something new in your booth. You want to protect yourself from the buyer walking by and thinking he or she knows what you have because he or she saw it last year." He also urges craftspeople to rearrange their booths and change their lighting from time to time. Arn's tip for new artists is to spend only what is necessary. "Treat every penny like it's your last," says Arn. "And don't max out your credit cards. You never know when you may need them!"

Linda Kaye-Moses:
Wholesale Shows As a Learning Experience

Linda Kaye-Moses realized that metalwork was her "thing" after taking a class at the local community college. With her husband, Evan Soldinger, Linda then started her craft business, Plumdinger Studio. The couple started small, selling their jewelry at a local music festival, then branching into other retail shows.

Next, Linda decided to give wholesale shows a try. Her first effort didn't go well. "At the end of the show, I sat on a crate and cried while Evan packed up our boxes." Instead of letting that frustration turn her off to the idea of wholesale shows, Linda learned from the experience. "On the drive home from that show, we talked about how lousy we felt, what had gone wrong, and what we had to do in the future," Linda says.

What Linda learned from that experience was that she needed to design a collection, not just present random pieces of jewelry. "I took that negative experience as a challenge to be more creative," says Linda. After that, Linda and Evan's wholesale show experience improved dramatically. Learning from your mistakes is the key, according to Linda. "Setbacks are setbacks, they don't feel good," says Linda. "But learn from your experiences and then move ahead."

▪ BEFORE YOU GO ▪

Before going to a show, there are both selling and non-selling objectives that you should consider. Selling objectives are those that can spark instant sales, while non-selling objectives are those that help you build for the future. It is crucial to remember that both of these categories should be weighed evenly in terms of importance.

Trade Show Tip:

Always visit a show before applying to exhibit there. This way you can eliminate all those shows that sound good—but don't really meet your needs. Call the promoter's office at least six weeks in advance and ask about their policy on visitors. When you arrive at the show, stop in the show office and introduce yourself. This is your chance to make a good first impression in person!

Selling Objectives:
- Stimulating sales
- Maintaining relationships
- Dispersing new information
- Remedying all service problems
- Scheduling special appearances at galleries

Non-selling Objectives:
- Determining needs
- Testing new ideas
- Making new contacts
- Gathering information on new trends
- Widening your exposure

■ SELECTING A SHOW ■

Many shows offer a new exhibitor packet—a brochure or kit supplied by show management to help you determine if a show meets your needs. In addition, you can usually obtain reliable information from people who have already exhibited at that show. Ask someone in the show management office to provide you with contact names of exhibitors in your media, or geographical area, and their addresses or telephone numbers. By relying on references, and the show's promoter, you should be able to find out the following information:

A. Audience. Who is coming? What kind of buyer will you be meeting at the show? Does the average buyer who visits the show fall into your target market? Do the attendees resemble your present customers? What is the track record of the show? How many attendees are expected? What organization sponsors the event? If the show brochure does not answer these questions directly, **ASK!** Don't waste valuable time and money on a show that isn't right for you. Again, the best way to investigate a show is to visit.

B. Costs. In addition to the exhibit space fee, are there membership fees involved? How about other costs, such as electricity, union labor, or jury fees? How much is the deposit? When is the balance due? What is the cancellation and refund policy?

C. Location. Is the show being held at a hotel or convention center? How far are local hotels? Is the hall in a downtown or suburban area? Can you get your display or booth in and out easily, and without additional union labor expense? Will the ceiling clearance and overhead lighting be satisfactory?

D. What is provided? Does your booth fee provide only a chalked-in floor space, or does it include: pipe and drape, electricity, chairs, tables, trash cans, a listing in the show program, union labor, and identification badges for you and your assistants?

E. Restrictions. Show management should spell out the restrictions it imposes on exhibitors. What can and

---

David & Mar Marcotte: Selecting a Show That Suits You

In the early seventies, David Marcotte joined his wife, Mar, in her jewelry business to expand their wholesale market. They started doing gift shows in their region of the country. The gift shows allowed the Marcottes to reach more people, thus expanding their customer base.

"To me, wholesale shows are the most productive, cost-efficient way to sell," says David. "You just have to determine specifically what your market is."

David believes that the more narrowly you can define your market, the better off you will be. "Let's say, for example, that you knit angora fuzzy dice to hang on the rear-view mirror of your car," David says. "This would be a handcrafted item. They might be the highest quality fuzzy dice in the world, but I think you would realize that they won't be sold in a craft gallery. They would probably do better at an auto supply shop, which would greatly change the type of show you would want to choose."

Right now the Marcottes' best accounts are in the Northeast and Mid-Atlantic states. "Most shows in this region are very good," says David, "though some are better than others." David's advice to artists just getting started is to begin conservatively. "Don't get in over your head," David says. "Make sure when you write orders, that you can fill them in an appropriate amount of time."

cannot be displayed? What are the exhibit height restrictions? Are there any restrictions on the type and size of sign used by exhibitors? What are the show hours? Is there a limit to the number of booth personnel covered by the booth rental fee? Are there restrictions on any promotions (some shows restrict the use of live models, live entertainment, music, or the demonstration of handcrafted instruments, and other activities within the booth)? What is the show policy on removing exhibits?

F. Timing. Make sure that the show in which you want to exhibit does not conflict with other big buying events important to your customers.

Stuart Abelman: Artist Finds His Place in Wholesale Shows

Stuart Abelman of Abelman Art Glass figured out which shows were right for him, and which were not, through trial and error. "In the beginning, I chose many shows incorrectly," says Stuart. "It is better to choose shows that are right for your product than to choose a 'successful show.' A show may truly be successful, but not for your product."

This was a lesson that Stuart also learned about retail shows. "I did a show once at a clam festival," says Stuart. "The clamming was successful; the crafts were not. This is why it's important to know about the show, and the people that it attracts."

Stuart now only does retail shows for product research, while his wholesale shows generate the largest part of his income. "I still do a few gift shows," says Stuart. "But my favorite shows are wherever I am most successful, and right now that would be the Buyers Markets in Boston and Philadelphia."

Stuart has two pieces of advice for other artists. "First, always look successful, even if you're not," he says. "It's a myth that people want to buy from starving artists. Also, always remember, the person who succeeds is the one who never quits. You stay with it and you win!"

WHAT YOU NEED TO KNOW ABOUT ▪ EXHIBIT SPACE ▪

Some show managers will tell you, "There is no such thing as a bad space." What they don't always tell you is that some spaces are better than others. Most shows assign spaces based on a seniority system. As a new exhibitor, you may have to take what you can get, at least for the first year. While it's understandable that long-time exhibitors should have a crack at the best spots, those who ask for something better, often get their wish. Even after contracts have been signed, and spaces have been allocated, exhibitors often drop out. It sometimes pays to be the squeaky wheel—though not too squeaky!

A bad location need not be the end of the world—in fact, it can turn out to be to your advantage. One exhibitor relegated to the back corner of a very large show printed maps of the floor layout, with his booth prominently marked; along with the map, he gave out a free compass. The map, accompanied by the novel give-away, turned a poor space into a productive sales tool! In most shows, your location matters much less than what you do with the booth, and how many buyers you invite prior to the show.

You can eliminate the space problem with a simple strategy—choose your shows carefully, and stay in the right one for several years. Eventually, the seniority system will work for you rather than against you, and you'll be in the center of all the action!

Tom Torrens: Getting the Most From Booth Space

While his philosophy is usually "less is more," Tom Torrens of Tom Torrens Sculptural Design doesn't believe that this applies to designing a display for booth space. "It is important to get as much as you can out of the space you have," says Tom, "without looking cluttered."

Tom has a "lucky spot" in his booth. "In the front of the booth there is a space, where no matter what we place there, it's always a bestseller," says Tom. Some of Tom's pieces, like his bells, need to be in an accessible location. "The bells really need to be placed where people can touch them," says Tom. "I think that this is important in the booth, and in store displays."

Some shows, as well as shops and galleries, have outdoor exhibit areas, or an outdoor display. This is something that Tom recommends asking about. "Many of my pieces are in their environment outdoors," says Tom. "An outdoor display communicates to the customer or buyer that the piece can be displayed outside." Tom's advice to beginning craftspeople: keep an eye on spending. "Finances are always the bottom line," Tom advises. "Whatever business you are in."

■ TRADE SHOW PROMOTION ■

It's a well-known fact that the average trade show attendee spends about thirty seconds at an exhibit before moving on. You are competing for the buyer's time and attention. It is the job of show management to bring buyers to the show. **It is your job to bring buyers into your booth!**

Begin your sales program long before the week of the show, with communication by mail and by telephone with your present and prospective buyers. Tell buyers ahead of time that you have new products to show, and that it will be worth their time and effort to stop by your booth. If you don't do your job before the show, it is possible that regular buyers will walk right by without stopping. They will think that they already know what you have, and that they can call in an order at another time, after the show.

The management may be able to offer you a list of buyer attendees who plan to visit the show. Send out a mailing to all prospective accounts. If the show management does not offer such a list, they may be able to

do a mailing for you, using their list. In the event that all else fails, find lists on your own.

Postcards make great direct mail pieces. They are inexpensive to mail, quick to send, and easy for the buyer to read. You can have a 4-color postcard preprinted on one side, and leave the second side blank for several different mailings. Promotional stickers are sometimes provided by show management for you to use on boxes, envelopes, and invoices.

EXHIBITOR KITS

Use the exhibitor kit to set up a timetable to accomplish all pre-show plans that need to be made. Call the show management office with any questions you have. Take care of all paperwork promptly. Order all electricity and other booth services at once. Remember: Hotel rooms in the area are at a premium, so make your reservations as soon as possible. Keep a photocopy of all checks to prove that these services were paid for in advance, storing these documents in your exhibitor kit.

Crafting As a Business

■ TRADE SHOW SELLING ■

Just as there is an art to developing your products for sale, there is also an art to selling what you make. Make the most of every minute at any show. Don't be discouraged by small numbers of buyers—it only takes one great order to make the trip worthwhile! Sometimes you won't know how successful a trade show is until years later, when you have had time to evaluate the number of steady, good customers you have derived from the experience.

Don't underestimate the power of your presence at a show. Buyers appreciate your active interest in their business. Sending a "rep" doesn't compare with meeting your customers in person. Your goal at a trade show is to find new customers, and to show current and former customers that their business is still important to you. Follow these helpful hints to make selling at trade shows more rewarding:

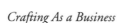

STEP 1

Set goals before the show begins. Decide on the maximum number of orders that you can possibly take. With a large calendar, create a tentative production and delivery schedule, and keep to it! Don't get in over your head with new customers. **Make a good impression by delivering on time!**

STEP 2

Prepare a short statement, briefly telling the buyer a few important points about your products. Begin with a cordial, personal introduction, and then make the necessary points. For example: "Hello, I'm Sue Smith, the designer of this work. My line consists of hand-thrown porcelain, with applied designs using materials such as wildflowers and foliage to create each unique piece."

STEP 3

Involve the buyer. If the buyer seems to be receptive to speaking with you, ask him or her a question that requires a response. For example: "Where is your store?" or "Do you sell porcelain?"

STEP 4

Begin selling your line. If the buyer seems to be comfortable with your conversation, it is time to sell your line. Offer a recommendation of your best sellers. Don't talk credit terms just yet. Explain your exchange policies, shipping procedures, and delivery schedule. "Our studio ships by UPS within five weeks. We can offer you an exchange policy for items that aren't selling as quickly as others."

STEP 5

Now is the time to ask for the order. If the buyer does not wish to write the order at this time, offer a brochure and order form to be used at a later date. Make sure you exchange information so that you can contact the buyer with additional information at another time. It's a good idea to follow up after the show by sending interested buyers and new accounts a short note. After you begin to take the order, you may begin to discuss credit terms, shipping, and packing charges. **Never, ever, forget to ask for the order!** A **legitimate** buyer will always respect and appreciate a direct and business-like approach. Be considerate of the buyer's time. Keep it short and sweet.

STEP 6

Follow up! After you return to the studio, send a note thanking your new accounts for their business. At this time, you may request additional credit information if you are unfamiliar with the account.

Super Buyer

A rough calculation of the total number of buying minutes available at the Buyers Markets will tell you how little time a hurried buyer might have to see your newest designs. At the Boston show, for example, there are three days of buying, adding up to 22 total buying hours for a buyer to work non-stop without a single break for meals.

This woman is "Super Buyer." She has over 900 exhibits to see, so we can make the following schedule for her:

Total show hours	*22*
Total minutes to buy	*1,320*
Average time per booth	*1.47 min.*
That's 1.47 minutes TOTAL including writing orders.	

This gives you far less than 90 seconds to capture this buyer's attention! That is a good argument for taking the largest booth you can afford, and then spending the necessary time to create the most dramatic display of your product possible.

■ ADVANCE ■ PLANNING

If you haven't done your homework before packing for the show, you might be wasting your time. Planning in advance is the key to success! The following is a sample checklist to help you prepare for a trade show.

1) Visit the show before applying to exhibit. This will help you understand who attends, who exhibits, and what your sales potential is. While there, ask questions!

2) Mail your completed application early. Include a self-addressed, stamped postcard for a return receipt. Many times, trade shows allot space on a seniority basis, with long-standing exhibitors given preference over newcomers. Check to see if the show's policies differ from your expectations.

3) Once you have been assigned a space, check the service order form and exhibition instructions to find out what items are furnished by show management, and what you need to order. Don't expect to arrive and find a booth with chairs and a table without having previously requested them. Order all the necessities—including electricity, carpeting, and a trash can! If you wait until you arrive at the show, a late fee may be added to the already steep rental fees.

4) When using last year's exhibit, erect it first at home to check it out ahead of time. It may need work or changes, or you may decide to plan a new booth. What is suitable for an outdoor show may not be appropriate for a trade show.

5) Consider how you will get your exhibit into the hall. Will you need a dolly, a freight elevator, or a labor assistant?

6) Learn the rules of the show and of the hall. Don't plan to hang things on walls or on the pipe and drape, unless you have verified that this is okay. Make sure that there are no restrictions on your booth design or planned activities (such as serving food to buyers, music, or other distractions).

7) Find out if the hall is a union or non-union facility. Services that you can do yourself may be free in a non-union hall (like plugging lights into the outlet), but they may carry a fee in a union hall, unless paid for by show management. Once again, **ASK!**

8) Consider a floater on your insurance policy to protect against damage, theft, or loss of goods at the show or in transit.

9) Mail in all forms in a timely fashion, to prevent delays at the show site.

10) **In case of emergency,** plan to make do without your freight. Carry samples with you, and be prepared to build a booth on-site with foam core or another acceptable material.

11) **Make and confirm hotel reservations** in advance. If necessary, make flight, train, or other travel arrangements at the same time.

12) **Purchase tickets to any seminars** or other events that you wish to attend.

13) **Set a specific sales objective** (by dollar amount, or number of orders). Purchase a sign-in guest book for leads. Determine which products should be emphasized, which new items should be introduced next time, and which items might be discontinued.

14) **Assemble all selling materials.** This should include price lists, promotional photos, press kits, brochures, reprinted articles, and color catalogs. Figure on 500 copies of printed literature, and 15-20 press kits.

15) **Design a booth with an efficient flow** of traffic in mind. Your products should be clearly visible. Provide a chair for buyers, but by all means, **don't sit in that chair!** Design a display area that is inviting—not intimidating.

16) **It is your responsibility** to create an exhibit that is non-flammable.

17) **Floor coverings are important.** Most hall floors are covered with stains and paint. In addition to the added visual impact, a floor covering provides extra comfort for you and your buyers.

18) **Plan lighting in advance,** checking to see that it will not exceed your electrical allotment. Strategic, effective lighting can increase sales. Pack extra bulbs!

19) **Consider color and other dramatic effects** for your booth such as moving parts, lighting, and music.

20) **Psych yourself up!** Be friendly and upbeat. Get to know the buyer, and ask them about their shop. Letting a buyer know you care about their customer is key. Remember, ask for the order, and write it up!

Stephan Roy: Returning to Wholesale After a Flood

Stephan Roy of Roy Designs has triumphed over a disaster that might have wiped out less hardy souls. After recently getting involved in wholesale craft shows, a move that Stephan credits

with really making a business out of his craft, Stephan's studio was flooded by twelve inches of rain in ten hours. He was able to salvage one kiln, but everything else in his studio was a loss. "The only other things that were saved were my booth and my samples that were already on their way to the Philadelphia show," Stephan says.

The shock of the flood, and what he had lost, left Stephan in a daze at the show, but that's when he found out how many friends he had. "At the show, all of the buyers who had bought from me before offered to pre-pay their new orders. Craft Emergency Relief Fund came to my rescue, and show management paid my booth fee for the upcoming Boston show."

Stephan is back to building his business again. The tragedy also had a bright side. "That Philadelphia show turned out to be one of my best shows ever," Stephan says.

Stephan advises fellow craftspeople to be patient. "It takes a long time to build a business," he says. "A long time, and a lot of hard work."

▪ EFFECTIVE EXHIBITS ▪

When doing a show with 500 to 2,000 other creative people, you need to do everything possible to catch the attention of buyers who are tired and glazed over from looking at exhibits. Create an exhibit that you can "live in" for three to six days, depending on the size and duration of the show. Here are some ideas for creating an exhibit that attracts attention.

SIZE

What are the booth size requirements for the show in which you will be participating? Are there freight elevators or narrow access doors that may prevent you from bringing in a large display? Most exhibits for craft markets and gift shows are built to fit an area 10' x 10'.

MERCURY VAPOR HALL LIGHTING

If you are exhibiting in a hall with mercury vapor lighting, consider a tent cover or canopy over your display. Mercury vapor lighting will cast a green color over your exhibit, washing out warm colors, while turning red to brown and yellow to green. Studies have also shown that mercury vapor lights can cause headaches, blurred vision, and fatigue. Take frequent breaks if possible to avoid harmful effects.

DESIGNING YOUR BOOTH

There are several different kinds of display designs and materials commonly used in trade shows. Each has its benefits—what works well for one artist might not be the right choice for another.

A) Architectural units with packing cases. These allow maximum freedom with form and materials. They are often used by companies doing numerous trade shows because they allow for the most protection during freight shipment from show to show. Each hard wall component of the exhibit fits into a protective case for quick and safe transport. Minimal maintenance is required.

B) Single-use exhibits. A creative mind can do wonders with inexpensive and disposable materials, such as foam core, gator board, contact paper, and other art supplies. You can order these items ahead of time to be delivered directly to a booth by a display company or local art supply store.

C) Modular pedestals. Often the most practical choice of craft exhibitors, they come in corrugated cardboard, plastic, or Formica™, and fold, stack, or nest neatly to transport. Pedestals can often be used like building blocks, stacked one on top of another for additional height.

D) Modular walls. Built of hollow-core door materials, lattice panels, metal or plastic tubing, they can be covered or adapted to carry shelves and to hang rods. Easily assembled and transportable, modulars are often hinged for folding during transport.

Thomas Markusen: Metalsmith Believes that Display is Crucial

When he first started exhibiting at shows, Tom Markusen quickly found out that the shows that were a combination of wholesale and retail didn't suit him. "It was difficult for me to create one display that would work in both retail and wholesale," Tom explains. For this reason, Tom participated in two shows each year (Philadelphia and Boston). "It's amazing to me that people don't realize how much time they lose out of their studios when they go to shows," Tom says. "The show is actually costing them twice as much."

Like a business, a display must evolve with time. This doesn't mean you have to change it constantly, just keep it interesting to the buyer. "My display keeps evolving," says Tom. "But I am still using the same modular units with the glass and the clips on the corners that I started using in 1976." Tom feels that attracting attention, so that

people will take a second look, is the display goal of the craftsperson. He also thinks it is important that the display invites people into the booth. "I firmly believe that until buyers break that plane of walking into and through the booth, they can ooh and ahh for hours, but

Tom's candlesticks were displayed as part of the permanent craft collection at the White House Christmas, 1993.

they're not going to buy anything," he stresses.

Vignettes are the secret to Tom's display success. "I think it's important to set up pieces in vignettes, or small groupings, so buyers can see how they can display the same items in their stores," says Tom. "This way, they can offer their customer a range of products and prices. My thinking is that the expensive pieces really sell the mid-priced pieces, because people will think, 'I really like that large bowl, but I can only afford the medium bowl.' You must give a customer an alternative to buying nothing."

Tom adds that the stores which successfully sell his work are those which sell the pieces in vignettes.

For artists just beginning to do shows, Tom recommends starting close to home. "It is better to start doing shows which don't involve a lot of travel," says Tom. "This way, your investment is smaller when you need to watch your spending."

The Gallery Relationship

Make yourself necessary to somebody.
—Emerson

THE GALLERY RELATIONSHIP: GETTING TO KNOW RETAILERS

Craft retailers. Where do they come from? Where can they be found? What do they expect from a craftsperson? What should I say to them? These are just a few of the questions asked by artists new to the wholesaling experience who are often anxious about meeting gallery owners, craft retailers, and buyers. What most people don't realize is that many craft retailers began their careers as working artists.

Developing a relationship with retailers is a two-way street. It is your responsibility as a craftsperson to respond to a retailer's praise of your work with genuine interest in what they have to say, and in their shop. Find out everything you can about the gallery's style (contemporary or traditional) and location (urban, sub-urban, or resort). Your interest in their business is welcome, and provides you with basic information that helps confirm whether your work will sell in the environment they have to offer.

Experienced retailers respond well to your guidance and suggestions as you write your first order. Remember—**you** are the expert when it comes to your work, and how it sells best! But realize that the retailer is the expert on knowing what his or her customers are looking for. Retailers will only buy what they can sell quickly. However, many retailers understand how important it is to invest in high-end, dramatic items that command a customers' attention, but may be slow sellers.

Arthur Grohe: Gallery Owner in Search of "Signature" Style

After fifteen years spent working in corporate positions for companies such as NCR and Western Union, Arthur Grohe, now co-owner of Signature, had grown tired, and was looking for a change. The decision to open a craft gallery came while Arthur and his sister, potter Gretchen Keyworth, were sitting on the beach in Hyannis, Massachusetts. "My sister was looking for a forum to sell her work, and was interested in starting a gallery," Arthur recalls. "We melded our ideas, and Signature was born," he says. Today Signature is a three-location venture.

Arthur explains that he locates new work for the galleries in several ways. "We

photo by Glenwood Jackson

find new artists at wholesale shows, but we also go to small, retail fairs in North Carolina, Seattle, and Michigan, for example." Another way that Arthur finds new artists is through Signature's reputation. "We are very fortunate that because we've been around so long, and we're as well known as we are, people approach us through the mail, sending us packets of information," Arthur states. "We probably receive five or ten requests a week."

The best way for artists to approach Signature is through the mail, sending clear photographs, or clear slides of your work, accompanied by a price list. "Nothing irritates me more than getting slides or photos, and not getting prices. Price is part of my decision, and so if there are no prices, part of that is lost." Having a full body of work is also important, from Arthur's perspective: "A display cannot be created properly with just one piece," Arthur says. "If that is all an artist does, I would probably pass on it."

To artists just getting started, Arthur passes on this advice: "Perceived value is something that one has to deal with. This means, that 'something extra' that is reflected in the price, better be evident. If a customer doesn't perceive its value, then it won't sell."

■ DECORATORS ■

Interior designers and decorators may routinely wish to purchase small amounts of your work for a specific customer's needs. Decorators and designers are identified, not by a business card (anyone can create a business card), but instead by an ASID or IBD membership card. The American Society of Interior Designers and the International Board of Design offer professional memberships at reasonable prices. As a supplier for interior designers, you may wish to join the Industry Foundation, a subsidiary of the ASID, which offers memberships to suppliers only.

Designers and decorators expect a retail discount (20-40%) for small purchases. However, if they actually have a storefront (and many do), then they may place a full minimum order, and expect the standard 50%-off-retail discount. Custom orders that require special fabrics or colors will include an extra charge for customization. Custom orders can require full payment in advance, or at the very least a sizable deposit.

GALLERIES AND EXCLUSIVITY ■ POLICIES ■

There are a few things your mother told you never to discuss— religion, politics, and sex! Some manufacturers would add territories and exclusivity to that list of unmentionable subjects.

Let's face it, you are not a manufacturer, and the reality of the marketplace is that wholesale craft buyers exist because of the demand for unique and unusual merchandise. If your work was available at five stores in every zip code throughout the country, it would no longer be unique.

There are many ways to establish a territory or exclusive arrangement. Here are some ideas that might be of help in creating a comfortable relationship for both buyer and seller:

• When establishing the terms of your relationship with any buyer, be specific and fair to both parties. When you deal fairly with a buyer, you will often be treated the same in return.

• A good customer, one who represents you well by stocking a reasonable amount of merchandise throughout the year, by advertising your work, and above all, by paying on time, deserves protection from a marketplace oversaturated with your work!

EXCLUSIVITY GUIDELINES

Establish the guidelines you desire early in the relationship. Use facts like previous ordering experiences and comparable information from other accounts to establish your basic structure. Offer only what you can live with—and no more! Be careful about any promises made in writing.

Be up-front and honest to earn the respect of the buyer. There will be times when you feel the need to expand, yet territories are controlling your growth. Try broadening a product line to attract different buyers.

EXCLUSIVITY STRATEGIES

A chain store with 95 locations has made an offer on one of your best-selling items. They like you, the work, and the price; there is only one problem—of the 95 stores, 75 of them fall within areas where you have territorial exclusivity agreements. What can you do?

The answer is simple—make a counter-offer to the chain store buyer. Design several new prototypes that can be theirs exclusively! Some of the new products could even be a bit less expensive than the item that they had selected. Make sure that the price includes packing and freight. Guarantee prompt delivery, and/or to drop-ship to each location. These new products won't compete with your established accounts. If necessary, rename the new line, or let the new account use its own name on the item!

It may take some time to develop new products, but your effort will be well rewarded. As a craft artist, you have the freedom to change a design, or produce new items— unlike larger manufacturers. Use this versatility to your advantage.

Phil Jurus: Career Change Leads to New Opportunities as an Artist and a Retailer

Before becoming a jeweler and a retailer, Phil Jurus made his living as a Lutheran minister. "I had been creating jewelry the entire time," says Phil. "Finally, I made the transition to full-time craft."

Phil's change in careers increased his personal freedom, but initially restricted his financial freedom. "At first, my financial situation went from bad to worse," Phil states. "But the good thing about being an artisan is that your ability to make money is in your own hands. There isn't anyone else dictating the terms, or parameters, or the time. I am literally my own boss."

Phil divides his time between his retail shop, where he works with his son, and his studio, where he works with his wife.

Phil has no regrets about leaving the ministry for a life as a jeweler and a retailer. To someone getting started as a craftsperson, or to a craft retailer, his advice is the same: "Learn basic business practices, or delegate that work to someone who already knows them. Many problems are easily resolved when you know the rules."

■ CUSTOMER SERVICE ■

The majority of businesspeople will acknowledge that the most critical ingredient in business is the customer. You can do almost anything wrong in business, but still succeed if you serve the customer. It is also possible that you can do everything else right in business, and still fail if the customer's needs, desires, and emotions are not taken care of.

This truism is known to every business executive. It is written in philosophies of operation, and has a chapter in every management book. But still, customer service seems to have a difficult time finding its way to the actual customer. Why is this so?

The common belief is that by declaring customer service to be a goal, and then "cheering on" employees, the goal will be accomplished. Although that strategy has done great things for customer service, it has done little for customers. A considerable amount of time, effort, and cost are needed to make real progress in improving the treatment of customers.

Pronouncements come down from the top of large companies, but customers are often handled by the people at the bottom of big organizations. Is it any wonder that the customer is the one who suffers? Lack of internal organizational management, not lack of communication, causes poor customer service. Here are some of the things that can be done to treat customers with the respect and care that they deserve:

• Don't let anybody near a customer until he knows what he is doing. Apprentices must be closely supervised, and then certified as able to assist customers.

• Dealing with a tired or overworked person is not in the best interest of the customer or the company. Make sure that customer service responsibilities are evenly distributed.

• Encourage and reward good customer contacts. Instead of asking customers what went wrong, ask what went right!

• Service overkill is the best remedy for a customer service problem. Try giving your customers more service than they would ever expect. This gives you the opportunity to see their reaction to the assistance, enabling you to analyze their position objectively.

Customers can sometimes have bad days, and there is nothing you can do about that. Often their problems will have nothing to do with you. When this happens, good communication is the best medicine.

What can you do when a customer truly gets a raw

deal? EVERYTHING! Throw out your procedures manual, and make it right. Cost is a relative concept. Think of what you spend on advertising to attract unidentified potential customers. Spend the same amount of money—and effort—on those people who are already your customers. When you are face-to-face with someone with a problem, solving that problem is your top priority.

Remember this rule: Everyone has an average of 200 personal friends or contacts. Good news, like a positive business experience, is likely to be shared with approximately one-tenth that number. On the other hand, when people are angry, or feel that they have been mistreated, they share that experience with at least twice that number—and the chain advances when these people talk!

A disgruntled customer is like a walking time bomb. Whether you get a positive or negative detonation depends on you! Customer service is not a cost, it's an investment. It produces returns that can be measured. If you don't believe that, go ask your customers!

Alexander Thomas: Offering the Retailer "Customized" Service

Alexander Thomas of Wood of a Kind produces functional woodwork ranging from picture frames to wine butlers. He got involved in the woodworking business on a whim, and has made that his living ever since (his previous career was as a musician, and he has played the trombone on approximately 500 albums).

Recently, Wood of a Kind began offering retailers products that can be customized through an in-house lasering process. "We can customize any of the woodwork with logos, signatures, or pictures," Alexander states. "This makes them even more desirable as gifts." One good example of the benefits of this service: "A store we do business with regularly had a client who needed gifts. The store's client had to have his company's name on the product for it to double as advertising. We were asked to provide something within a certain price range. The item chosen was a yo-yo. We had it in stock in the quantity ordered (75). That day, we personalized them with lasering for the client. The next day, they were shipped out second-day air. And all was done with no overhead for the store. This would not have been possible for the store to accomplish without our in-house lasering."

Lasering is just one more service that convinces the retailer that Alexander is prepared to meet his or her needs. Alexander encourages all young people, especially minorities, to consider a career in craft: "Craft is such a great thing to be into, because it is so inexpensive to get started. You can start in your garage, or at the kitchen table, and then expand as you get orders."

photo by Glenwood Jackson

■ METHODS ■ OF PAYMENT

The method of payment that you use with each retail account should be determined in advance. The following are three suggestions for getting paid (terms):

Cash On Delivery (C.O.D.): A craft retailer who approaches you at a trade show or fair gives you the advantage. Generally, any first order is C.O.D., unless you make an exception based on excellent credit references from other craftspeople. If the retailer wishes to continue the relationship and receive orders on a regular basis, he may ask for **30-day terms**. At this time, it is appropriate to have the retailer fill out a complete credit application, or provide you with credit references that meet your approval. A line of credit should then be offered to the retailer, and only then should 30-day terms be extended.

Pro Forma: Retailers often have many valid reasons to refuse C.O.D. terms. Many retailers cannot be present at delivery times, or they do not have the time to check a shipment against the purchase order at the time of the delivery. Stores with more than one location, or owners who are not always at one location, find C.O.D. an impossible business relationship. If C.O.D. doesn't work, pro forma is the next best option. Pro forma requires you to phone the shop or gallery before shipping an order, giving the exact total of the shipment, including freight costs. The retailer then mails you a check for that amount prior to the shipment of the merchandise. If you want to be extra cautious, deposit the check and wait for it to clear before sending the order.

> *The method of payment that you use with each retail account should be determined in advance. Three suggestions for payment terms are:*
> - *Cash on Delivery (C.O.D.)*
> - *Pro Forma*
> - *Consignment*

Consignment: For most craftspeople, consignment is only plausible for galleries or shops near home, because they can be personally monitored on a regular basis. Other than that, consignment should be reserved for expensive pieces (those over $500 retail) that retailers would otherwise not risk purchasing outright. If a retailer suggests consignment, your best counter-offer is a guarantee to exchange or trade the item for other items in your line at a predetermined time. Some artists require buyers to purchase a predetermined amount of merchandise before a consignment of additional pieces is considered.

Christopher Jupp: Artist Gained New Perspective for Retailers When He Became One

Christopher Jupp of Jupp-Spoon Metalsmiths used to believe that the life of a retailer was easy—that they just profited off the sweat of artists. Now he knows that nothing is further from the truth. "When I first got started in business, retailers were asking for 30% off the retail price. At that time, I thought they were greedy, and refused to sell to them, saying that I needed all of the profit for myself—

that I would do my own retail. Now, I realize that 30% off was a great deal, and that successful craft retailing is a tough business," Christopher says.

After he became a retailer, Christopher realized that after all the bills were paid, the profit margin wasn't that great. "Today, I would rather give 50% off the top, and let someone else have all of the hassles that go into selling the piece."

The advice that Christopher gives to new artists is: "Be aware of what your goals are, and be prepared to change with them. Doing crafts has a lot of warm, fuzzy feelings about it, but business is a whole different ballgame; it can be difficult at first."

■ CREDIT & COLLECTION ■

In our business lives we encounter many potential customers. Seeking out the best possible clients is everyone's goal. A good customer is one who pays according to the agreements made at the time of the order.

Most customers are indeed good customers. Very few buyers are out to take advantage of or to cheat a craft supplier. But the only way to prevent a bad experience is to avoid one with a thorough check of all credit references. Although your customers are good customers, they may not always be fast-paying customers. In this overview, we will attempt to encourage good customers to pay their bills promptly.

THE VALUE OF THE UNCOLLECTED BILL

The Shrinking Dollar:

1 month	.983
2 months	.966
3 months	.949
4 months	.932
5 months	.915
6 months	.898
7 months	.800

The probability of collections diminishes in direct proportion to time:

60 days past due	90%
90 days past due	80%
180 days past due	50%
360 days past due	0%

CONSUMER LAWS

Equal Credit Opportunity Act. If you can prove that a creditor has discriminated against you, a court will award you court costs and a reasonable amount for attorney's fees. You may also sue for punitive damages up to $10,000.

Fair Credit Reporting. You may sue any credit reporting agency or creditor for violating the rules about who may have access to your credit records and correcting errors in your file. An unauthorized person who secures a credit report—or any employee of a credit reporting agency who supplies a credit report to unauthorized persons—may be fined up to $5,000 or imprisoned for one year, or both.

Credit and Collection Methods Today. Know your customer thoroughly before you OK the order or raise the credit line. Once the order is filled and becomes past due, use the best techniques available for collecting or protecting the open balance. Get this information from the customer <u>before extending credit</u>:

1. Current financial statements or current estimates of sales, net profit, net worth, or working capital.

2. Average bank balance and bank loan experience.

3. The name of the owner of the company.

4. The customer's major suppliers.

5. The amount of mark-up on products sold in the store.

6. Information on whether the organization is "clean," efficient, and well run.

7. The credibility of the company's officers.

8. The number and amount of outstanding loans, including SBA loans.

COLLECTION TIPS FOR OVER THE PHONE

The most sensitive collecting is done by telephone—even though, on a sizable customer base, letters may actually produce more total dollars. Telephone collecting requires mental agility, the ability to react instantly to changing situations, plus innovation and flexibility in negotiating. Successful collectors take pains to remove all possible surprise elements from the process by thorough pre-call planning.

1. Know your customer, including the type of business, success factor, pattern and trend of debtor payments, and previous collection experience with the account.

2. The first few seconds of a call are the most important. Use three short calls rather than a single, lengthy conversation.

3. Do not disclose the purpose of the call to anyone but the creditor. If your call poses an embarrassment, you'll have added another hurdle.

4. When debtors launch into a tirade, let them talk

themselves out (it may be the first time anyone's listened). Only then will they be inclined to listen to your message.

5. There's a place for an aggressive, insistent, demanding, forceful effort. Some debtors understand—and react to—no other approach. Still, it can be done without abusing the debtor.

6. Silence is a powerful weapon. In phone work, state your case, and then wait. Don't bow to temptation to fill the void. Eventually, the debtor will respond, sometimes blurting out causes or reasons you'd get no other way.

7. Always be prepared with a substitute payment plan (and at least one alternative) if the debtor indicates that the full amount, in a single payment, is not possible.

8. Once a payment plan is accepted, restate the details immediately. After the call, write a letter confirming the details.

9. Claims of non-payment for reasons of incorrect billing, short shipment, or damaged goods can be put right with an adjusted invoice mailed that same day. Immediately advise the debtor of your action and ask for full payment by return mail.

PUTTING IT IN WRITING

A simple letter can be an effective method of collection. If a few simple rules are followed, a letter can help you clear up an old debt.

1. Keep form letters fresh. Review, revise, and re-write letters at least once a year.

2. To forestall claims that an invoice was never received, attach a photocopy to your letter.

3. Final demand letters signed by your attorney, on his or her letterhead, will likely produce more results than the same letter with your signature.

4. Keep letters brief and to the point, just two or three short paragraphs, on a single page.

5. To "spotlight" delinquency, place the amount and exact number of days overdue (as of the letter date) in full caps at top center of the letter—before the salutation or a single word of body copy.

6. When you are unsure that letters are reaching the proper party, send at least one piece via certified mail with a return receipt requested.

7. Don't bury the message in long words, jargon, or flowery phrases.

8. The consequences of failure to pay are negative. Put the message in terms of positive benefit statements.

9. Take the "form" out of form letters by adding quick, brief, handwritten comments to catch the reader's eye.

10. All collection letters should be personally signed.

STANDARD PRACTICES

1. Whether in letters, phone calls, or personal visits, *always* ask for first or full payment, now.

2. Intersperse letters and calls. Unless the situation is critical, use letters to set up your subsequent calls, if necessary.

3. Avoid arguments. They reduce your chances for a reasonable discussion.

4. Control the conversation, but learn more through questioning and listening.

5. In probing, ask open-ended questions requiring "essay" answers, not yes or no responses.

6. Ask for return of remaining goods (at debtor's expense) and bill for the portion used.

7. Personal visits can not only clean up a current delinquency but may forestall future problems. Once the debtor has seen you face-to-face, he will usually try harder to meet your future bills.

8. Build goodwill with annual "thank you" letters to good customers.

9. Occasionally, send final demand letters in plain, invitation-sized envelopes with the address individually typed (or handwritten) and stamped with an actual stamp (not metered).

The most important part of any collection call is to always ask: "Will you send me a check for the full amount today?" If you get no committment restate the question, "When will you send me a check for the full amount?"

THE CREDIT CHECK

Terms are a gift to an established account that has proven itself as a good and potential long-term customer. Have a good reason for extending terms, such as the store owner not being able to be present for the delivery. This is common for stores with many locations, or stores in tourist locations that may have stock delivered off-season.

Check references carefully. Get a promise of prompt payment from the store owner and accounts payable clerk. Many buyers for large stores realize the artists' need for prompt payment and have set up special payment programs for craft artists—ask the buyer if you can be included in a similar program.

Your best reason for declining credit may be one that is on the store's credit reference sheet. It's amazing how many buyers aren't familiar with the accounts they use on their credit reference sheet. Check references by sending out a pre-paid postcard requesting the information you need. It's becoming more and more common to ask if the account is troublesome. Craft stores and galleries will generally be your better paying accounts as they are sympathetic to the artist's need for prompt payment.

A Picture is Worth...

Ask the gallery owner for a photo of the inside of the store. Know your marginal credit customers and look for ways to help them with sales and help them pay on time. A successful store is a well-paying customer. A store that is dependent upon your merchandise is a good customer—it can't afford not to be.

Elisa Drumm Van Auken: Artist Finds that Strict Retail Guidelines Make for Good Business

Elisa Drumm Van Auken comes from a craft business family. Her father, Don Drumm, is a metalsmith, so she grew up in the industry. Now a married mother of fraternal twins (a boy and a girl), Elisa produces handprinted and appliquéd wearables in wool, silk, and cotton. Her philosophy is to work with each retailer to develop a collection. "Working with each shop as an individual allows me to make a perfect match between the work, and the final customer," Elisa believes. "This method also helps to encourage re-orders."

The road to success was not always so smooth. Along the way, Elisa encountered problems with a retailer, and ended having to use a collection agent. Now it is her procedure to make all first orders C.O.D., and then run a credit check. "I learned quickly that it is important to ask around within the craft community to see if a retailer pays on time, and plays by the rules, and has a good reputation," she stresses.

To get new accounts, Elisa checks out shops that she is interested in, and sends them one of her catalogs. "After sending out materials, I follow up with a phone call in about two weeks. The call is the important touch, because shop owners get a lot of mail, and you want to stand out."

CREDIT APPLICATION
Sample

Company Name _____

Address _____

Telephone _____

Fax _____

Check One: ❏ Proprietorship   ❏ Partnership   ❏ Corporation

State Incorporated In _____

How Long in Business? _____ Type of Business _____

List Officers, Partners, or Owners:

Name	Title	Home Address
_____	_____	_____
_____	_____	_____
_____	_____	_____

Bank Reference:

Name of Institution _____ Branch _____

Address _____ Phone (_____) _____

Bank Contact _____ Type of Account _____

Account # _____

Business Credit References:

Name *(company & business)*	Full Address	Phone
_____	_____	_____
_____	_____	_____
_____	_____	_____

Does your company require purchase orders? ❏ Yes   ❏ No

Authorized Purchasers:

_____   _____   _____

The undersigned agrees that the information herein contained is true and correct. The previously mentioned company understands that any false information may result in cancellation of any account which may be established.

Company _____ Date _____

Authorized Signature _____

Print Name _____ Title _____

It is suggested that you have this form, and all others, reviewed by an attorney, for it may not be legal and binding.

OUTLINE OF UNDERSTANDING

By Gail Sustare

The following outline is in its formative stage, but can be used as a means to keep track of agreements between craftspeople and various retailers. It should be used with the idea that it will open lines of communication, but it is not a legal document.

Artist's Name _____   Buyer's Name _____

Business Name _____   Business Name _____

Address _____   Address _____

City _____ State ____ Zip _____   City _____ State ____ Zip _____

Phone _____   Phone _____

Artist Checklist

❏ 1. I charge___% additional packing and shipping.

❏ 2. I charge__% of unpaid balance after 30 days.

❏ 3. I agree to ship within two weeks of the shipping date specified.

❏ 4. I will exchange anything within the first___days.

❏ 5. I will exchange only with prior approval by my studio.

❏ 6. I agree to notify you if I do a retail show in your area.

❏ 7. I agree not to discount my work at a retail show in your area.

❏ 8. I agree to exchange pieces if they haven't sold within__ months.

❏ 9. I am willing to give an exclusive on a certain item or items in my line.

❏ 10. I am willing to give an exclusive in your zip code (watch out—some competitors may face each other on a main thoroughfare, but may actually have different zip codes).

❏ 11. I am willing to give an exclusive in your city, including zip codes _____.

❏ 12. I am willing to give an exclusive with an annual minimum purchase of $_____.

❏ 13. I am not willing to give an exclusive.

❏ 14. I am willing to bill net __ with three credit references.

❏ 15. All first orders are C.O.D.

❏ 16. I can supply individual cards or tags with each piece.

❏ 17. I am available for one-of-a-kind or commission work.

❏ 18. I produce individual art pieces, and may be interested in a show at your gallery.

❏ 19. Special information_____

Gallery Checklist

❏ 1. I have had a retail outlet for __ years.

❏ 2. I have had a retail outlet at this address for __ years.

❏ 3. My gallery or shop is more than 50% American handcrafts.

❏ 4. I agree to notify you if there is a delay in payment.

❏ 5. I keep regular store hours:_____.

❏ 6. The shipping address is my retail outlet address.

❏ 7. I mail to my customers __ times a year.

❏ 8. I have special events __ times a year.

❏ 9. I publish a catalog.

❏ 10. I am the bookkeeper of my business. I am not the bookkeeper—contact: _____.

❏ 11. I am a partner, sole proprietor, buyer, for the store (circle one).

❏ 12. I advertise in the following publications:

_____

❏ 13. Additional retail outlets:

_____

❏ 14. Special information_____

_____

Gail Sustare is the co-owner of The Studio Gallery in Manlius, NY.

10

Craft as a Family Business

*One travels the world over in search of what he needs
and returns home to find it.*
–George Moore

CRAFT: A BUSINESS ▪ TO KEEP ▪ IN THE FAMILY

Craftwork is a business that the whole family can enjoy, while playing an important role in its development. Most successful craft businesses are headed by partners who are husband and wife, mother and daughter, or parent and child. The crucial point to remember is that a craft business is not only the product, but includes everything from sales to public relations to booth construction. When members of your family realize that what benefits one, benefits all, your business will run like a well oiled machine.

THREE STEPS FOR COMBINING ▪ FAMILY AND ▪ BUSINESS

Every business encounters problems. Whether they are personality conflicts or financial difficulties, these problems are made worse if those in conflict are related—or worse yet if they happen to be living in the same house. Following are three steps that can help you map out your business, and better define each family member's role. The bottom line is that communication and expectations are always better on the table than in the back of your mind.

What duties go along with each job? The best way to create resentment is to have an overlap in assigned responsibilities. For each person, create a list of duties, or departments he or she controls. This defines each person's turf, so there is never a question about whose is the final word. Christopher Jupp, a metalsmith, explains that his partner, in all definitions of the

The Ayre Family: Building a Business Together

Most members of the Ayre family are now involved in some way with the family business, Ayre & Ayre Silversmiths. Each Ayre plays an important role that keeps the family, and the business, running smoothly. Bob Ayre started the business with his son, Bill, who for now does most of the production, while Bob works with the computer and repairs the equipment.

The other branch of the family business is an H&R Block office. Early in his career, Bob thought that he was taken advantage of by his C.P.A. His wife, Patty, had just finished taking a tax course, so they decided to buy a local H&R Block franchise. Later, their oldest daughter joined Patty, and now, business is booming. The team of mother and daughter ably take care of all the bookkeeping for Ayre & Ayre Silversmiths. Bill's wife helps out assembling earrings, and Bob and Patty's other daughter (who is in the Air Force) lends a hand for any east coast shows. Currently, everyone on the payroll is named Ayre.

Working with family members isn't always a breeze. "In working with your family, disputes elevate into real arguments," Bob says. "With regular employees, you don't get into those kinds of arguments; they quit. With family, you want to strangle each other for a few days, and then it calms down."

Bob believes that the only job more difficult than being a craftsperson is being a mother. "Being a mother, you are never finished, you can never stop."

Kyle McKeown Mansfield: Artist Finds the Right Combination for Family and Business

Kyle McKeown Mansfield believes that she has the best of both worlds—a family involved in the business of craft, but not directly involved in her business, Kyle Design, Inc. Her father, the late artist Robert McKeown, and her mother, Lee McKeown, worked in the craft industry (in woodworking) from the time she was young, so Kyle grew up in the craft community.

Kyle began her career painting on silk—mostly scarves and wall pieces—and later turned to creating silk jewelry, and then metal jewelry. "Having family in the same type of business is a great asset," Kyle says. "They can be used as a constant source of feedback—a great sounding board." But there was also a time when having family in the business caused conflict. After her father died, Kyle and her mother tried working together.

It took some time before both women decided it would be best to pursue their own businesses separately. They still brainstorm regularly, however, and confer on product development. "My mom is my best source for advice," says Kyle.

"Kyle Design, Inc. evolved differently because my parents were in the business," Kyle says. "I have known many of the buyers since I was a teenager, and that certainly helped on one hand, but made things tougher on another." At a show in 1988, for example, a buyer asked Kyle: "When did Bob start doing jewelry?" Kyle replied that her father never made jewelry, that the jewelry was her own work. Fellow artists were still asking Kyle is she was at the show helping her dad. Kyle has to keep reminding people that she is an artist in her own right.

Being able to ask the veterans for advice, though, was one of the perks of being in a craft family. For those craftspeople who might not have that advantage, Kyle has this advice: "Ask a lot of questions. Also, shop as many shows as possible to find out where you fit in."

word, is Lois Wacholtz. "As the artist, for artistic decisions, I get 51% of the vote when conflicts arise," Christopher says. "But on the other hand, when it's a question of business, Lois gets the 51% vote."

Map out future plans for the business. Do you want to keep the business small and personal, while your sister has expectations of adding twenty employees and selling your work in department stores across the country? These are the differences that need to be worked out now, rather than later. Plans that you believe are understood may not be. Arguments over purchasing a new kiln versus a used one might be about the growth of the business rather than kilns. If everyone involved has helped create a plan for the future of the business, many of these arguments can be easily avoided.

A chain is only as strong as its weakest link. Sure, everyone knows someone who has gotten a job because he or she was the boss's sister, brother, mother, or nephew—and the situation works out anyway. But everyone also hears about those times when working with relatives is a disaster. Mixing family with business can be the perfect solution to everyone's problems, or it can be the final blow to an already precarious relationship. From the start, the ground rules must be that each person carries his or her own weight. If not, resentment won't be left at the office, it will creep into your home life. Make sure that each person is right for his particular job, and that he feels comfortable in that role. If you have additional employees who are not family members, it is important that blatant favoritism isn't shown. If the rule is that no personal calls can be made at the office, then that rule goes for everyone—family included.

All businesses must be based on honesty, communication, and performance, and this is most important in family businesses. Everyone makes mistakes, loses his temper, and has differences of opinion, but realize that in working with family, you have a lot more to lose than your business.

Janice Chesnik & Sheryl Koch: Mother-Daughter Team Create Kaleidoscopes Together— in Different States

Janice Chesnik and Sheryl Koch are the mother-daughter team that comprise Chesnik-Koch, Ltd. Having had experience in a variety of crafts, Janice took a class on kaleidoscopes, and thought, "I can do better than that." And she did. Together with her daughter, Sheryl, Janice began creating and selling kaleidoscopes.

When Sheryl got married and moved to Nevada, the two could have gone their separate ways. "But since we design very different lines, and have different price lists, it's really no problem," Janice says. The distance in miles allows both Janice and Sheryl to create on their own without any interruption during the designing process. Wholesale shows provide the opportunity for the two women to mesh their two small companies into a united Chesnik-Koch, Ltd.

As individual artists, and as a mother-daughter team, Janice and Sheryl continue to provide new and exciting designs to the world of kaleidoscopes. Janice's suggestion to artists just getting started is not to grow too fast. "Let your business grow at a natural pace."

■ CRAFT ■ BUSINESSES: SOMETHING FOR EVERYONE

Even if your spouse or significant other isn't artistically gifted, there still is a place for him or her in your craft business. Regardless of what his or her day job entails, your partner can play a key role in making the business end of your craft enterprise run smoothly.

If your partner's career involves writing or editing, these skills can come in handy when creating printed materials. A good writer can add that extra something to a public relations campaign, and editing skills are crucial when designing business forms. A partner who works with numbers is a valuable asset. Accounting, bookkeeping, and even making change at retail shows is easier when someone you trust is there to lend a hand. If your partner is a retail professional—you've hit the jackpot! Getting the inside track on the world of retail, in addition to having an in-house sounding board, can improve your chances of being a successful wholesaler.

At the very least, your partner is a warm body who can help you pack for shows, load the van, and boothsit when you need to use the restroom! Perhaps the most important role a partner can play is as emotional support. The more you let this person know about your business and what you do, the better prepared he or she is to come to the rescue when times are tough.

A. John & Judith Rose: Craft Couple's Skills Complement Each Other

A. John and Judith Rose's business, Textillery, developed after John bought Judith a small loom as a birthday present. Soon after, the Roses were preparing to move to Indiana from Ohio, and friends started asking if they could purchase some of Judith's creations. "That was the spark for the business," Judith explains.

The transition into full-time craft was a rocky one. "John is the idea man," says Judith. "He had always wanted to have his own business." The first five years, Textillery only broke even, because the Roses were still trying to find their niche. Finally, they settled into selling in the home furnishings market, where they found success. John and Judith still do wholesale shows, but they also rely heavily on their network of independent sales representatives that they have built over the years.

Judith believes strongly that a craft business must be treated with professionalism. "Too many people do not treat their craft like a business. You have to be able to give your customers what they want; this is something that people don't often do."

photo by DeJohn Rose

■ CHILDREN AND THE ■ CRAFT PROFESSIONAL

Craft is one of the best businesses to be involved in if you have babies or young children. How many other jobs allow you to stay around the house, or actually be at home when school lets out? Depending on your chosen craft, you can work in a home studio, or even at the kitchen table. Craft is also one of the few professions that allows children to get involved.

If you design jewelry, whose opinion is better than that of a teenage girl? Product testing can be done at home if you create dolls or wooden toys. If your business involves wearables, you have models at your disposal! Children can also pitch in with cleanup, product development, and many other tasks that, while simple, are easier when there is another set of hands (albeit little ones).

The only time when small children can be a handful is at a show or a craft fair. If your children are young enough to need constant attention, then they don't belong anywhere near your booth. A spouse or other caretaker who can keep an eye on the child is an added plus. A booth can feel like a prison to a three-year-old. The bottom line is that you don't want your child to suffer because of your business, and you don't want your business to suffer because of your child. A baby-sitter is often the best solution for everyone.

Wayne Reynolds & Caryn Fried: Husband and Wife Artists Sell Their Pottery, Bonsai, and Christmas Trees

Wayne Reynolds and Caryn Fried of North Eagle Pottery live and work together on property that includes their home, their studio, a retail shop which sells their pottery and bonsai trees, and a two-acre Christmas tree farm. This unusual combination works well for Wayne and Caryn. "I incorporated bonsai into the business about five years ago," Wayne says. "The Christmas tree farm was here when we got here, so that, too, is now a part of the business."

Because the public schools in their area are making cutbacks, arts and crafts are no longer available during school time. For this reason, a teacher at his daughter Maya's school asked Wayne if he could offer pottery classes for kids. This idea worked out so well that Wayne started a second class for adults. Wayne believes that working together in business is the best thing for his relationship with Caryn. "Because pottery is so labor-intensive, we work long hours," says Wayne. "If we worked separate jobs, we wouldn't see much of each other, and I think that would be detrimental to our relationship." Wholesale shows are also easier because Wayne and Caryn work together "We think of wholesale shows as pleasure trips, where we get to see our friends, and the people who buy from us," says Wayne.

For a craft artist just starting out, Wayne recommends an apprenticeship. "Apprenticeships are the most ideal form of education. Find someone whose work you like, and ask to work with him. Even if you have to pay for the experience, it's a great education."

The Wise Family: Combining Child Rearing and Craft

Kathy Wise works in business with her husband, Patrick, her brother-in-law, Steven, and his wife, Helen. Together they are Wise Studios. Before they got together, creating fantasy sculptures out of porcelain, stoneware, bronze, and silver, they all held different jobs. As the parents of eight children, collectively, the Wises feel that they are lucky to have a business where they can work at home, and often work with their children.

"Before we started the business full-time, I was working as a nurse in pediatric intensive care, Patrick was teaching the second grade, Steven was a photographer, and Helen had a variety of jobs," Kathy says. "We were sculpting on the side for a year before we got involved in wholesaling, and made this our full-time work."

In Wise Studios there is a play table, because the partners have had kids almost as long as they've had a business. "We feel fortunate that we can work, and have the kids with us," Kathy says. When asked if their work is fragile, Kathy explains that if it can survive a studio filled with children, it can survive anything. Kathy sees many benefits in the business of craft. "The good thing about craft is that it is something you can combine with a family. Having kids around is really a good thing; they make you take a break."

Notes

Notes

Notes

Notes

Craft Resources

Educational Opportunities for Craftspeople

A

Anderson Ranch Arts Center
Contact: Frances Chaves
P.O. Box 5598
Snowmass, CO 81615
(303)923-3181
Classes Available:
Classes available in ceramics, woodworking, sculpture, photography, and interdisciplinary studies. Most courses are offered in the summer only.

Archie Bray Foundation
Contact: Carol Roorbach
2915 Country Club Avenue
Helena, MT 59601
(406)443-3502
Classes Available:
A ceramics artists' residence program is offered. The deadline for applying is March 1st each year. Classes are offered in throwing and hand-building by the artists in residence.

Arrowmont School
Contact: Sandra Blain
P.O. Box 567
Gatlinburg, TN 37738
(615)436-5860
Classes Available:
One- and two- week sessions in all variations of art media.

Art Farm
Contact: Janet Williams
1306 West 21st Road
Marquette, NE 68854
(402)854-3120
Classes Available:
Provides a worksite, resources and support for artists, giving them time to experiment with new projects while working and living in a rural environment.

B

Baltimore Clayworks
Contact: Director
5706 Smith Avenue
Baltimore, MD 21209
(410)578-1919
Classes Available:
Classes offered throughout the year for adults and children at various levels of skill.

Brookfield Craft Center
Contact: John I. Russell
P.O. Box 122
Brookfield, CT 06804
(203)775-4526
Classes Available:
Offers extensive classes, workshops, seminars, and exhibitions involving: ceramics, fibers/weaving, metal-smithing/jewelry, woodworking, glass, paper/book arts, photography, and business, design, and marketing.

C

Cranbrook
Contact: Director
500 Lone Pine Road, P.O Box 801
Bloomfield Hills, MI 48013
(313)645-3303
Classes Available:
Private graduate art school offering the Master of Architecture degree and the Master of Fine Arts degree in eight disciplines.

F

Farmington Valley Art Center
Contact: Betty Friedman
25 Arts Center Lane
Avon, CT 06001
(203)678-1867
Classes Available:
Classes are offered throughout the year in decorative arts, fiber arts, weaving, quilting, basketry, pottery, and jewelry. Children's classes are also offered.

Foothills Artists
Contact: Pam Meade
P.O. Box 264
White Oak, KY 41472
(606)743-7510
Classes Available:
Exhibits of artwork from local and regional artists are held throughout the year. Classes in ceramics, quilting, and watercolors are also offered.

G

Glass Workshop
Contact: Director
647 Fulton Street
Brooklyn, NY 11217-1112
(718)625-3685
Classes Available:
Offers classes, workshops, exhibitions, studio access, and residencies.

H

Haystack Mountain School of Crafts
Contact: Stuart Kestenbaum
P.O. Box 518
Deer Isle, ME 04627
(207)348-2306
Classes Available:
An international arts center providing two and three week summer sessions in diverse craft/fine arts mediums.

I

Isomata (Idlewild School)
Contact: Director
P.O. Box 38
Idyllwild, CA 92349
(714)659-2171
Classes Available:
Offers courses in writing, visual arts, music (orchestra, bands, jazz workshops, chamber music and solo performance) theatre, dance, and Native American arts (weaving, pottery, jewelry making).

J

John Campbell Folk Art School
Contact: Virginia Bledsoe
John Campbell Folk Art School
Brasstown, NC 28902
(704)837-2775
Classes Available:
Classes offered for craft artists of all levels. Basketry, blacksmithing, beadwork, broommaking, clay, dollmaking, enameling, glass, knitting, jewelry, kaleidoscopes, and much more.

K

Kentucky Folklife Program
Contact: Bob Gates
P.O. Box H
Frankfurt, KY 40601
(502)564-3016
Classes Available:
Apprenticeship program available in all facets of folkcraft.

M

Mary Anderson Center For the Arts
Contact: Sarah Yates
101 St. Francis Drive
Mt. St. Francis, IN 47146
(812)923-8602
Classes Available:
The Mary Anderson Center is an artist's residence and retreat, offering stays from one day to several weeks.

Mudflat Studio
Contact: Director
149 Broadway
Sommerville, MA 02145
(617)628-0589
Classes Available:
Offers a full range of ceramic courses and workshops in wheelthrowing, handbuilding , and technical topics in a fully equipped studio.

N

Northern Clay Center
Contact: Joanne Kelly
2375 University Avenue West
St. Paul, MN 55114
(612)642-1735
Classes Available:
Classes are available in ceramics from pre-schoolers to advanced artists. Rental studio space is also available.

NY Glass Experimental
Contact: Director
647 Fulton Street
Brooklyn, NY 11217
(212)966-1808
Classes Available:
Classes in all facets of glasswork offered throughout the year. Studio space is also available.

O

Oregon School For Arts & Crafts
Contact: Christina Kahn
8245 SW Barnes Road
Portland, OR 97225
(503)297-5544
Classes Available:
Offers classes and workshops in book arts, ceramics, drawing, fiber arts, metal, photography, and wood.

P

Penland School of Crafts
Contact: Ken Botnick
Penland Road
Penland, NC 28765
(704)765-2359
Classes Available:
Classes are offered in ceramics, book arts, fiber, glass, iron, metal and wood for artists of all levels.

Peters Valley Craft Center
Contact: Jeanie Eberhardt
19 Kuhn Road
Layton, NJ 07851
(201)948-5200
Classes Available:
Offers summer workshops in: blacksmithing/metals, ceramics, fibers, fine metals, photography, and wood-working for beginning, intermediate, and advanced levels.

Phoenix City Arts Center
Contact: Sylvia Vielma
1202 North 3rd Street
Phoenix, AZ 85004
(602)262-4627
Classes Available:
Classes available in the visual arts for artists of all ages/abilities.

Pilchuck Glass School (Summer)
Contact: Marge Levy
1201 316th Street
Stanwood, WA 98292
(206)445-3111
Classes Available:
Classes offered throughout the summer in all facets of glasswork. Classes available for beginners and advanced artists.

Pilchuck Glass School (Winter)
Contact: Marge Levy
107 South Main Street
Seattle, WA 98104
(206)621-8422
Classes Available:
Winter address for information only. Classes available in the summer only.

R

Revere Academy of Jewelry Arts
Contact: Alan Revere
760 Market Street
San Fransisco, CA 94102
(415)391-4179
Classes Available:
Offers a wide range of short, intensive hands-on classes for working professionals and serious beginners.

S

School For the Arts
Contact: Richard E. Gilson, Director
1395 Lexington Avenue
New York, NY 10128
(212)427-6000
Classes Available:
Offers courses and workshops in fine art, fine crafts, music and dance for children, teens and adults.

Shockoe Bottom Arts Center
Contact: Rusty Davis
1632 West Grace Street, #2
Richmond, VA 23220
(804)359-2931
Classes Available:
The Shockoe Bottom Arts Center rents studio space to craft and fine artists. Craft shows are also sponsored by the center.

Southwest Craft Center
Contact: Ric Collier
300 Augusta
San Antonio, TX 78205
(512)224-1848
Classes Available:
Offers workshops in surface design, papermaking, photography, fibers, ceramics and metals.

T

The Torpedo Factory
Contact: Director
105 North Union Street
Alexandria, VA 22314
(703)838-4565
Classes Available:
Year-round art school offering classes in various media for artists of all ability levels.

Touchstone Center For Crafts
Contact: Marianne Filiaggi
R.D. #1 Box 60
Farmington, PA 15437
(412)329-1370
Classes Available:
Workshops for all levels of experience are taught by
nationally acclaimed artists in blacksmithing, clay, fiber,
wood, jewelry, printmaking, glass, drawing and painting.

V

Vermont State Craft Center
Contact: Pamela Siers
Frog Hollow
Middlebury, VT 05753
(802)388-3177
Classes Available:
100-plus classes each year for children & adults; release-
time pottery programs for area schools; art administration
internships.

W

Watershed
Contact: Holly Walker
RR1 Box 845, Cochran Road
Edgecomb, ME 04556
(207)882-6075
Classes Available:
Independent study retreat for ceramic artists and small
groups.

Wesleyan Potters
Contact: Melissa Schilke
350 South Main Street
Middletown, CT 06457
(203)347-5925
Classes Available:
Offers classes and workshops in pottery, basketry, jewelry,
weaving, and children's art.

West Virginian Cultural Center
Contact: Director
State Capital Complex, 1900 Washington Street NE
Charleston, WV 25305
(304)558-0220
Classes Available:
Offering classes in most craft media throughout the year.

Education–
Improving Your
Craft Through Schooling

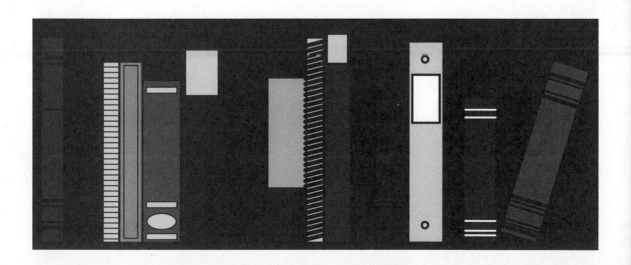

Craft Suppliers

Basketry Suppliers & Equipment

Bamboula
27 West 20th Street
New York, NY 10011
(212)675-2714
Merchandise Includes:
Basketry supplies and equipment

Basket Works, The
77 Mellor Avenue
Baltimore, MD 21228
(410)747-8300
Merchandise Includes:
Basketry supplies and equipment

Cane & Basket Supply Co.
1283 South Cochran Avenue
Los Angeles, CA 90019
(213)939-9644
Merchandise Includes:
Basketry supplies and equipment

Canyon Records & Indian Arts
4143 North 16th Street
Phoenix, AZ 85016
(602)266-4823
Merchandise Includes:
Basketry supplies and equipment

Country Seat, The
Box 24A, Road # 2
Kempton, PA 19529
(215)756-6124
Merchandise Includes:
Basketry supplies and equipment

CT Care & Reed Co.
134 Pine Street
Manchester, CT 06040
(203)646-6586
Merchandise Includes:
Basketry supplies and equipment

Hansa
4315 Upton Avenue South
Minneapolis, MN 55410
(612)925-6014
Merchandise Includes:
Basketry supplies and equipment

Inter Mares Trading Co., Inc.
1064 Route 109
Lindenhurst, NY 11757
(516)957-3467
Merchandise Includes:
Basketry supplies and equipment

JHB International
1955 South Quince Street
Denver, CO 80231
(303)751-8100
Merchandise Includes:
Basketry supplies and equipment

John McGuire Basket Supplies
398 South Main Street
Geneva, NY 14456
(315)781-1251
Merchandise Includes:
Basketry supplies and equipment

Loew-Cornell, Inc.
563 Chestnut Avenue
Teaneck, NJ 07666
(201)836-7070
Merchandise Includes:
Basketry supplies and equipment

Maurice Goldman & Sons, Inc.
22 West 48th Street
New York, NY 10036
(212)575-9555
Merchandise Includes:
Basketry supplies and equipment

Melanie Collection, The
12105 Bermuda Northeast
Albuquerque, NM 87111
(505)298-7036
Merchandise Includes:
Basketry supplies and equipment

Name Game, The
P.O. Box 1732
Matthews, NC 28106
(704)847-8278
Merchandise Includes:
Basketry supplies and equipment

Plymouth Reed & Cane Supply
1200 West Ann Arbor Road
Plymouth, MI 48170
(313)455-2150
Merchandise Includes:
Basketry supplies and equipment

Renaissance, Inc.
P.O. Box 130
Oregon House, CA 95962
(916)692-1663
Merchandise Includes:
Basketry supplies and equipment

Western Trading Post
32 Broadway
Denver, CO 80209
(303)777-7750
Merchandise Includes:
Basketry supplies and equipment

Winona Trading Post
P.O. Box 324
Santa Fe, NM 87504
(505)988-4811
Merchandise Includes:
Basketry supplies and equipment

Ceramics Suppliers & Equipment

Aim Kilns Manufacturing
350 Southwest Wake Robin Avenue
Corvallis, OR 97333
(800)647-1624
Merchandise Includes:
Ceramics equipment

American Art Clay Co.
4717 West 16th Street
Indianapolis, IN 46222
(317)244-6871
Merchandise Includes:
General ceramics supplies and
equipment

Axner Pottery Supply
P.O. Box 1984
Guiedo, FL 32765
(800)843-7057
Merchandise Includes:
Ceramics supplies, equipment, and
craft books.

C&F Wholesale Ceramics
3241 East 11th Avenue
Hilaleah, FL 33013
(305)835-8200
Merchandise Includes:
General ceramics supplies and
equipment

Ceramic Supply of NY & NJ
7 Route 46 West
Lodi, NJ 07644
(201)340-3005
Merchandise Includes:
General ceramics supplies and
equipment

Claymaker
1240 North 13th Street
San Jose, CA 95112
(408)295-3352
Merchandise Includes:
General ceramics supplies and
equipment

Columbus Clay Co.
1049 West Fifth Avenue
Columbus, OH 43212
(614)294-1114
Merchandise Includes:
General ceramics supplies and
equipment

Coneart Kilns, Inc.
15 W. Pearce Street Unit 7
Richmond Hill, Ontario
CAN L4B 1H6
(416)889-7705
Merchandise Includes:
Ceramics equipment

Cornell Studio Supply
1025 North Main Street
Dayton, OH 45405
(513)228-6777
Merchandise Includes:
General ceramics and copper ena-
maling supplies and equipment.

Georgie's Ceramic & Clay Co.
P.O. Box 820
Portland, OR 97211
(800)999-CLAY
Merchandise Includes:
General ceramics supplies and
equipment

H.C. Spinks Clay Co., Inc.
P.O. Box 820
Paris, TN 38242
(901)642-5414
Merchandise Includes:
General ceramics supplies and
equipment

Laguna Clay Company
14400 Lomitas Avenue
City of Industry, CA 91746
(818)330-0631
Merchandise Includes:
General ceramics supplies and
equipment

Ohio Ceramic Supply, Inc
P.O. Box 630, 286 State Route 59
Kent, OH 44240
(216)296-3815
Merchandise Includes:
General ceramics supplies and
equipment

Perma-Flex Mold Co., Inc.
1919 E. Livingston Avenue
Columbus, OH 43209
(614)252-8034
Merchandise Includes:
Molds for ceramics

Polyform Products Co., Inc.
P.O. Box 2119
Schillar Park, IL 60176
(708)678-4836
Merchandise Includes:
Polymers for sculpture and jewelry
in various colors

Standard Ceramic Supply Co.
P.O. Box 4435
Pittsburgh, PA 15205
(412)276-6333
Merchandise Includes:
General ceramics supplies and
equipment

Computer Software Suppliers ⎯⎯⎯⎯

E.E.S. Companies
2 Vernon Street, #404
Framingham, MA 01701
(508)653-6911
Merchandise Includes:
Computer software for craftspeople

Industriouss Software Solutions
500 West Florence Avenue
Inglewood, CA 90301
(310)672-8700
Merchandise Includes:
Display and exhibit manufacturers

Mate Systems
Wayne Stahnke
16 Technology Drive, Suite 113
Irvine, CA 92718
(714)453-2759
Merchandise Includes:
Computer and computer software
for small manufacturers

Mine Your Own Business
Gold Mine Plus Series
Silver Lining
1320 Standiford, Suite 170
Modesto, CA 92350
(800)828-4143
Merchandise Includes:
Computer software for the
wholesale craftsperson

Credit Card Systems ⎯⎯⎯

Arts & Crafts Business Solutions
2804 Bishopgate Drive
Raleigh, NC 27613
(800)873-1192
Merchandise Includes:
Credit card services and equipment
for the craft industry

U.S. Wireless Data, Inc.
4888 Pearl East Circle, Suite 110
Boulder, CO 80301
(303)440-5464
Merchandise Includes:
Mobile credit card processors and
services for small business people

Display, Exhibit & Canopy Suppliers _____

Abstracta Structures, Inc.
347 Fifth Avenue
New York, NY 10016
(212)532-3710
Merchandise Includes:
Display and exhibit manufacturers

Armstrong Products
P.O. Box 979, Dept. C
Guthrie, OK 73044
(405)282-7584
Merchandise Includes:
Display and exhibit manufacturers

Creative Energies, Inc.
1609 North Magnolia Avenue
Ocala, FL 34475
(904)351-8889
Merchandise Includes:
Canopies for display and exhibit

Dealer's Supply
P.O. Box 717
Matawan, NJ 07747
(800)524-0576
Merchandise Includes:
Display supplies and security aids

Downing Displays, Inc.
115 West McMicken
Cincinnati, OH 45210
(800)883-1800
Merchandise Includes:
Display and exhibit manufacturers

Elaine Martin Company
P.O. Box 274
Deerfield, IL 60015
(800)642-1043
Merchandise Includes:
Canopies and accessories for display and exhibit

Exhibit Builders, Inc.
9119 Carpenter Freeway
Dallas, TX 75427
(214)638-6297
Merchandise Includes:
Display and exhibit manufacturers

ExpoSystems
3203 Queen Palm Drive
Tampa, FL 33619
(813)623-2402
Merchandise Includes:
Display and exhibit manufacturers

F.W. Dixon Co.
55 Salem Street
Woburn, MA 01801
(617)935-8855
Merchandise Includes:
Display and exhibit manufacturers

Flourish Company
5763 Wheeler Road
Fayetville, AR 72703
(501)444-8400
Merchandise Includes:
Canopies and display materials

Fred's Studio
74 Lake Avenue
Stillwater, NY 12170
(800)99-TENTS
Merchandise Includes:
Tents and canopies for display

Gibson Holders, Inc.
P.O. Box 23504
3922 West 1st Avenue
Eugene, OR 97402
(800)444-2944
Merchandise Includes:
Display and exhibit manufacturers

Graphic Display Systems
1243 Lafayette Street
Lebanon, PA 17042
(717)274-3954
Merchandise Includes:
Display and exhibit manufacturers

Haaga & Associates
100 Ebbtide Avenue, Suite 11
Sausalito, CA 94965
(415)332-6560
Merchandise Includes:
Display and exhibit manufacturers

Intex, International Exhibits
3812 North Mississippi
Portland, OR 97227
(503)249-0400
Merchandise Includes:
Display and exhibit manufacturers

John Mee Canopies
P.O. Box 11220
Birmingham, AL 35202
(800)TOP-TENT
Merchandise Includes:
Canopies and equipment for display and exhibit

M.D. Enterprise Display Systems
9738 Abernathy
Dallas, TX 75220
(214)350-5765
Merchandise Includes:
Display and exhibit manufacturers

Millrock, Inc.
P.O. Box 974
Sanford, ME 04073
(207)324-0041
Merchandise Includes:
Display and exhibit manufacturers

Mobilite Exhibit Systems
617 East 28th Street
Charlotte, NC 28205
(704)375-3184
Merchandise Includes:
Display and exhibit manufacturers

Moss, Inc.
Box 309
Camden, ME 04843
(207)236-8368
Merchandise Includes:
Tents and canopies for display and exhibit

New Venture Products, Inc.
7441 11th Avenue, Suite 605
Largo, FL 34643
(800)771-SHOW
Merchandise Includes:
Canopy and display products

Newton Display Products
122 Fifth Street
Ft. Myers, FL 33907
(800)678-8677
Merchandise Includes:
Canopies and display panels

Rogers Display Co.
7550 Tyler Boulevard
Mentor, OH 44060
(216)951-9200
Merchandise Includes:
Display and exhibit manufacturers

Schacht Lighting
5214 Burleson Road
Austin, TX 78744
(800)256-7114
Merchandise Includes:
Lighting for displays and exhibits

Skyline Displays, Inc.
12345 Portland Avenue South
Burnsville, MN 55337
(612)894-3240
Merchandise Includes:
Display and exhibit manufacturers

Supply Source
8805 North Main Street
Dayton, OH 45415
(513)274-4688
Merchandise Includes:
Canopies for display and exhibit

Fiber Arts Suppliers & Equipment

Allied Felt Group
46 Star Lake Road
Bloomingdale, NJ 07403
(800)631-8969
Merchandise Includes:
Fiber supplies

Atlanta Thread & Supply
695 Red Oak Road
Stockbridge, GA 30281
(800)331-7600
Merchandise Includes:
General sewing tools and supplies

Azar Industries
225 5th Avenue Suite 410
New York, NY 10010
(908)351-2255
Merchandise Includes:
General sewing supplies

Country Ribbon Co., Inc.
349 Essex Road
Tintonfolds, NJ 07753
(800)FOR-LACE
Merchandise Includes:
Lace, ribbons, and other fabric
supplies

Crystal Palace Yarns
3006 San Pablo
Berkeley, CA 94702
(510)548-9988
Merchandise Includes:
Yarn and knitting supplies

Designs by Gloria & Pal, Inc.
P.O. Box 2318
Sumter, SC 29151
(803)775-8525
Merchandise Includes:
Knitting and needlework supplies

Dharma Trading Co.
P.O. Box 150916
San Rafael, CA, 94915
(415)456-7657
Merchandise Includes:
Fabric, dyes, and fiber art supplies

Far Eastern Fabrics Ltd.
171 Madison Avenue
New York, NY 10016
(212)683 2623
Merchandise Includes:
Fiber and fabric supplies

Fiber Studio, The
9 Foster Hill Road, P.O. Box 637
Henniker, NH 03242
(603)428-7830
Merchandise Includes:
Fiber supplies

Great Northern Weaving
P.O. Box 361-D
Augusta, MI 49012
(616)731-4487
Merchandise Includes:
Weaving supplies and equipment

IMC Needlecraft
55 Railroad Avenue
Garnerville, NY 10923
(914)429-2102
Merchandise Includes:
Knitting and needlework supplies

Kreinik Mfg. Co., Inc.
P.O. Box 1966
Parkersburg, WV 26102
(304)422-8900
Merchandise Includes:
Fiber and fabric supplies

Lana Moro, Inc.
1865 Broadway
New York, NY 10023
(212)757-1500
Merchandise Includes:
Knitting and needlework supplies

Margaret Perl Yarns
Box 21R Big Laurel Road
Sias, WV 25563
(304)778-3772
Merchandise Includes:
Yarn and knitting supplies

Mary Lu's Knitting World
101 West Broadway
St. Peter, MN 56082
(800)622-5433
Merchandise Includes:
Knitting and needlework supplies

Money Arts, Inc.
P.O. Box 17441
Jackonsville, FL 32245
(800)722-2890
Merchandise Includes:
Fabric and sewing supplies

Needlecraft Corp. of America, Inc.
P.O. Box 1599
Calhoun, GA 30701
(800)227-1340
Merchandise Includes:
General sewing supplies

Pattern Works
P.O. Box 1690
Poughkeepsie, NY 12601
(914)462-8000
Merchandise Includes:
Knitting and needlework supplies

Plymouth Yarn Co., The
P.O. Box 28
Bristol, PA 19007
(215)788-0459
Merchandise Includes:
Yarn and knitting supplies

River Farm, The
Rt. 1 Box 471
Fulks Run, VA 22830
(703)896-5833
Merchandise Includes:
Weaving supplies

Robin & Russ Handweavers
533 North Adams Street
McMinnville, OR 97128
(503)472-5760
Merchandise Includes:
Weaving supplies

Rupert, Gibbon & Spider, Inc.
P.O. Box 24
1147 Healdsburg Avenue
Healdsburg, CA 95448
(707)433-9577
Merchandise Includes:
Silk dyes, paints, and general supplies for dyeing fabric

Simtex Yarns, Inc.
P.O. Box 56
Armonk, NY 10504
(914)273-5300
Merchandise Includes:
Knitting and needlework supplies

Spring House Yarns
649 Wexford Bayne Road
Wexford, PA 15090
(412)935-5266
Merchandise Includes:
Yarn and knitting supplies

Straw Into Gold
3006 San Pablo Avenue
Berkeley, CA 94702
(510)548-5247
Merchandise Includes:
Fabric, yarn, and fiber arts supplies

Target Care & Trims
915 South Santa Fe Avenue
Los Angeles, CA 90021
(800)248-LACE
Merchandise Includes:
Lace, ribbons, and fabric supplies

The Fiber Studio
P.O. Box 637
Henniker, NH 03242
(603)428-7830
Merchandise Includes:
Weaving and knitting supplies and equipment

Tomorrow's Heirlooms
33 Buckmanville Road
Newton, PA 18940
(215)598-7070
Merchandise Includes:
Knitting and needlework supplies

Twin Birch Products
P.O. Box 327
Pittsboro, NC 27312
(919)742-3325
Merchandise Includes:
Knitting and needlework supplies

Glass Suppliers & Equipment

Adventure Art Glass, Inc.
46364 Dequindre
Utika, MI 48317
(313)254-0650
Merchandise Includes:
Glass supplies and equipment

Delphi Stained Glass
2116 East Michigan Avenue
Lansing, MI 48912
(800)248-2048
Merchandise Includes:
Glass supplies and equipment

Joppa Glassworks, Inc.
Box 202
Warner, NH 03278
(603)456-3569
Merchandise Includes:
Glass supplies and equipment

Glues & Adhesives

Aleene's Division of Arts, Inc
85 Industrial Way
Buelton, CA 93427
(800)825-3363
Merchandise Includes:
Glue & adhesives only

Red Hill Corporation
P.O. Box 4234
Gettysburg, PA 17325
(800)822-4003
Merchandise Includes:
Glue, adhesive, and abrasives for woodworking and metalworking

Insurance for Craftspeople

Associated Underwriters, Inc.
877 Executive Center Drive West, #305
St. Petersburg, FL 33742
(800)328-2317
Merchandise Includes:
Amusement insurance specialists

Connell Howe
P.O. Box 640
Kimberling City, MO 65686
(417)739-2491
Merchandise Includes:
Insurance for craftspeople only

Jewelry Suppliers & Equipment

ARE, Inc.
Route 16, Box 8
Greensboro Bend, VT 05842
(802)533-7007
Merchandise Includes:
General jewelry-making supplies
and equipment

B. Nathan & Sons
50 West 47th Street
New York, NY 10036
(212)391-2885
Merchandise Includes:
Gems and stones for jewelry-
making

Beadworks
139 Washington Street
South Norfolk, CT 06854
(203)852-9194
Merchandise Includes:
Beads and supplies for beaded
jewelry

Benmark and Margola Co.
48 West 37th Street
New York, NY 10018
(212)564-9180
Merchandise Includes:
General jewelry supplies including
many beads and stones

Canadia Enterprises
P.O. Box 394
Canadia, NH 03034
(603)483-2545
Merchandise Includes:
Jewelry castings for precious metals

Heher, Bill Fine Gemstones
Box 158
West Redding, CT 06869
(203)378-8672
Merchandise Includes:
Gems and stones for jewelry-
making

Jaco Import Corporation
1156 Avenue of the Americas
New York, NY 10036
(212)398-9220
Merchandise Includes:
Gems and stones for jewelry-
making

James Alger Co., Inc.
P.O. Box 3648
Manchester, NH 03105
(603)625-5947
Merchandise Includes:
Gems and stones for jewelry-
making

Makens
Box 130
Sausalito, CA 94966
(415)332-2744
Merchandise Includes:
General jewelry supplies

New England Gemstone Supply
P.O. Box 3204
Vernon, CT 06066
(203)871-0098
Merchandise Includes:
Gems and stones for jewelry-
making

Olive Glass
Rt 2, Box 3196
Lopez, WA 98261
(206)468-2821
Merchandise Includes:
Hand-blown glass beads for
jewelry-making

P. Aiello Casting Co., Inc.
15 Joy Street
Johnston, RI 02919
(401)944-3695
Merchandise Includes:
Jewelry castings for precious and
non-precious metals

Pachamama
125 East Palace Avenue, Suite 10A
Santa Fe, NM 87501
(505)983-4020
Merchandise Includes:
General jewelry supplies and
equipment

Pearl and Bead Service
373 Washington Street #304
Boston, MA 02108
(617)542-9442
Merchandise Includes:
Gems and stones for jewelry-
making

Rare Colored Gems
P.O. Box 3181
Melvindale, MI 48122
(313)382-3412
Merchandise Includes:
Gems and stones for jewelry-
making

Rings & Things of Spokane
P.O. Box 450
Spokane , WA 99210
(509)624-8565
Merchandise Includes:
General jewelry supplies and
equipment

Stern, Lucien L., Inc.
1500 Broadway
New York, NY 10036
(212)768-7500
Merchandise Includes:
Gems and stones for jewelry-
making

Together, Inc.
P.O. Box 52528
Tulsa, OK 74152
(918)587-2405
Merchandise Includes:
General jewelry supplies and
equipment

Virginia Corant
38 West 48th Street
New York, NY 10036
(212)869-4530
Merchandise Includes:
Gems and stones for jewelry-
making

Metalwork Suppliers & Equipment ────────

Caprock, The
1524 38th Street
Rock Island, IL 61201
(309)794-0010
Merchandise Includes:
Metal supplies and equipment

Danforth Pewter
52 Seymour Street
Middlebury, VT 05753
(802)388-8666
Merchandise Includes:
Metal supplies and equipment

Hoover, Torrance D.
10700 Trade Road
Richmond, VA 23236
(800)759-9997
Merchandise Includes:
Metal supplies and equipment

Miscellaneous Craft Supplies ────────

A and B Smith Company
4250 Old William Penn Hwy
Monroeville, PA 15146
(800)288-1776
Merchandise Includes:
Miscellaneous craft supplies

American Int'l Trading Co.
260 Newhall Street
San Francisco, CA 94124
(415)285-6566
Merchandise Includes:
Miscellaneous craft supplies

Audria's Inc.
6821 McCart
Ft. Worth , TX 76133
(817)346-2497
Merchandise Includes:
Miscellaneous craft supplies

Back Street
P.O. Box 1213
Athens, AL 35611
(205)232-2708
Merchandise Includes:
Cutting tools and miscellaneous
craft supplies

Canterbury Designs, Inc.
P.O. Box 204060
Martinez, GA 30917
(706)860-1674
Merchandise Includes:
Miscellaneous craft supplies

Coit Pen System
P.O. Box 472742
Charlotte, NC 28247
(704)542-5165
Merchandise Includes:
Miscellaneous craft supplies

Decart, Inc.
Lamoille Industrial Park Box 309
Morrisville, VT 05661
(802)888-4217
Merchandise Includes:
Miscellaneous craft supplies

Dick Blick Co.
P.O. Box 1267
Galesburg, IL 61401
(309)343-6181
Merchandise Includes:
Miscellaneous art and craft supplies

Eagle Feather Trading Post
168 West 12th Street
Ogden, UT 84404
(801)393-3991
Merchandise Includes:
Miscellaneous craft supplies

Earth Guild
33 Haywood Street
Shelville, NC 28801
(704)255-7818
Merchandise Includes:
Miscellaneous craft supplies

Enterprise Art
2860 Roosevelt Boulevard
Clearwater, FL 34620
(813)536-3568
Merchandise Includes:
Miscellaneous art and craft supplies

Filardo Products Co.
6105 South 108th Street
Hales Corners, WI 53130
(414)425-3510
Merchandise Includes:
Miscellaneous art and craft supplies

Flatlander Sculpture Supply
11993 East U.S. 223
Blissfield, MI 49228
(800)234-4591
Merchandise Includes:
Miscellaneous art and craft supplies

Good Earth Farm Inc.
RR1 Box 210 Pleasant Hill Road
Freeport, ME 04032
(207)865-9544
Merchandise Includes:
Miscellaneous art and craft supplies

Griffin Mfg. Co., Inc.
1656 Ridge Road East
Webster, NY 14580
(716)265-1991
Merchandise Includes:
Cutting tools and miscellaneous
craft supplies

J.W. Etc.
2205 1st Street #103
Simi Valley, CA 93605
(805)526-5066
Merchandise Includes:
Miscellaneous art and craft supplies

Lank Horst Distributors, Inc.
11583 K-Tel Drive
Hopkins, MN 55343
(612)933-4876
Merchandise Includes:
Miscellaneous art and craft supplies

Priority Supply Company
2127 Lake Lansing Road
Lansing, MI 48912
(517)374-8573
Merchandise Includes:
Miscellaneous art and craft supplies

S. Levine & Sons, Inc.
P.O. Box 148
Allentown, PA 18105
(215)398-2204
Merchandise Includes:
Miscellaneous art and craft supplies

Sax Arts & Crafts
2405 South Calhoun Road
New Berlin, WI 53151
(414)784-6880
Merchandise Includes:
Miscellaneous art and craft supplies

W.N. deSherbinin Products, Inc.
P.O. Box 63
Hawleyville, CT 06440
(203)791-0494
Merchandise Includes:
Miscellaneous art and craft supplies

Packing & Packaging Materials

Action Bag Co.
501 North Edgewood Avenue
Wood Dale, IL 43209
(614)252-8034
Merchandise Includes:
Packing materials

Boas Box Co.
5610 Lancaster Avenue, POB 15577
Philadelphia, PA 19131
(800)262-7269
Merchandise Includes:
Packing materials

Gaylord Specialities Corp.
225 5th Avenue
New York, NY 10010
(212)683-6182
Merchandise Includes:
Packing materials

Gift Box Corporation of America
225 5th Avenue
New York, NY 10010
(212)684-5113
Merchandise Includes:
Packaging materials

Springfield Corrugated Box, Inc.
P.O. Box 714
Agawan, MA 01001
(413)593-5211
Merchandise Includes:
Packing materials

Paint & Enamel Supplies

Art Hardware
1135 Broadway
Boulder, CO 80302
(303)444-3063
Merchandise Includes:
Paint and painting equipment

M. Swift & Sons
10 Love Lane
Hartford, CT 06141
(203)522-1181
Merchandise Includes:
Paint and painting equipment

Thompson Enamel
Box 310
Newport, KY 41072
(606)291-3800
Merchandise Includes:
Enamel and paint supplies

Portrait and Product Photographers

Jerry Anthony
3952 Shattuck Avenue
Columbus, OH 43220
(614)451-5207

Bob Barrett
323 Springtown
New Paltz, NY 12561
(914)255-1591

Chuck Bateman
1407 Newport Place
Lutherville, MD 21093
(410)296-2777

Judith Bellisari
4424 Castleton Road West
Columbus, OH 43220
(614)457-9077

David Egan
1606 Portugal Street
Baltimore, MD 21231
(410)563-0043

Glenwood Jackson
3000 Chestnut Avenue, Suite 10
Baltimore, MD 21211
(410)366-0049

Media Image Photography
21 SE Second Place
Gainesville, FL 32601
(904)375-1911

Don Schwarz
28 Essex Circle Drive
Shrewsbury, PA 17361
(717)235-2491

Printers: Promotional Materials

Aquarius Printing
5525 Wilkins Court
Rockville, MD 20852
(800)794-0203
Specialties:
1, 2 & 3-color printing for brochures, stationery, business cards, etc.

ASAP Reprints
851 Dairy Ashford
Houston, TX 77079
(800)327-2162
Specialties:
Custom reprints from existing film

Beckett Corporation
219 Wesch Pool Road
Lionville, PA 19341
(215)363-9600
Specialties:
Stickers

Forms One
3 Greenwood Place, Suite 104
Baltimore, MD 21208
(800)698-1142
Specialties:
Business forms, commercial printing, advertising specialties

Globe Screen Print
875 Hollins Street
Baltimore, MD 21201
(800)755-6757
Specialties:
All types of screen printing

McGrew Color Graphics
1615 Grand Avenue
Kansas City, MO 64108
(800)877-7700
Specialties:
Full-color postcards and brochures

Modern Postcards
6354 Corte del Abeto #E
Carlsbad, CA 92009
(800)959-8365
Specialties:
Full-color postcards

Piedmont Group
8753 Mylander Lane
Baltimore, MD 21286
(410)825-3600
Specialties:
Design, printing and mailing

US Press
P.O. Box 640
Valdosta, GA 31603
(800)227-7377
Specialties:
4-color postcards and brochures

Whitmore Printing
1982 Moreland Parkway
Annapolis, MD 21401
(800)327-1982
Specialties:
2- & 3-color printing, specializing in split-fountain color

Quilting Supplies & Equipment

Buffalo Batt & Felt Corp.
3307 Walden Avenue
Depew, NY 14043
(716)683-4100
Merchandise Includes:
Filling and inserts for quilting

Edmonds, Frank A. & Co., Inc.
6111 South Sayre
Chicago, IL 60638
(312)586-2772
Merchandise Includes:
Quilting supplies and equipment

Fairfield Processing Corp.
P.O. Box 1130
Danbury, CT 06813
(800)243-0989
Merchandise Includes:
Quilting supplies and equipment

Gettinger Feather Corp.
16 West 36th Street
New York, NY 10018
(212)695-9470
Merchandise Includes:
General assortment of feathers for quilting and fiber arts

Hobbs Industry
1000 North Highway 14
Groesbeck, TX 76642
(817)729-3223
Merchandise Includes:
Quilting supplies and equipment

Mountain Mist-Sterns Textile
100 Williams Street
Cincinnati, OH 45215
(513)948-5276
Merchandise Includes:
Quilting supplies and equipment

New England Quilt Supply
158 Center Street
Pembroke, MA 02539
(617)293-6401
Merchandise Includes:
Quilting supplies and equipment

White Sewing and Craft Products
11750 Berea Road
Cleveland, OH 44111
(216)252-3300
Merchandise Includes:
Quilting supplies and equipment

Wickham Wristen, Inc.
3308 Leonard Road
St. Joseph, MO 64503
(816)233-5106
Merchandise Includes:
Quilting supplies and equipment

Specialty Tools

Kestrel Tool
Rt. 1 Box 1762
Lopez, WA 98261
(206)468-2103
Merchandise Includes:
Specialty tools

Wilke Machinery Co.
3230 Susquehanna Trail
York, PA 17402
(717)764-5000
Merchandise Includes:
Specialty tools

Woodworking Supplies & Equipment

Artistry in Veneers, Inc.
450 Oak Tree Avenue
South Plainfield, NJ 07080
(908)668-1430
Merchandise Includes:
Wood and woodworking supplies

Cherry Tree Toys, Inc.
P.O. Box 369-140
Belmont, OH 43718
(800)848-4363
Merchandise Includes:
Wood and woodworking supplies

Driftwood House Mfg. & Whls.
P.O. Box 67
Brookings, OR 97415
(503)469-6055
Merchandise Includes:
Wood and woodworking supplies

Exotic Woods Company
444 Erial-Williamstown Road
Sicklerville, NJ 08081
(609)728-6055
Merchandise Includes:
Wood and woodworking supplies

Heartwood Design, Inc.
Rt. 2 Box 343
Afton, VA 22920
(804)361-1262
Merchandise Includes:
Wood and woodworking supplies

Loeffer-Valac Industries
2557 Forbestown Road
Oroville, CA 95966
By mail only
Merchandise Includes:
Wood and woodworking supplies

McFeely Hardwoods and Lumber
P.O. Box 3
Lynchburg, VA 24505
(804)846-2729
Merchandise Includes:
Wood and woodworking supplies

Woodcraft Supply Corp.
7845 Emmerson Avenue
Parkersburg, WV 26101
(304)464-5286
Merchandise Includes:
Wood and woodworking supplies

Craft Guilds & Organizations

A

Albuquerque Arts Alliance
1650 University North East
Albuquerque, NM 87102
(505)243-4971
Contact: H. Barker
Information Available:
Woodturning enthusiasts are welcome to open memberships.

American Art Pottery Association
125 East Rose
Webster Groves, MO 63119
(314)968-0708
Contact: Director
Information Available:
Open membership for ceramics artists.

American Association of Woodturners
667 Harriet Avenue
Shoreview, MN 55126
(612)484-9094
Contact: Alan Lacer, President
Information Available:
Woodturning enthusiasts are welcome to join.

American Craft Council
72 Spring Street
New York, NY 10012
(212)274-0630
Contact: Elected board
Information Available:
Open membership for craft artists and craft enthusiasts.

American Society of Furniture Artists (ASOFA)
Box 270188
Houston, TX 77277
(713)660-8855
Contact: Adam St. John, President
Information Available:
Open membership. Fees are $40 for individuals and $100 for a business. Contributing and student memberships are available.

Arizona Blacksmith Association
Route 1 Box 647
Buckley, AZ 85326
(602)938-1495
Contact: Mike Cooper
Information Available:
Hosts five demonstrations per year teaching in subjects ranging from basic blacksmith skills to design theory. Open membership.

Arizona Designer Craftsman
136 Voltaire
Phoenix, AZ 85022
(602)863-1212
Contact: Jane Metzger
Information Available:
Open membership. Designer craftsman will be selected by a jury.

Arkansas Arts Council
1500 Tower Building,323 Center Street
Little Rock, AK 72201
(501)324-9150
Contact: Sally Williams
Information Available:
Arkansas Arts Council offers grants to craft artists living in the state.

Arkansas Craft Guild
P.O. Box 800
Mountain View, AR 72560
(501)746-4396
Contact: Linda Van Trump
Information Available:
Must be an Arkansas resident, products must be handmade, no two-dimensional art, juried.

Artist-Blacksmiths' Association of North America
P.O. Box 1181
Nashville, IN 47448
(812)988-6919
Contact: Dorothy Stiegler, President
Information Available:
Membership open to all interested in blacksmithing.

ArtsPlace
161 North Mill Street
Lexington, KY 85030
(606)233-1469
Contact: John White, LACC Marketing Advisor
Information Available:
Open membership. Grants are available to craft artists.

C

Corning Museum of Glass, The
One Museum Way
Corning, NY 14830-2253
(607)937-5371
Contact: David Whitehouse, Director
Information Available:
Open memberships for glass enthusiasts.

Craft Alliance of Missouri
6640 Delmar Boulevard
St. Louis, MO 63130
(314)725-1177
Contact: Jim Reed, Executive Director
Information Available:
Open membership for Missouri residents. Classes
offered in various craft media.

Creative Glass Center of America
1501 Glentown Road
Millville, NJ 08332-1566
(609)825-6800
Contact: Paul J. Stankard, President
Information Available:
Open memberships to those interested in creative glass.

E

Empire State Crafts Alliance, Inc.
511 Broadway
Saratoga Springs,NY 12885
(518)584-1819
Contact: Jeff Cox, Board President
Information Available: Open memberships for craft
artists and craft enthusiasts.

F

Farmington Valley Art Center
25 Arts Center Lane
Avon, CT 06001
(203)678-1867
Contact: Betty Friedman, Executive Director
Information Available:
Open memberships. Additional benefits available to the
1,000 members who pay a fee.

First Nations Arts
69 Kelley Road
Falmouth, VA 22405
(703)371-5615; Fax: (703)371-3505
Contact: Andrea Coron or Debra Lew
Information Available:
Offers marketing workshops to educate Native
American artists on the fundamental business and mar-
keting principals necessary to develop a healthy arts-
related career.

Florida Craftsmen
235 3rd Street South
St. Petersburg, FL 33701
(813)821-7391
Contact: Michelle Tuegel
Information Available:
Offers an annual conference featuring hands-on workshops, exhibits and symposiums, a traveling exhibition
program, and statewide workshops and gallery lectures.

G

Glass Art Society
1305 Fourth Avenue, Suite 711
Seattle, WA 98101-2401
(206)382-1305
Contact: Alice Rooney, Executive Director
Information Available:
Open memberships for glass enthusiasts both nationally
and internationally.

H

Hand Workshop
1812 West Main Street
Richmond , VA 23220
(804)353-0094
Contact: Director
Information Available:
Open membership based on donation.

Handweavers Guild of America, Inc.
120 Mountain Avenue
Bloomfield, CT 06002
(203)242-3577
Contact: Norma Smayda, President
Information Available:
Any fiber artist can become a member for a fee of $25
or $29 outside of the U.S.

K

Kentucky Art and Craft Foundation
609 West Main Street
Louisville, KY 40207
(502)589-0102
Contact: Rita Steinberg, Director
Information Available:
Any Kentucky craftsperson can be a member for a fee.
Juried members can have work in the gallery, and must
be chosen by a committee, based on creativity,
originality, and quality of work.

Kentucky Craft Marketing Program
39 Fountain Place
Frankfort, KY 40601
(502)564-3757
Contact: Fran Redmon, Program Manager
Information Available:
Sponsors annual workshop series, provides technical
and marketing assistance for Kentucky craftspeople.

L

League of New Hampshire Craftsmen
205 North Main Street
Concord, NH 03301
(603)224-3375
Contact: Mary G. White
Information Available:
Open memberships. Must be state juried to exhibit in
the League Marketing system.

M

Maine Products Marketing Program
187 State Street
Augusta, ME 04333
(207)289-3153
Contact: Joan Anderson Cook, Director
Information Available:
A panel chooses member companies, who plan to
expand and wholesale their products, by reviewing
applications and samples to ensure the products are
high quality and handcrafted.

Michigan Guild of Artists & Artisans
118 North Fourth Avenue
Ann Arbor, MI 48104-1402
(313)662-2787
Contact: Mary Strope, Executive Director
Information Available:
Open memberships. Associate memberships are available to professional artists and craftspeople who meet
certain qualifying standards.

N

National Council on Education for the Ceramic Arts
P.O. Box 1677
Bandon, OR 97411
(503)347-4394
Contact: Joe Bova, President
Information Available: Membership fee. All ceramic
artists within the United States are welcome to join.

National Ornamental & Miscellaneous Metals Association
804-10 Main Street, Suite E
Forest Park, GA 30050
(508)999-8921
Contact: Barbara Cook, Executive Director
Information Available:
Membership is available to all metalsmiths.
Membership fee.

New Jersey Designer Craftsmen
65 Church Street
New Brunswick, NJ 08901-1242
(908)246-4066
Contact: Maxine Van Arsdale, Director
Information Available:
Open membership. Membership fee. Juried members
must go through a review process. Membership is not a
requirement to exhibit in guild shows.

O

Ohio Designer Craftsmen
2164 Riverside Drive
Columbus, OH 43221
(614)486-7119
Contact: JoAnn Stevens, Executive Director
Information Available:
Membership open to all.

P

Pennsylvania Guild of Craftsmen
P.O. Box 820
Richboro, PA 18954
(215)860-0731
Contact: Lyn Jackson, Director
Information Available:
Open membership to all craft enthusiasts within the state. Workshop series and newsletter available.

R

Resources and Counseling For the Arts
75 West Fifth Street
St. Paul, MN 55102
(612)292-4381
Contact: Director
Information Available:
All craft artists are encouraged to contact the organization to gain information from their arts information clearing house.

S

Society of American Silversmiths
P.O. Box 3599
Cranston, RI 12910
(401)461-3156
Contact: Jeffrey Herman
Information Available:
To become an artisan member, submit work to be judged on technical merit; the fee is $35; supporting members, who pay $40. Students can join associate members for $20. Open memberships for all who are interested.

Society of North American Goldsmiths (SNAG)
5009 Londonderry Drive
Tampa, FL 33647-1069
(813)977-5328
Contact: Peter Jagoda, President
Information Available:
Open membership. Membership fee is $45, and a subscription to the magazine is $26.

Southern Highlands Handicraft Guild
P.O. Box 9545
Asheville, NC 28815
(704)298-7928
Contact: Robert Gabriel, Executive Director
Information Available:
Members must be juried by a standards committee. Non juried members pay a yearly fee of $25.

Southwest Craft Center
300 Augusta
San Antonio, TX 78205
(512)224-1848
Contact: Ric Collier, Director
Information Available:
Open to all. Membership fees from $25 to $1000.

Stained Glass Association of America
6 SW 2nd Street, Suite 7
Lee's Summit, MO 64063
(816)524-9430
Contact: Kathy Murdock, Executive Secretary
Information Available:
Open memberships for those interested in stained and decorative glass may join one of the six categories of membership ranging from no criteria to juried members.

V

Vermont State Craft Center
Frog Hollow
Middlebury , VT 05753
(802)388-3177
Contact: Pamela Siers, Executive Director
Information Available:
Vermont state residents selected through a jury process.

W

Wesleyan Potters
350 South Main Street
Middletown, CT 06457
(203)347-5925
Contact: Melissa Schilke, Director
Information Available:
After taking classes for at least one year, one can be invited to become a member. The jury selects three to five people each year.

Retail & Wholesale Shows & Fairs

RETAIL & WHOLESALE SHOWS & FAIRS

KEY TO SHOW LISTINGS

R = Retail
W = Wholesale
C = Country
F = Fine Craft
M = Mixed
T = Contemporary
I = Indoor
O = Outdoor

ARIZONA

Scottsdale Festival of the Arts
Code: R,F,O **Average Attendance:** 75,000
Month of Show: March
Contact: Center for the Arts
                            7383 Scottsdale Mall
                            Scottsdale, AZ 85251
                            (602)994-2301

Festival in the Pines (Flagstaff)
Code: R,F,O **Average Attendance:** 80,000
Month of Show: August
Contact: Mill Avenue Merchants Association
                            Box 3084
                            Tempe, AZ 85281
                            (602)967-4877

Old Town Tempe Fall Festival of the Arts
Code: R,M,O **Average Attendance:** 200,000
Month of Show: December
Contact: Mill Avenue Merchants Association
                            P.O. Box 3084
                            Tempe, AZ 85280
                            (602)967-4877

ARKANSAS

War Eagle Fair at War Eagle Mill
Code: R,M,I **Average Attendance:** 150,000
Month of Show: October
Contact: Ozark Arts & Crafts Fair Assoc. Inc.
                            Route 1 Box 157
                            Hindsville, AR 72738
                            (501)789-5398

CALIFORNIA

Beverly Hills Affaire in the Garden at Beverly Gardens Park
Code: R,F,O **Average Attendance:** 60,000
Month of Show: May
Contact: City of Beverly Hills Parks & Recreation
                            La Cienega Commerce Center
                            8400 Gregory Way
                            Beverly Hills, CA 90211
                            (310)550-4628

Contemporary Crafts Market (Malibu)
Code: R,M,O **Average Attendance:** 12,000
Month of Show: November
Contact: Roy Helms & Associates
                            1142 Auahi Street, Suite 2820
                            Honolulu, HI 96814
                            (808)422-7362

Contemporary Crafts Market (San Francisco)
Code: R&W,F,I&O **Average Attendance:** 15,000
Month of Show: March
Contact: Roy Helms & Associates
                            1142 Auahi Street, Suite 2820
                            Honolulu, HI 96814
                            (808)422-7362

Gilroy Garlic Festival
Code: R,M,O **Average Attendance:** 130-140,000
Month of Show: July
Contact: Gilroy Garlic Festival Association
                            P.O. Box 2311
                            Gilroy, CA 95021
                            (408)842-1625

Harvest Festival Fall Tour (San Francisco location)
Code: R,M,I **Average Attendance:** 25,000
Month of Show: November
Contact: General Expositions Inc.
                            601 North McDowell Boulevard
                            Petaluma, CA 94954
                            (707)778-6300

Winter Gift Market (Los Angeles)
Code: W,M,I **Average Attendance:** 11,000
Month of Show: January
Contact: Industry Productions of America Inc.
                            Beckman's Gift Show, Box 27337
                            Los Angeles, CA 90027
                            (213)962-5424

La Jolla Festival of Arts & Food Fair
Code: R, M, O, **Average Attendance:** 20,000
Month of Show: June
Contact: Kiwanis Foundation
4130 La Jolla Village Drive,
Suite 10717
La Jolla, CA 92037
(619)456-1268

San Francisco Gift Show
Code: W,T,I **Average Attendance:** 10,000
Month of Show: August
Contact: George Little Management, Inc.
10 Bank St., Suite 1200
White Plains, NY 10606
(914)421-3200

Sausalito Art Festival
Code: R, F, O **Average Attendance:** 50,000
Month of Show: September—Labor Day Weekend
Contact: Sausalito Art Festival
P.O. Box 566
Sausalito, CA 94966
(415)332-3555

Half Moon Bay Pumpkin Festival
Code: R,M,O **Average Attendance:** 100,000
Month of Show: October
Contact: MIA Productions
1384 Western Road
Scotts Valley, CA 95066
(408)438-4751

COLORADO

Cherry Creek Arts Festival (Denver)
Code: R,F,O **Average Attendance:** 250,000
Month of Show: July
Contact: Cherry Creek Arts Festival
201 Fillmore Street, Suite 200
P.O. Box 6265
Denver, CO 80206
(303)355-2787

CONNECTICUT

Guilford Handcraft Exposition on Guilford Green
Code: R,M,O **Average Attendance:** 50,000
Month of Show: July
Contact: Guilford Handcraft Expo
P.O. Box 412
Guilford, CT 06437
(203)453-5947

DISTRICT OF COLUMBIA

Smithsonian Craft Show at Andrew W. Mellon Auditorium (Washington, D.C.)
Code: R,F,I **Average Attendance:** 14,000
Month of Show: April
Contact: Smithsonian Women's Committee
A&I Building, Room 1465
Smithsonian
Washington, DC 20560
(202)357-4000

FLORIDA

Coconut Grove Arts Festival
Code: R,F,O **Average Attendance:** 750,000
Month of Show: February
Contact: Coconut Grove Arts Festival
P.O. Box 330757
Coconut Grove, FL 33233
(305)447-0401

Museum of Art Las Olas Art Festival (Ft. Lauderdale)
Code: R&W,M,O **Average Attendance:** 50,000
Month of Show: March
Contact: Las Olas Art Festival
P.O. Box 2211
Ft. Lauderdale, FL 33303
(305)525-5500

Festival of the Masters at Disney Village (Orlando)
Code: R,F,O **Average Attendance:** 110,000
Month of Show: November
Contact: Walt Disney Company
P.O. Box 10000
Lake Buena Vista, FL 32830
(407)934-6743

Miami Beach Festival of the Arts
Code: R,M,O **Average Attendance:** 150,000
Month of Show: February
Contact: Miami Beach Festival,
Walter Erickson
P.O. Bin O
Miami Beach, FL 33119
(305)673-7733

Lowe Museum Beaux Arts Festival (Miami)
Code: R,M,O **Average Attendance:** 75,000
Month of Show: January
Contact: Lowe Art Museum
                     P.O. Box 431216
                     South Miami, FL 33143
                     (305)284-3536

Mount Dora Arts Festival
Code: R,T,O **Average Attendance:** 200,000
Month of Show: February
Contact: Mount Dora Arts Festival
                     138 East 5th Avenue
                     Mount Dora, FL 32757
                     (904)383-0880

Boca Museum Festival at Crocker Center (Boca Raton)
Code: R,W,M,O **Average Attendance:** 50,000
Month of Show: February
Contact: Meladie Shoop
                     801 West Palmetto Park Road
                     Boca Raton, FL 33486
                     (407)392-2500

GEORGIA

Yellow Daisy Festival at Stone Mountain Park
Code: R,M,O **Average Attendance:** 450,000
Month of Show: September
Contact: Stone Mountain Park,
                     Public Relations
                     Box 778
                     Stone Mountain, GA 30086
                     (404)498-5633

IDAHO

A&C Festival by the Center for the Arts (Sun Valley)
Code: R,M,O **Average Attendance:** 10,000
Month of Show: August
Contact: A&C Festival
                     P.O. Box 656
                     Sun Valley, ID 83353
                     (208)726-9491

ILLINOIS

Fountain Square Arts Festival (Evanston)
Code: R,F,O **Average Attendance:** 15-20,000
Month of Show: June
Contact: 807 Davis Street
                     Evanston, IL 60201
                     (708)328-1500

KENTUCKY

Kentucky Apple Festival (Paintsville)
Code: R,M,O **Average Attendance:** 65,000
Month of Show: October
Contact: Ray Tosti
                     Kentucky Apple Festival
                     P.O. Box 879
                     Paintsville, KY 41240
                     (606)789-4355

Kentucky Craft Market (Louisville)
Code: W,M,I **Average Attendance:** 12,000
Month of Show: January
Contact: Fran Redmon
                     Kentucky Craft Market
                     39 Fountain Place
                     Frankfort, KY 40601
                     (502)564-8076

MARYLAND

ACE Craft Fair Baltimore
Code: R&W,T,I **Average Attendance:** 35,000
Month of Show: February
Contact: ACE
                     South Eltings Corner Road
                     Highland, NY 12528
                     (800)836-3470

Autumn-Winter Craft Festival (Gaithersburg)
Code: R&W,M,I&O **Average Attendance:** 45,000
Month of Show: November
Contact: Sugarloaf Mountain Works Inc.
                     Deann Verdier
                     200 Orchard Ridge Drive #215
                     Gaithersburg, MD 20878
                     (301)990-1400

National Craft Fair (Gaithersburg)
Code: R,F,I&O **Average Attendance:** 20,000
Month of Show: October
Contact: National Crafts Ltd.
4845 Rumler Road
Chambersburg, PA 17201
(717)369-4810

Spring Arts & Crafts Festival (Gaithersburg)
Code: R,F,I&O **Average Attendance:** 35,000
Month of Show: April
Contact: Sugarloaf Mountain Works Inc.
Deann Verdier
200 Orchard Ridge Drive #215
Gaithersburg, MD 20878
(301)990-1400

Sugarloaf Craft Festival (Timonium)
Code: R,F,I **Average Attendance:** 21,000
Month of Show: April
Contact: Sugarloaf Mountain Works Inc.,
Deann Verdier
200 Orchid Ridge Drive #215
Gaithersburg, MD 20878
(301)990-1400

Maryland Crafts Festival (Timonium)
Code: R,F,I **Average Attendance:** 32,000
Month of Show: October
Contact: Sugarloaf Mountain Works Inc.,
Deann Verdier
200 Orchard Ridge Drive #215
Gaithersburg, MD 20878
(301)990-1400

MASSACHUSETTS

Boston Buyers Market at Bayside Expo
Code: W,F,I **Average Attendance:** 8,000
Month of Show: July
Contact: The Rosen Group, Inc.
3000 Chestnut Avenue, Suite 300
Baltimore, MD 21211
(410)889-2933

MICHIGAN

Ann Arbor Summer Art Fair
Code: R,F,O **Average Attendance:** 450,000
Month of Show: July
Contact: Michigan Guild, Shary Brown
118 North 4th Avenue
Ann Arbor, MI 48104
(313)662-3382

Ann Arbor State Street Area Art Fair
Code: R,M,O **Average Attendance:** 500,000
Month of Show: July
Contact: State Street Area Association
P.O. Box 4128
Ann Arbor, MI 48106
(313)663-6511

NEW JERSEY

Morristown Craft Market
Code: R,M,I **Average Attendance:** 10,000
Month of Show: October
Contact: Craft Market
Michael Feno
P.O. Box 2305
Morristown, NJ 07962
(201)263-8332

NEW MEXICO

South West Arts & Crafts Festival (Albuquerque)
Code: R,F&C,OI **Average Attendance:** 30,000
Month of Show: November
Contact: South West Arts & Crafts Festival
525 San Pedro NE, Suite 107
Albuquerque, NM 87108
(505)262-2448

NEW YORK

Crafts Park Avenue (New York City)
Code: R,T,I **Average Attendance:** 10,000
Month of Show: October
Contact: Artrider Productions Inc., Stacey Jarit
4 Camelot Road
Woodstock, NY 12498
(914)679-7277

WBAI Craft Fair (New York City)
Code: R&W,F,I **Average Attendance:** 16,500
Month of Show: December
Contact: WBAI Craft Fair
Box 889 Times Square Station
New York, NY 10108
(212)279-0707

New York International Gift Fair (New York City)
Code: W,T,O **Average Attendance:** 25,000
Month of Show: January
Contact: George Little Management
Deborah Hartstein
10 Bank Street, Suite 1200
White Plains, NY 10606
(914)421-3287

Fall Crafts at Lynhurst (New York City)
Code: R,F,O **Average Attendance:** 20,000
Month of Show: September & May
Contact: Artrider Productions Inc., Stacey Jarit
4 Camelot Road
Woodstock, NY 12498
(914)679-7277

American Crafts Festival at Lincoln Center
Code: R,F,O **Average Attendance:** 100,000
Month of Show: July
Contact: ACAC, Maureen Mullin
20 East 79th Street
New York, NY 10021
(201)746-0091

NORTH CAROLINA

Christmas Made in the South (Charlotte)
Code: R,M,I **Average Attendance:** 30,000
Month of Show: October
Contact: Carolina Shows Inc.
P.O. Box 853
Matthews, NC 28106
(704)847-9480

Carolina Craftsmen's Christmas Classic (Greensboro)
Code: R,M,I **Average Attendance:** 30,000
Month of Show: November
Contact: Gilmore Enterprises Inc.
1240 Oakland Avenue
Greensboro, NC 27403
(910)274-5550

OHIO

Crafts Affair (Cincinatti)
Code: R&W,T,I Average Attendance: 40-60,000
Month of Show: November
Contact: Ohio Designer Craftsmen
1665 West 5th Street
Columbus, OH 43221
(614)486-7119

Winterfair of Crafts (Columbus)
Code: R&W,T,I **Average Attendance:** 50,000
Month of Show: December
Contact: Ohio Designer-Craftsmen,
Gregory Phelps
1665 West 5th Avenue
Columbus, OH 43212
(614)486-7119

33rd Columbus Arts Festival
Code: R,M,O Average Attendance: 15,000
Month of Show: Beginning of Summer
Contact: Greater Columbus Art Council
Vicki Schultz
55 East State Street
Columbus, OH 43215
(614)224-2606

OKLAHOMA

Oklahoma Festival of Arts (Oklahoma City)
Code: R&W,M,O **Average Attendance:** 750,000
Month of Show: April
Contact: Arts Council
400 West California
Oklahoma City, OK 73102
(405) 236-1426

PENNSYLVANIA

Philadelphia Buyers Market at The Pennsylvania Convention Center
Code: W,F,I **Average Attendance:** 10,000
Month of Show: February
Contact: The Rosen Group, Inc.
3000 Chestnut Avenue, Suite 300
Baltimore, MD 21211
(410)889-2933

Long's Park Art & Craft Festival (Lancaster)
Code: R,F,O **Average Attendance:** 25,000
Month of Show: September
Contact: Long's Park Arts & Craft Festival
541 North Mulberry Street
Lancaster, PA 17603
(717)295-7001

Philadelphia Craft Show
Code: R,F,I **Average Attendance:** 27,000+
Month of Show: November
Contact: Philadelphia Museum of Art
Terry Hoff
P.O. Box 7046
Philadelphia, PA 19101
(215)763-8100

Three Rivers Arts Festival (Pittsburgh)
Code: R,F,I&O **Average Attendance:** 20,000
Month of Show: June
Contact: Carnegie Museum of Art
207 Sweetbriar Street
Pittsburgh, PA 15211
(412)481-7040

SOUTH CAROLINA

Craft Show at Piccolo Spoleto (Charleston)
Code: R,M,I **Average Attendance:** 15,000
Month of Show: Late Spring
Contact: Office of Cultural Affairs
133 Church Street
Charleston, SC 29401
(803)724-7305

TENNESSEE

Pink Palace Crafts Fair (Memphis)
Code: R,F/M,O **Average Attendance:** 50,000
Month of Show: October
Contact: Pink Palace Crafts Fair
3050 Central Avenue
Memphis, TN 38111
(901)320-6320

TEXAS

Laguna-Gloria Fiesta (Austin)
Code: R,F,O **Average Attendance:** 40,000
Month of Show: Late Spring
Contact: Laguna-Gloria Chairman
4821 Spicewood Springs Road
Austin, TX 78759
(512)499-8802

Dallas 500 Artfest
Code: R,M,I **Average Attendance:** 20,000
Month of Show: Late Spring
Contact: 500 Inc, Cynthia Armstrong
8300 Douglas, Suite 800
Dallas, TX 75225
(214)361-2011

WASHINGTON

Best of the Northwest (Seattle)
Code: R,M,I **Average Attendance:** 8,000
Month of Show: November
Contact: Crafts Alliance
P.O. Box 9937
Seattle, WA 98109
(206)781-1903

Rest of the Best Fest (Seattle)
Code: R,F,O **Average Attendance:** 250,000
Month of Show: July
Contact: Craft Cooperative of the Northwest
1916 Pike Place, Suite 146
Seattle, WA 98101
(206)363-2048

WEST VIRGINIA

Mountain Heritage Art & Craft Festival
Code: R,M,O **Average Attendance:** 30,000
Month of Show: June
Contact: Jefferson County Chamber
of Commerce
P.O. Box 426
Charles Town, WV 25414
(304)725-2055

Craft Retailers
& Galleries

A

A Different Drummer, Inc.
2 Town Square
Hollidaysburg, PA 16648
(814)696-4141
Owner(s):
Mary Ann Bloom and
Barbara Titelman
Buyer(s):
Mary Ann Bloom and
Barbara Titleman
Primary Focus:
Contemporary craft gallery
Founded: 1983

A Touch of Earth
6580 Richmond Road
Williamsburg, VA 23090
(804)565-0425
Owner(s):
Lianne Lurie and Paul Pittman
Buyer(s):
Lianne Lurie and Paul Pittman
Primary Focus:
Fine American crafts
Founded: 1977

Aaron Faber Gallery
666 Fifth Avenue
New York, NY 10103-0094
(212)735-5600
Owner(s):
Patricia and Edward Faber
Buyer(s):
Jennifer Hermann, Gallery Assistant
Primary Focus:
Jewelry
Founded: 1974

Abacus
44 Exchange Street
Portland, ME 04101
(207)772-4880
Owner(s):
Dana Heacock and Sal Scaglione
Buyer(s):
Dana Heacock and Sal Scaglione
Primary Focus:
American crafts and jewelry
Founded: 1971

Acropolis Now
1933 South Broadway, Suite 1010
Los Angeles, CA 90007
(213)396-7611
Owner(s):
Michelle Stein
Buyer(s):
Michelle Stein
Primary Focus:
Furniture
Founded: 1989

Adrien Linford
1320 Madison Avenue
New York City, NY 10128
(212)289-4427
Owner(s):
Morgan Allard and Gary L. Yee
Buyer(s):
Morgan Allard and Gary L. Yee
Primary Focus:
Functional crafts
Founded: 1987

Alianza
154 Newbury Street
Boston, MA 02116
(617)262-2385
Owner(s):
Karen and Michael Rotenberg
Buyer(s):
Karen and Michael Rotenberg
Primary Focus:
Contemporary crafts with a heavy
concentration on pottery, glass and
jewelry
Founded: 1968

Ambitious Endeavors
11 Union Avenue
Bala Cynwyd, PA 19004
(215)667-7377
Owner(s):
Philis Mason-Rosenberg and Janice
Milstien
Buyer(s):
Philis Mason-Rosenberg and Janice
Milstien
Primary Focus:
Contemporary craft
Founded: 1980

American Artisan, The
4231 Harding Road
Nashville, TN 37205
(615)298-4691
Owner(s):
Nancy Saturn
Buyer(s):
Nancy Saturn
Primary Focus:
American handcrafts
Founded: 1971

American Details
3107 Grand Avenue
Coconut Grove, FL 33133
(305)448-6163
Owner(s):
Lynn Allinger and Gary Stam
Buyer(s):
Lynn Allinger and Gary Stam
Primary Focus:
Contemporary American crafts
Founded: 1987

American Hand Plus
2906 M Street, NW
Washington, DC 20007
(202)965-3273
Owner(s):
Ken Deavers
Buyer(s):
Ken Deavers
Primary Focus:
Contemporary American crafts
Founded: 1968

American Hand, The
125 Post Road East
Westport, CT 06880
(203)226-8883
Owner(s):
Susan Hirsch
Buyer(s):
Susan Hirsch
Primary Focus:
Mid to high quality production
crafts, some one-of-a-kind
Founded: 1983

American Pie
327 South Street
Philadelphia , PA 19147
(215)922-2226
Owner(s):
Peter and Kristen Kreider Ebert
Buyer(s):
Peter and Kristen Krieder Ebert
Primary Focus:
Jewelry and crafts
Founded: 1988

An Artisan's Marketplace
120 East Street
Plainville, CT 06062
(203)747-4121
Owner(s):
Martha Couture and Cynthia
Couture-Logan
Buyer(s):
Martha Couture and Cynthia
Couture-Logan
Primary Focus:
Jewelry accompanied by stained
glass, pottery and fine crafts
Founded: 1980

Applause
1141 Pearl Street
Boulder, CO 80302
(303)442-7426
Owner(s):
Charles and Jody Hunker
Buyer(s):
Marybeth Thomas, Jackie
Rundquist,Tracey Duncan
and Jody Hunker
Primary Focus:
Womens contemporary wear, chil-
drens colorful and creative wear
Founded: 1981

Arcadia
10 Bridge Street
Frenchtown, NJ 08825
(908)996-7570
Owner(s):
Stephen Thompson
Buyer(s):
Sherry Thompson
Primary Focus:
Craft and furniture
Founded: 1991

Ariana Gallery
119 S. Main Street
Royal Oak, MI 48067
(810)546-8810
Owner(s):
Ann E. Kuffler
Buyer(s):
Ann E. Kuffler
Primary Focus:
Contemporary crafts and glass
Founded: 1987

Art A La Carte
1911 Chestnut Street
Philadelphia, PA 19103
(215)963-0767
Owner(s):
David Decca, Ronnie Smash and
Tony Mecca
Buyer(s):
David Decca
Primary Focus:
Contemporary American craft
Founded: 1981

Art Effect
651 West Armitage
Chicago, IL 60614
(312)664-0997
Owner(s):
Esther Fishman
Buyer(s):
Esther Fishman and Mary
Schakowsky
Primary Focus:
Clothing, jewelry, and home
accessories
Founded: 1984

Art Mecca
3352 North Halsted
Chicago, IL 60657
(312)935-3255
Owner(s):
Melanee Cooper
Buyer(s):
Melanee Cooper
Primary Focus:
Contemporary crafts
Founded: 1988

Artcrafters Gallery
472 Elmwood Avenue
Buffalo, NY 14222
(716)881-4320
Owner(s):
Ellen Drexler-Caughill
Buyer(s):
Ellen Drexler-Caughill
Primary Focus:
American crafts
Founded: 1989

Arteffects
1101 St. Gregory Street
Cincinnati, OH 45202
(513)381-2783
Owner(s):
Hillary Carter
Buyer(s):
Hillary Carter
Primary Focus:
Contemporary American crafts
Founded: 1990

Artes
6510 West Mequon Road
Mequon, WI 53092
(414)242-1121
Owner(s):
Will Stolen
Buyer(s):
Will and Hoja Stolen
Primary Focus:
Contemporary American crafts
Founded: 1980

Artful Eye, The
1333 A Lincoln Avenue
Calistoga, CA 94515
(707)942-4743
Owner(s):
Paula Camacho
Buyer(s):
Paula Camacho
Primary Focus:
Contemporary crafts
Founded: 1985

Artful Hand Gallery
36 Copley Place
Boston, MA 02116
(617)262-9601
Owner(s):
Joseph and Mary Porcari
Buyer(s):
Joseph and Mary Porcari
Primary Focus:
Multi-media craft gallery
Founded: 1981

Artisan Center
815 Blooming Grove
TPK Route 94
New Windsor, NY 12553
(914)569-0406
Owner(s):
Ted Tanner
Buyer(s):
Jane Tanner
Primary Focus:
Handmade crafts
Founded: 1990

Artisan Shop and Gallery, The
Plaza Del Lago
1515 Sheridan Road
Wilmette, IL 60091
(708)251-3775
Owner(s):
Lynn and Allan Hansen
Buyer(s):
Lynn and Allan Hansen
Primary Focus:
American crafts
Founded: 1968

Artisans Alley
10 Rainbow Boulevard
Niagara Falls, NY 14303
(716)282-0196
Owner(s):
Joyce Dannels
Buyer(s):
Lisa Osborn
Primary Focus:
High quality craft gallery—
all American crafts
Founded: 1980

Artisans Gallery
Peddlers Village
Lahaska, PA 18931
(215)794-3112
Owner(s):
Helen Cuff
Buyer(s):
Verna De Flavees and Susan
Snyder-Johnson
Primary Focus:
Contemporary American crafts fea-
turing jewelry, pottery, wood, glass,
kaleidoscopes and fiber
Founded: 1981

Artisans Three
The Village Center, P.O. Box 550
Spring House, PA 19477
(215)643-4504
Owner(s):
Helens Highley
Buyer(s):
Helens Highley
Primary Focus:
Gallery of distinctive American
crafts
Founded: 1979

Artist's Proof Inc.
Harrison Avenue and
High School Road
Elkins Park, PA 19117
(215)635-6166
Owner(s):
Margo Weiner
Buyer(s):
Margo Weiner
Primary Focus:
Crafts, jewelry and custom framing
Founded: 1978

Artists Market
163 Main Street
Norwalk, CT 06851
(203)846-2550
Owner(s):
Nancy and Jeff Price
Buyer(s):
Nancy and Jeff Price
Primary Focus:
Crafts, art and framing
Founded: 1970

Arts and Artisans, Ltd.
108 South Michigan Avenue
Chicago, IL 60603
(312)641-0088
Owner(s):
David and Jeanine Hoffmann
Buyer(s):
Amy, David and Jeanine Hoffman
Primary Focus:
Contemporary American crafts
Founded: 1988

Artworks
P.O. Box 1186, 121 East State Street
Kennett Square, PA 19348
(215)444-6544
Owner(s):
Liz Reilly
Buyer(s):
Liz Reilly
Primary Focus:
Creative multi-media exhibitions
Founded: 1986

Artworks Gallery
155 South Main
Seattle, WA 98104
(206)625-0932
Owner(s):
M.J. Rehm
Buyer(s):
M.J Rehm
Primary Focus:
Art and fine crafts
Founded: 1987

Artworks, The
3677 College Road
Fairbanks, AK 99709
(907)479-2563
Owner(s):
Gloria Fischer
Buyer(s):
Susan Cridge, Judy Wilson and
Gloria Fischer
Primary Focus:
Art and craft
Founded: 1974

Atelier Studio/Gallery
P.O. Box 2034
New Milford, CT 06776
(203)354-0453
Owner(s):
Beth Collings
Buyer(s):
Beth Collings
Primary Focus:
Contemporary American crafts
Founded: 1980

B

Barston's Craft Gallery
1331 Pennsylvania Avenue NW
Suite 300
Washington, DC 20004
(202)737-0569
Owner(s):
Steven Aarons
Buyer(s):
Laura Parr
Primary Focus:
American made crafts
Founded: 1984

Baubles and Beads
381 Elliot Street
New Upper Falls, MA 02164
(617)969-5656
Owner(s):
Sallie Macintosh and Doreen Glazer
Buyer(s):
Sallie Macintosh and Doreen Glazer
Primary Focus:
International gallery featuring
American handcrafted jewelry
Founded: 1979

Baubles and Beads
25 West King Street
Lancaster, PA 17603
(717)299-3931
Owner(s):
Frank Thomas
Buyer(s):
Doris Risley
Primary Focus:
Primarily American crafts
Founded: 1984

Bea Hive Craft and Gift Gallery
472 Cedar Lane
Teaneck, NJ 07666
(201)836-1366
Owner(s):
Bea Westin
Buyer(s):
Bea Westin
Primary Focus:
Contemporary American crafts
Founded: 1975

Beautiful Things
1838 East Second Street
Scotch Plains, NJ 07076
(908)322-1817
Owner(s):
Henri Leighton
Buyer(s):
Nell Goodin
Primary Focus:
Contemporary American crafts
Founded: 1975

Bellagio
5 Biltmore Plaza
Asheville, NC 28803
(704)277-8100
Owner(s):
John Cram
Buyer(s):
Nancy Beyer and John Cram
Primary Focus:
Specializes in fine jewelry and
wearable art.
Founded: 1991

Benchworks Gallery and Cafe
2563 North High Street
Columbus, OH 43202
(614)263-2111
Owner(s):
Bonnie Moseley
Buyer(s):
Bonnie Moseley and Jack Southal
Primary Focus:
Handcrafted jewelry by Bonnie
Mosely.
Founded: 1978

Benet, Inc.
247 Washington Street, Route 138
Stoughton, MA 02072
(617)341-3909
Owner(s):
Bonnie Pike
Buyer(s):
Bonnie Pike
Primary Focus:
Contemporary craft
Founded: 1968

Best Wishes, Inc.
190 Route 10 West
Whippany, NJ 07981
(201)267-6394
Owner(s):
Maxine and Jed Beck
Buyer(s):
Maxine and Jed Beck
Primary Focus:
Gifts for children and home
accessories
Founded: 1985

Bhadon Gallery
1075 Pleasant Street
Worcester, MA 01602
(508)798-0432
Owner(s):
Jacqueline Ford
Buyer(s):
Jacqueline Ford
Primary Focus:
American and international crafts
and collectibles
Founded: 1977

Bibelot Shops, The
1082 Grand Avenue
St. Paul, MN 55105
(612)222-0321
Owner(s):
Roxy Freese
Buyer(s):
Roxy Freese and Peggy Merril
Primary Focus:
Handmade arts and crafts
Founded: 1966

Black Cat, The
3424 Sansom Street
Philadelphia, PA 19104
(215)386-9224
Owner(s):
Judy Wicks
Buyer(s):
Eric Tucker
Primary Focus:
Eclectic mix of contemporary crafts,
jewelry and antiques
Founded: 1989

Bloom's
98 Albany Street
New Brunswick, NJ 08901
(908)246-0818
Owner(s):
Jeff Bloom
Buyer(s):
Brett Wilson, Amy Wallace,
Jeff Bloom
Primary Focus:
Craft gallery
Founded: 1984

Blue Spiral One
38 Biltmore Avenue
Asheville, NC 28801
(704)251-0202
Owner(s):
John Cram
Buyer(s):
John Cram
Primary Focus:
Specializes in painting and
sculpture
Founded: 1991

Bohemian
2112 Devine Street
Columbia, SC 29205
(803)256-0629
Owner(s):
Karen Murphey and Bruce Schultz
Buyer(s):
Karen Murphey and Bruce Schultz
Primary Focus:
Eclectic natural fiber wearables, and
contemporary furniture and crafts
Founded: 1980

Bramhall and Dunn
16 Federal Street
Nantucket, MA 02554
(508)228-4688
Owner(s):
Sharon Dunn and Emily Bramhall
Buyer(s):
Sharon Dunn and Emily Bramhall
Primary Focus:
Home furnishings, handmade crafts
Founded: 1983

Breit Crafts
1701 Coley Avenue
Norfolk, VA 23517
(804)640-1012
Owner(s):
Barbara Savage Breit
Buyer(s):
Barbara Savage Breit
Primary Focus:
Handmade craft
Founded: 1989

Brooke Pottery, Inc.
223 North Kentucky Avenue
Lakeland, FL 33801
(813)668-6844
Owner(s):
Gloria and David Brooke
Buyer(s):
Mary Patterson, Assistant
Primary Focus:
Fine craft
Founded: 1988

Brookfield Craft Center Gallery
Route 25, Box 122
Brookfield, CT 06804
(203)775-4526
Owner(s):
Non-profit corporation
Buyer(s):
Judith T. Russell, Manager
Primary Focus:
American handmade crafts
Founded: 1954

By Hand Fine Craft Gallery
142 Kings Highway East
Haddonfield, NJ 08033
(609)429-2550
Owner(s):
Marjorie Harris
Buyer(s):
Marjorie Harris
Primary Focus:
Contemporary American craft
gallery featuring decorative and
wearable crafts
Founded: 1977

By Hand South
308 West Ponce de Leon #E
Decatur, GA 30030
(404)378-0118
Owner(s):
Brenda Leder
Buyer(s):
Brenda Leder
Primary Focus:
Fine American crafts
Founded: 1989

C

Calico Bow, The
247 Wentworth Road
Wayne, PA 19087
(215)687-1672
Owner(s):
Walter Schmitt
Buyer(s):
Judy Schmitt
Primary Focus:
Unique gift shop featuring
hand-made American crafts
Founded: 1978

Calla Lilly, The
5901 North Prospect Road
Peoria, IL 61614
(309)693-2988
Owner(s):
Stephen Gauwitz
Buyer(s):
Stephen Gauwitz
Primary Focus:
General crafts and gifts
Founded: 1986

Caprice Gifts
10775 Bustleton Avenue
Philadephia, PA 19116
(215)969-0101
Owner(s):
Martin Friedman
Buyer(s):
Martin Friedman
Primary Focus:
Handmade arts and crafts
Founded: 1979

Carol Saunders Gallery
922 Gervais Street
Columbia, SC 29201
(803)256-3046
Owner(s):
Carol Saunders
Buyer(s):
Carol Saunders
Primary Focus:
Contemporary crafts and jewelry
Founded: 1984

Carolina Moon
P.O. Box 1060, Nags Head Station
Nags Head, NC 27959
(919)441-4000
Owner(s):
Louann Barcher
Buyer(s):
Louann Barcher
Primary Focus:
Pottery and jewelry
Founded: 1982

Cascabel Ltd.
10 Chase Road
Scarsdale, NY 10583
(914)725-8922
Owner(s):
Arlene Kolbert
Buyer(s):
Arlene Kolbert
Primary Focus:
Home accessories and gifts
Founded: 1991

Casual Cat
112 Route 101A
Amherst, NH 03031
(603)882-1443
Owner(s):
Cynthia Doyle and B.J. Lownie
Buyer(s):
Cynthia Doyle and B.J. Lownie
Primary Focus:
Fine art and fine craft
Founded: 1987

Catch the Wind
23 South Main Street
Medford, NJ 08055
(609)654-9393
Owner(s):
Charles Gaylord
Buyer(s):
Charles Gaylord
Primary Focus:
Handmade gifts
Founded: 1982

Catskill House
69 Tinker Street
Woodstock, NY 12498
(914)679-8819
Owner(s):
Cru Chase
Buyer(s):
Cru Chase
Primary Focus:
Kaleidoscopes, blown glass, exotic
instruments and rare Woodstock
memorabilia
Founded: 1976

Cedanna
1925 Fillmore Street
San Francisco , CA 94115
(415)474-7152
Owner(s):
Cedric Koloseus, Mimi Haas, and
Zoe Koloseus
Buyer(s):
Cedric Koloseus, Mimi Haas, and
Zoe Koloseus
Primary Focus:
American craft
Founded: 1987

Cedar Creek Gallery
1150 Fleming Road
Creedmoor, NC 27522
(919)528-1041
Owner(s):
Sid and Pat Oakley
Buyer(s):
Lisa Oakley
Primary Focus:
Fine American craft
Founded: 1969

Centre Gallery
103 East Carmel Drive
Carmel, IN 46032
(317)844-6421
Owner(s):
Mark Wientraut
Buyer(s):
Mark Wientraut
Primary Focus:
Multi-media craft gallery
Founded: 1984

Chestnut House
25 West King Street Hager Arcade
Lancaster, PA 17603
(717)393-0111
Owner(s):
Lola and Frank Thomas
Buyer(s):
Lola and Frank Thomas
Primary Focus:
Fine American crafts and bonsai
Founded: 1981

Chiaroscuro
700 North Michigan Avenue
Chicago, IL 60611
(312)988-9253
Owner(s):
Peggy Wolf and Ronna Isaacs
Buyer(s):
Peggy Wolf and Ronna Isaacs
Primary Focus:
Contemporary functional crafts
Founded: 1987

Chimneyville Crafts Gallery
1150 Lakeland Drive
Jackson, MS 39216
(601)981-2499
Owner(s):
Non-Profit, Craftman's Guild of
Missouri, Inc.
Buyer(s):
JoLynn Vaughan
Primary Focus:
Fine crafts
Founded: 1973

Choices Gallery
11 Pleasant Street
Newburyport, MA 01950
(508)462-5577
Owner(s):
Carly Levinson and Jan Jones
Buyer(s):
Carly Levinson and Jan Jones
Primary Focus:
Fine American crafts
Founded: 1987

Church Street Trading Co.
19 Church Street
New Milford, CT 06776
(203)355-2790
Owner(s):
Gay Parise and Bob Rush
Buyer(s):
Gay Parise and Bob Rush
Primary Focus:
Conceptual multi-media crafts
Founded: 1979

Clarksville Pottery Gallery
Arboretum Market, Great Hills Trail
Austin, TX 78759
(512)794-8580
Owner(s):
Sydelle and Arnold Popinsky
Buyer(s):
Sydelle and Arnold Popinsky
Primary Focus:
Craft gallery, specialty pottery
Founded: 1977

Clay Lady, The
Font Road and Route 100
Eagle , PA 19480
(215)458-8262
Owner(s):
Polly Gable
Buyer(s):
Polly Gable
Primary Focus:
Eclectic gifts, contemporary clay,
paper and jewelry
Founded: 1986

Clay Pigeon, The
601 Ogden Street
Denver, CO 80218
(303)832-5538
Owner(s):
Peggy and Tom Forte
Buyer(s):
Peggy and Tom Forte
Primary Focus:
Clay only
Founded: 1970

Clay Place, The
5416 Walnut Street, Mineo Building
Pittsburgh, PA 15232
(412)682-3737
Owner(s):
Elvira Peake
Buyer(s):
Elvira Peake
Primary Focus:
Ceramics both functional and
decorative, some glass, enamel and
jewelry
Founded: 1973

Clay Pot, The
162 Seventh Avenue
Brooklyn, NY 11215
(718)788-6564
Owner(s):
Robert and Sally Silberberg
Buyer(s):
Tara Silberberg
Primary Focus:
American crafts
Founded: 1969

Common Wealth Gallery, The
Hyatt Regency 313 4th Avenue
Louisville, KY 40202
(502)589-4747
Owner(s):
Kathy and Rick Davidson
Buyer(s):
Rick Davidson
Primary Focus:
Fine American crafts
Founded: 1980

Company of Craftsmen
43 West Main Street
Mystic, CT 06355
(203)536-4189
Owner(s):
Jack Steel
Buyer(s):
Jack Steel
Primary Focus:
Pottery, fiber, iron, jewelry, glass,
and wood
Founded: 1980

Compliments
Dock Square, P.O. Box 567A
Kennebunkport, ME 04046
(207)967-2269
Owner(s):
David A. Betses
Buyer(s):
David A. Betses
Primary Focus:
Contemporary and decorative crafts
Founded: 1981

Compositions Gallery
2801 Leavenworth (The Cannery)
San Francisco, CA 94133
(415)693-9111
Owner(s):
Siegfried Ehrmann
Buyer(s):
Siegfried Ehrmann
Primary Focus:
Contemporary glass art and designs
in wood
Founded: 1979

Contemporary Center
2630 West Sepulveda Boulevard
Torrance, CA 90505
(310)539-1933
Owner(s):
Sharon Fowler, Director
Buyer(s):
Sharon Fowler
Primary Focus:
All crafts except wearables
Founded: 1953

Contemporary Crafts Gallery
3934 SW Corbett Avenue
Portland, OR 97201
(503)223-2659
Owner(s):
Non-profit organization
Buyer(s):
Marlene Gabel
Primary Focus:
Arts and crafts
Founded: 1937

Continuity, Inc.
P.O. Box 999, Market Square
U.S. Hwy 19
Maggie Valley, NC 28751
(704)926-0333
Owner(s):
Shy and Elizabeth Lurie
Buyer(s):
Elizabeth Lurie and Joy Nelson
Primary Focus:
Multi-media and fine craft
Founded: 1984

Country Artisans, Inc.
Colony Hill Market Place
Keene, NH 03431
(603)352-6980
Owner(s):
Megan Kidder, Cornelia Jenness and
Florence Rosestock
Buyer(s):
Megan Kidder, Cornelia Jenness and
Florence Rosenstock
Primary Focus:
Contemporary and traditional crafts
Founded: 1973

**Country Heritage Antiques
and Crafts**
Main Street, P.O. Box 148
Washington, VA 22747
(703)675-3738
Owner(s):
Mary Simons
Buyer(s):
Mary Simons
Primary Focus:
Antiques, American crafts
and folk art
Founded: 1982

Country Studio, The
590 Georgetown Road
Hadley, PA 16130
(412)253-2493
Owner(s):
Lynn Linton, Jack Linton and
Evelyn Linton
Buyer(s):
Lynn Linton
Primary Focus:
Contemporary and traditional
American art and handcrafts
Founded: 1972

Courtyards Ltd.
3980 Main Road
Tiverton, RI 02878
(401)624-8682
Owner(s):
Dean and Sharon Prazak
Buyer(s):
Dean and Sharon Prazak
Primary Focus:
Shop representing most areas
of fine craft
Founded: 1986

Craft Alliance Gallery
6640 Delmar
St. Louis, MO 63130
(314)725-1177
Owner(s):
Not for profit
Buyer(s):
Barbara Jedda
Primary Focus:
Fine crafts
Founded: 1964

Craft Company Number 6
785 University Avenue
Rochester, NY 14607
(716)473-3413
Owner(s):
Lynn Allinger and Gary Stam
Buyer(s):
Lynn Allinger and Gary Stam
Primary Focus:
Contemporary American crafts
Founded: 1980

Craft Concepts
Green Spring Station-Falls and
Joppa Roads
Lutherville, MD 21093
(410)823-2533
Owner(s):
Carol Brody-Luchs and Carole Finn
Halverstadt
Buyer(s):
Carol Brody-Luchs and Carole Finn
Halvertstadt
Primary Focus:
Craft
Founded: 1979

Crafters Gallery
Route 10 Box 97
Charlottesville, VA 22903
(804)295-7006
Owner(s):
Bob Leiby
Buyer(s):
Bob Leiby
Primary Focus:
Pottery, fiber, metal, glass, leathers,
brooms, and toys
Founded: 1975

Craftmen's Gallery
H.C. 6 Box 6950
Hawley, PA 18428
(717)226-4111
Owner(s):
Rose-Marie and John Chapman
Buyer(s):
Rose-Marie Chapman
Primary Focus:
American crafts
Founded: 1985

Craftsman, The
Poughkeepsie Plaza
Route 9 South Road
Poughkeepsie, NY 12601
(914)454-2336
Owner(s):
Gloria Turk
Buyer(s):
Gloria Turk and Lisa Casowitz
Primary Focus:
Handmade American crafts
Founded: 1974

Crafty Yankee, The
1838 Massachusetts Avenue
Lexington, MA 02173
(617)863-1219
Owner(s):
Dottie Simpson and Carla Fortman
Buyer(s):
Dottie Simpson and Carla Fortman
Primary Focus:
Handcrafted pottery
Founded: 1980

Crate, The
1200 K Street Mall #9
Sacramento, CA 95814
(916)441-4136
Owner(s):
Betty D. Mast
Buyer(s):
Karen Mast
Primary Focus:
Craft gallery
Founded: 1973

Creative Hands
P.O. Box 264 Route 206
Rocky Hill, NJ 08553
(609)924-3355
Owner(s):
Deborah Sands
Buyer(s):
Deborah Sands
Primary Focus:
American handcrafts
Founded: 1987

Creator's Hands, The
336 Arnett Boulevard
Rochester, NY 14619
(716)235-8550
Owner(s):
Carleen Wilenius
Buyer(s):
Marilee Elash
Primary Focus:
American handcraft specializing in
Christian and Judaica items
Founded: 1979

Crock-R-Box Craft Gallery
73425 El Paseo
Palm Desert, CA 92260
(619)568-6688
Owner(s):
John Wenzell
Buyer(s):
John Wenzell
Primary Focus:
100% American craft
Founded: 1979

Croma Gallery
94 Central Street
Wellesley, MA 02181
(617)235-6230
Owner(s):
Irene Chung
Buyer(s):
Irene Chung
Primary Focus:
Jewelry
Founded: 1989

D

Dandelion 2
1618 Latimer Street
Philadelphia, PA 19103
(215)546-7655
Owner(s):
Beth Fluke
Buyer(s):
Beth Fluke
Primary Focus:
Handcrafted gifts and
international art
Founded: 1969

Decoart
815 First Street
Menominee, MI 49858
(906)863-3300
Owner(s):
Alexandria Thomas
Buyer(s):
Alexandria Thomas
Primary Focus:
Custom frames and matting, hand-
made jewelry and gifts
Founded: 1987

Del Mano Gallery
11981 San Vincente Boulevard
Los Angeles, CA 90049
(310)476-8508
Owner(s):
Jan Peters and Ray Leier
Buyer(s):
Jan Peters and Ray Leier
Primary Focus:
Contemporary crafts
Founded: 1973

Design Concern
1420 5th Avenue #201
Seattle, WA 98101
(206)623-4444
Owner(s):
Steve Okawa
Buyer(s):
Steve Okawa
Primary Focus:
Gift shop
Founded: 1989

Designer Crafts
448 Lafayette Road
Hampton, NH 03842
(603)926-0716
Owner(s):
Lucille Marston
Buyer(s):
Lucille Marston
Primary Focus:
Pottery, jewelry, glass lamps,
stained glass
Founded: 1983

Designer's Circle
52 Church Street
Burlington, VT 05401
(802)864-4238
Owner(s):
Dennis Bosch
Buyer(s):
Chandelle Trahan
Primary Focus:
Retail jeweler and manufacturer
Founded: 1975

Designers Studio
492 Broadway
Saratoga Springs, NY 12866
(518)584-0987
Owner(s):
Jill Marvin
Buyer(s):
Jill Marvin
Primary Focus:
Contemporary crafts
Founded: 1983

Designs in Silver, Etc.
230 East Main Street
Port Jefferson, NY 11777
(516)928-2037
Owner(s):
Charles Kohn
Buyer(s):
Charles Kohn
Primary Focus:
Contemporary crafts
Founded: 1975

Details
40 Brattle Street
Cambridge, MA 02138
(617)354-4255
Owner(s):
Carolyn Fantasia
Buyer(s):
Carolyn Fantasia
Primary Focus:
Arts and crafts
Founded: 1986

Detroit Gallery of Contemporary Crafts
104 Fisher Building
Detroit, MI 48202
(313)873-7888
Owner(s):
Judith Primak and
Lorraine Bookstein
Buyer(s):
Judith Primak and
Lorraine Bookstein
Primary Focus:
American crafts
Founded: 1976

Dexterity, Ltd.
26 Church Street
Montclair, NJ 07042
(201)746-5370
Owner(s):
Shirley Zafirau
Buyer(s):
Shirley Zafirau
Primary Focus:
Contemporary American crafts
Founded: 1974

Dina Porter Gallery
3900 Hamilton Boulevard
Allentown, PA 18103
(215)434-7363
Owner(s):
Susan Coker
Buyer(s):
Connie Paisley and Cindy Sadler
Primary Focus:
Pottery, jewelry, accessories, glass, leather, kaleidoscopes, and metal
Founded: 1983

Dining In
2 West Northfield Road
Livingston, NJ 07039
(201)992-8300
Owner(s):
Linda Levitt
Buyer(s):
Linda Levitt
Primary Focus:
Home accessories
Founded: 1973

Discoveries
P.O. Box 1552, 2nd and
Penn Streets
Reading , PA 19603
(215)372-2595
Owner(s):
Douglas Fischer
Buyer(s):
Douglas Fischer
Primary Focus:
Handmade art
Founded: 1986

Discoveries
Columbia Mall
Columbia, MD 21044
(410)740-5800
Owner(s):
Sally Tennant
Buyer(s):
Sally Tennant
Primary Focus:
American crafts
Founded: 1982

Don Drumm Studios and Gallery
437 Crouse Street
Akron, OH 44311
(216)253-6268
Owner(s):
Don Drumm
Buyer(s):
Don Drumm
Primary Focus:
American crafts and sculpture
Founded: 1984

Dorothy Weiss Gallery
256 Sutter Street
San Francisco, CA 94108
(415)397-3611
Owner(s):
Dorothy Weiss
Buyer(s):
Dorothy Weiss
Primary Focus:
Contemporary ceramic and glass sculpture
Founded: 1984

Douglas Albert Gallery
107 McAllister Alley Walkway
State College, PA 16801
(814)234-9822
Owner(s):
Douglas Albert
Buyer(s):
Douglas Albert
Primary Focus:
Original fine art, graphics, better crafts and glass
Founded: 1981

Dr. Livingston's Finds
Kings Highway
Sugar Loaf, NY 16801
(914)469-5577
Owner(s):
Robin Fremon
Buyer(s):
Robin Fremon
Primary Focus:
Jewelry and gifts
Founded: 1988

E

E. Gelb Jewelers
224 Constitution Plaza
Hartford, CT 06103
(203)247-4335
Owner(s):
E. Gelb
Buyer(s):
E. Gelb
Primary Focus:
Handcrafted jewelry
Founded: 1963

Earthly Pleasures
610 North Maple Avenue
Ho-Ho-Kus, NJ 07423
(201)444-4834
Owner(s):
Norma E. Rappaport
Buyer(s):
Norma E. Rappaport
Primary Focus:
Gift shop
Founded: 1984

East Bay Gallery
280 Coleman Boulevard
Mount Pleasant, SC 29464
(803)849-9602
Owner(s):
John Guthrie
Buyer(s):
John Guthrie
Primary Focus:
American crafts
Founded: 1987

Electric Glass Company
1 East Mellen Street
Hampton, VA 23663
(804)722-6200
Owner(s):
Bob and Bobo Vines
Buyer(s):
Bob and Bobo Vines
Primary Focus:
Glass
Founded: 1977

Elements
338 Commercial Street,
P.O. Box 1205
Provincetown, MA 02657
(508)487-4351
Owner(s):
Claudia Gal and Ben Kettlewell
Buyer(s):
Claudia Gal and Ben Kettlewell
Primary Focus:
Jewelry, crafts and artwork
Founded: 1988

Elizabeth and Harriet
Old Mystic Village
Mystic, CT 06355
(203)536-0316
Owner(s):
Suzanne E. Rummel-Lane
Buyer(s):
Suzanne E. Rummel-Lane
Primary Focus:
American handcrafts
Founded: 1987

Elvid Gallery, The
P.O. Box 5267
Englewood, NJ 07631-5267
(201)871-8747
Owner(s):
Elissa Goldstein
Buyer(s):
Elissa Goldstien
Primary Focus:
Contemporary mixed-media
Founded: 1987

Enchanted Forest, The
85 Mercer Street
New York, NY 10012
(212)925-6677
Owner(s):
David Wallace
Buyer(s):
David Wallace
Primary Focus:
Handcrafted toys, folk art and books
Founded: 1985

Endleman Gallery
1014A Chapel Street
New Haven, CT 06510
(203)776-2517
Owner(s):
Sally-Ann Endleman
Buyer(s):
Sally-Ann Endelman
Primary Focus:
Jewelry
Founded: 1983

Engel Pottery
51 Main Street
East Hampton, NY 11937
(516)324-6462
Owner(s):
Wendy Engel
Buyer(s):
Wendy Engel
Primary Focus:
American crafts
Founded: 1973

Epitome
611 East Cooper Avenue
Aspen, CO 81611
(303)925-7966
Owner(s):
Richard and Jane Kelley
Buyer(s):
Richard and Jane Kelley
Primary Focus:
Fine jewelry, art glass, porcelain
Founded: 1986

Estal Specialties
433 Medford Avenue
Patchogue, NY 11772
(516)289-3311
Owner(s):
Michael Mizrahi
Buyer(s):
Michael Mizrahi
Primary Focus:
Crafts
Founded: 1965

Esther Saks Fine Art, Ltd.
P.O. Box 14169
Chicago, IL 60614
(312)751-0911
Owner(s):
Esther Saks
Buyer(s):
Esther Saks
Primary Focus:
Contemporary art, ceramics,
sculpture
Founded: 1984

Evergreen
291 Main Street
Great Barrington, MA 01230
(413)528-0511
Owner(s):
Barbara Watkins
Buyer(s):
Barbara Watkins
Primary Focus:
American crafts
Founded: 1980

Evergreen Gallery
21 Boston Street
Guilford, CT 06437
(203)453-4324
Owner(s):
Diane Robinson and Sharon
Silvestrini
Buyer(s):
Diane Robinson and Sharon
Silvestrini
Primary Focus:
American crafts
Founded: 1983

F

Fanny Garver Gallery, The
230 State Street
Madison, WI 53703
(608)256-6755
Owner(s):
Fanny and John Garver
Buyer(s):
Fanny and John Garver
Primary Focus:
Fine art and craft
Founded: 1972

Fine Lines
304 South Stratford Road
Winston-Salem, NC 27103
(910)723-8066
Owner(s):
Sandy Steele
Buyer(s):
Sandy Steele
Primary Focus:
Crafts
Founded: 1981

Fire Opal
7 Pond Street
Jamaica Plains, MA 02130
(617)524-0262
Owner(s):
Susannah R. Gordon
Buyer(s):
Susannah R. Gordon
Primary Focus:
Contemporary jewelry, ceramics,
clothing and cards
Founded: 1984

Fireburst
R.F.D. #2
Orange, MA 01364
(508)575-0493
Owner(s):
Genevieve Morley
Buyer(s):
Genevieve Morley
Primary Focus:
American jewelry
Founded: 1978

FireWorks Gallery
Westlake Center, 400 Pine Street
Seattle, WA 98101
(206)682-8707
Owner(s):
Michelle Manasse
Buyer(s):
Michelle Manasse
Primary Focus:
Fine crafts galleries
Founded: 1983

Fisher Gallery Shop
Farmington Valley Arts Center
Art Center Lane
Avon, CT 06001
(203)678-1867
Owner(s):
Betty Friedman
Buyer(s):
Sally Bloomberg
Primary Focus:
American contemporary crafts
Founded: 1972

Flying Shuttle
607 First Avenue
Seattle, WA 98104
(206)343-9762
Owner(s):
Judith Jester
Buyer(s):
Judith Jester
Primary Focus:
Wearable art
Founded: 1982

Folk Art Gallery
4138 University Way NE
Seattle, WA 98105
(206)634-1795
Owner(s):
Leslie Grace
Buyer(s):
Leslie Grace
Primary Focus:
Jewelry, clothing, ceramics, puppets, musical instruments, cards
Founded: 1962

For Decor
1458 Plum Lane
East Meadow, NY 11554
(516)489-4363
Owner(s):
Holly Chalnick
Buyer(s):
Holly Chalnick
Primary Focus:
Handmade two and three
dimensional art
Founded: 1988

FreeFlight Gallery
603 Munger #309, West End
Marketplace
Dallas, TX 75202
(214)720-9147
Owner(s):
Ed and Sandy Smith
Buyer(s):
Ed and Sandy Smith
Primary Focus:
Contemporary American crafts
Founded: 1986

Freewheel Pottery, The
7 Tinker Street
Woodstock, NY 12498
(914)679-7478
Owner(s):
Philip Bresler
Buyer(s):
Philip Bresler
Primary Focus:
Handmade pottery and jewelry
Founded: 1979

Frick & Frack
1480 Route 23 North
Wayne, NJ 07470
(201)696-8266
Owner(s):
Eileen Anatro
Buyer(s):
Eileen Anatro
Primary Focus:
Multi-media
Founded: 1986

Fumie Gallery
19 South La Salle Street
Chicago, IL 60603
(312)726-0080
Owner(s):
John and Fumie Madden
Buyer(s):
Richard M. Hartnett
Primary Focus:
Contemporary American crafts
Founded: 1982

G

Gail Severn Gallery
620 Sun Valley Road,
P.O. Box 1679
Ketchum, ID 83340
(208)726-5079
Owner(s):
Gail Severn
Buyer(s):
Gail Severn
Primary Focus:
Multi-media fine art
Founded: 1987

Gallery 10
7 Greenwich Avenue
New York, NY 10014
(212)206-1058
Owner(s):
Marica Lee Smith
Buyer(s):
Robert Chiampas
Primary Focus:
Craft gallery
Founded: 1972

Gallery 3
213 Market Street
Roanoke, VA 24011
(703)343-9698
Owner(s):
Ted and Sandy Beindorf
Buyer(s):
Lee Baker
Primary Focus:
Original two dimensional art
Founded: 1973

Gallery 500
Church & Old York Roads
Elkins Park, PA 19117
(215)572-1203
Owner(s):
Harriet Friedberg and Rita
Greenfield
Buyer(s):
Harriet Friedman and Rita
Greenfield
Primary Focus:
Contemporary fine arts, crafts, and
art jewelry
Founded: 1968

Gallery Alexander
7850 Girard Avenue
La Jolla, CA 92037
(619)459-9433
Owner(s):
Roberta and Stephen Edelstein
Buyer(s):
Roberta and Stephen Edelstein
Primary Focus:
Contemporary American crafts
Founded: 1968

Gallery Collection, The
693 Boston Post Road
Madison, CT 06443
(203)245-4442
Owner(s):
Lorene Sholl
Buyer(s):
Lorene Sholl
Primary Focus:
Crafts, jewelry and original art
Founded: 1990

Gallery Eight
7464 Girard Avenue
La Jolla, CA 92037
(619)454-9781
Owner(s):
Ruth Newmark, Florence Cohen,
Barbara Saltman
Buyer(s):
Ruth Newmark, Florence Cohen,
Barbara Saltman and Sheryl
Stougaard
Primary Focus:
Contemporary crafts
Founded: 1978

Gallery Five
363 Tequesta Drive
Tequesta, FL 33469
(407)747-5555
Owner(s):
Paul and Paula Coben
Buyer(s):
Paul and Paula Coben
Primary Focus:
Wearable art and American crafts
Founded: 1982

Gallery Riggione
130 Almshouse Road
Richboro, PA 18954
(215)322-5035
Owner(s):
Joe and Addie Riggione
Buyer(s):
Joe and Addie Riggione
Primary Focus:
Contemporary American crafts
Founded: 1984

Gallery Wear
6741 Reynolds Street
Pittsburgh, PA 15206
(412)661-WEAR
Owner(s):
Patti Haskell
Buyer(s):
Patti Haskell
Primary Focus:
Handmade clothing, jewelry
Founded: 1990

Gallimaufry Gallery
3345 North Halsted Street
Chicago, IL 60657
(312)348-8090
Owner(s):
Michael Merkle and Pat Rodarte
Buyer(s):
Michael Merkle and Pat Rodarte
Primary Focus:
Crafts
Founded: 1975

Gango Gallery
205 SW 1st Street
Portland, OR 97204
(503)222-8350
Owner(s):
Debi Gango Teschke and Jackie
Gango
Buyer(s):
Cathy Rocque
Primary Focus:
Crafts, fine art
Founded: 1977

Gazelle
Village of Cross Keys,
5100 Falls Road
Baltimore, MD 21210
(410)433-3305
Owner(s):
Amanda Black
Buyer(s):
Amanda Black
Primary Focus:
Wearable art, fine jewelry and
museum-quality crafts
Founded: 1981

Gifted Hands Gallery
Tiaquepaque Village,
P.O. Box 1388
Sedona, AZ 86336
(602)282-4822
Owner(s):
Byron Mckeown
Buyer(s):
Byron Mckeown
Primary Focus:
Fiber and pottery
Founded: 1989

Glass Act
10 Sylan Drive #15
St. Simons Island, GA 31522
(912)634-1228
Owner(s):
Chris Coleman
Buyer(s):
Chris Coleman
Primary Focus:
American craft
Founded: 1988

Glass Eye, The
Main Street Mercantile, Route 6
North Eastham-Cape Cod, MA
02651
(508)255-5044
Owner(s):
Donna and John Knight
Buyer(s):
Donna and John Knight
Primary Focus:
American crafts representing over
100 artists
Founded: 1971

Glass Gallery, The
4720 Hampden Lane
Bethesda, MD 20814
(301)657-3478
Owner(s):
Sarah Hansen
Buyer(s):
Sarah Hansen
Primary Focus:
Sculpture, primarily glass
Founded: 1981

Glass Growers Gallery
701 Holland Street
Erie, PA 16501
(814)453-3758
Owner(s):
Debra Vahanian
Buyer(s):
Debra Vahanian and Heidi
Lombardo
Primary Focus:
Arts and crafts
Founded: 1974

163

Goldart
930 Walnut Street
Allentown, PA 18102
(215)433-1220
Owner(s):
Robert Singley
Buyer(s):
Robert Singley
Primary Focus:
Creative jewelry
Founded: 1984

Goldsmith, The
49 Court Street
Binghampton, NY 13901
(607)723-0001
Owner(s):
Gina Mchugh
Buyer(s):
Gina Mchugh
Primary Focus:
Jewelry: custom designed
Founded: 1986

Grey Dove, The
159 South Livingston Avenue
Livingston, NJ 07039
(201)994-2266
Owner(s):
Gail Gold and Audrey Weinstock
Buyer(s):
Gail Gold and Audrey Weinstock
Primary Focus:
Gift gallery, mixed-media— clay,
glass, fiber, wood, and jewelry
Founded: 1981

Grohe Glass Gallery
24 North Street
Boston, MA 02109
(617)227-4885
Owner(s):
Arthur Grohe, Jr. and Donna Grohe
Buyer(s):
Priscilla Merritt
Primary Focus:
Glass, pottery, jewelry, and other
American crafts
Founded: 1979

Guilford Handcrafts, Inc.
P.O. Box 589, 411 Church Street
Guilford, CT 06437
(203)453-5947
Owner(s):
Fern Hubbard, Director
Buyer(s):
Patricia Seekamp, shop/gallery
coordinator
Primary Focus:
American handcrafts
Founded: 1950

H

Habatat Galleries
32255 Northwestern Highway
Farmington Hills, MI 48334
(313)851-9090
Owner(s):
Ferdinand Hampson
Buyer(s):
Ferdinand Hampson
Primary Focus:
Fine art
Founded: 1974

Hand of Man-A Craft Gallery, The
The Curtis Shops
Lenox, MA 01240
(413)443-6033
Owner(s):
Stephen and Marilyn Shannon, and
Heather Barry
Buyer(s):
Stephen and Marilyn Shannon, and
Heather Barry
Primary Focus:
Fine crafts
Founded: 1984

Hand of the Craftsman
5 South Broadway
New York, NY 10960
(914)358-6622
Owner(s):
Janet and Sheldon Haber
Buyer(s):
Janet and Sheldon Haber
Primary Focus:
Original American crafts
Founded: 1971

Handblock
860 Lexington Avenue
New York, NY 10021
(212)570-1816
Owner(s):
Chris Cornell
Buyer(s):
Paul Mardall
Primary Focus:
Bed and table linens
Founded: 1989

Handcrafters, The
57 Main Street
Chatham, NY 12037
(518)392-5484
Owner(s):
Sally and Dan Block
Buyer(s):
Sally and Dan Block
Primary Focus:
American crafts
Founded: 1971

Handmade and More
6 North Front Street
New Paltz, NY 12561
(914)255-6277
Owner(s):
Marge Schanck
Buyer(s):
Marge Schanck
Primary Focus:
Gift shop
Founded: 1974

Hands All Around
986 Lexington Avenue
New York, NY 10021
(212)744-5070
Owner(s):
Addie Havemeyer
Buyer(s):
Addie Havemeyer
Primary Focus:
Hand decorated home furnishings
Founded: 1983

Handworks, Inc.
161 Great Road
Acton, MA 01720
(508)263-1707
Owner(s):
Ken and Karen Singmaster
Buyer(s):
Ken and Karen Singmaster
Primary Focus:
American crafts
Founded: 1977

Hanson Galleries
800 West Sam Houston Parkway
North G137
Houston, TX 77024
(713)984-1242
Owner(s):
Art and Donna Milstein
Buyer(s):
Larry Williams
Primary Focus:
Sell American handcrafted items in
all media
Founded: 1977

Hattie's Parlor
4915 Plum Run Court
Wilmington, DE 19808
(302)737-9751
Owner(s):
Suzanne Young
Buyer(s):
Jim Young
Primary Focus:
American crafts specializing in
environmentally-oriented wooden
products
Founded: 1988

Heartland Gallery
4006 South Lamar, Suite 950
Austin, TX 78704
(512)447-1171
Owner(s):
Holly Plotner
Buyer(s):
Holly Plotner
Primary Focus:
Fine crafts
Founded: 1984

Heartworks Gallery
820 Lomax
Jacksonville, FL 32204
(904)355-6210
Owner(s):
Ellain Wheeler
Buyer(s):
Ellain Wheeler
Primary Focus:
Eclectic mix of arts and crafts
Founded: 1987

Helen Winnemore's
Winter and Elizabeth Street
Delaware, OH 43015
(614)444-5850
Owner(s):
Helen Winnemore
Buyer(s):
Jack Barrow
Primary Focus:
Focus on display of mixed media
Founded: 1940

Heller Gallery
71 Greene Street, Soho
New York City, NY 10012
(212)966-5948
Owner(s):
Douglas Heller
Buyer(s):
Douglas Heller
Primary Focus:
Specialize in contemporary glass
sculptures
Founded: 1973

Hibberd McGrath Gallery
101 North Main Street
P.O. Box 7638
Breckenridge, CO 80424
(303)453-6391
Owner(s):
Terry McGrath and Martha Hibberd
Buyer(s):
Terry McGrath and Martha Hibberd
Primary Focus:
Clay, fiber, glass and folk art
Founded: 1982

Hibiscus
114 Main Street
Gloucester, MA 01930
(508)283-3848
Owner(s):
Sandy and Michael Koolkin
Buyer(s):
Sandy and Michael Koolkin
Primary Focus:
Contemporary gifts and decorative
accessories
Founded: 1987

Hillyer House, Inc.
207 East Scenic Drive
Pass Christian, MS 39571
(601)452-4810
Owner(s):
Katherine Reed and Paige Reed
Buyer(s):
Katherine Reed and Paige Reed
Primary Focus:
Jewelry, pottery and glass
Founded: 1970

Hodgell Gallery
46 South Palm Avenue South
Sarasota, FL 34236
(813)366-1146
Owner(s):
Kate O'Connell
Buyer(s):
Kate O'Connell
Primary Focus:
Fine glass and paintings
Founded: 1974

Hoffman Gallery
2000 East Sunrise Boulevard
Level 2
Fort Lauderdale, FL 33304
(305)763-5371
Owner(s):
William S. Hoffman
Buyer(s):
William S. Hoffman
Primary Focus:
Furniture and accessories
Founded: 1986

Hoot Inc., The
East Brook Mall
Willimantic, CT 06226
(203)456-2775
Owner(s):
Kathy and Robin Chesner
Buyer(s):
Kathy and Robin Chesner
Primary Focus:
Gift shop
Founded: 1967

Hudson River Gallery
217 Main Street
Ossining, NY 10562
(914)762-5300
Owner(s):
Pat Lawrence
Buyer(s):
Pat Lawrence
Primary Focus:
Contemporary art and craft
Founded: 1985

Hyacinth
40-04 Bell Boulevard
Bayside, NY 11361
(718)224-9228
Owner(s):
Sara Quart
Buyer(s):
Sara Quart
Primary Focus:
American contemporary crafts
Founded: 1981

I

Ilona and Gallery
6385 Orchard Lake Road
West Bloomfield, MI 48322
(313)855-4488
Owner(s):
Hirschel Levine
Buyer(s):
Hirschel Levine
Primary Focus:
Arts and fine craft
Founded: 1980

Image Gallery and Gifts
3330 West 26th Street,
Village West #1
Erie, PA 16506
(814)838-8077
Owner(s):
Eugene and Nancy Ware
Buyer(s):
Eugene and Nancy Ware
Primary Focus:
Arts and fine craft
Founded: 1980

Interiors and Extras
324 Metairie Road
Metairie, LA 70005
(504)835-9902
Owner(s):
Nancy Lassen
Buyer(s):
Nancy Lassen
Primary Focus:
Interior design, furniture, gifts and
accessories
Founded: 1986

International Gallery
643 G Street
San Diego, CA 92101
(619)235-8255
Owner(s):
Stephen Ross
Buyer(s):
Stephen Ross
Primary Focus:
Contemporary, folk, and primitive
crafts
Founded: 1984

Iowa Artisans Gallery
117 East College, Pedestrian Mall
Iowa City, IA 52240
(319)351-8686
Owner(s):
Artist Owner
Buyer(s):
Christiane Knorr
Primary Focus:
Fine craft
Founded: 1984

J

J.C. Glassworks
990 Main Street
Branford, CT 06405
(203)488-6615
Owner(s):
Janet Carlin and Jayne Crowley
Buyer(s):
Janet Carlin and Jane Crowley
Primary Focus:
Contemporary craft gallery
Founded: 1980

J. Cotter Gallery
234 Wall Street
Vail, CO 81657
(303)476-3131
Owner(s):
Jim Cotter
Buyer(s):
Jim Cotter
Primary Focus:
Contemporary jewelry
Founded: 1970

Jackie Chalkley Gallery
5301 Wisconsin Avenue NW
Washington, DC 20015
(202)537-6100
Owner(s):
Jackie Chalkley
Buyer(s):
Jackie Chalkley
Primary Focus:
Crafts, womens' wearables and
accessories
Founded: 1978

James Meyer Company
441 Market Street
Williamsport, PA 17701
(717)326-4874
Owner(s):
James I. Meyer
Buyer(s):
James I. Meyer
Primary Focus:
Handmade jewelry and
American crafts
Founded: 1970

Jewelry Design
63 Haywood Street
Asheville, NC 28801
(704)254-5088
Owner(s):
Paula Dawkins and Carol
Schniedewin
Buyer(s):
Paula Dawkins and Carol
Schniedwin
Primary Focus:
Jewelery
Founded: 1986

Joanie's Place
55 Main Street
Millburn, NJ 07041
(201)564-8555
Owner(s):
Angela Zamora
Buyer(s):
Angela Zamora
Primary Focus:
Clothing and accessories
Founded: 1991

**Joanne Rapp Gallery-The Hand
and The Spirit**
4222 North Marshall Way
Scottsdale, AZ 85251
(602)949-1262
Owner(s):
Joanne Rapp
Buyer(s):
Joanne Rapp
Primary Focus:
Craft gallery with displays of fiber,
glass, ceramics, jewelry, metal,
wood, and baskets
Founded: 1971

Joel Schwalb Gallery
12 South Broadway
Nyack, NY 10960
(914)358-1701
Owner(s):
Joel Schwalb
Buyer(s):
Joel Schwalb
Primary Focus:
Jewelry, crafts, pottery, lamps, and
perfume bottles
Founded: 1975

John Christopher Gallery
43 Main Street
Cold Spring Harbor, NY 11724
(516)367-3978
Owner(s):
John Chandler and Christopher
Deveau
Buyer(s):
John Chandler and Christopher
Deveau
Primary Focus:
American crafts
Founded: 1978

Joie de Vivre
1792 Massachussetts Avenue
Cambridge, MA 02140
(617)864-8188
Owner(s):
Linda Given
Buyer(s):
Linda Given
Primary Focus:
Gift shop that sells craftwork with
whimsy
Founded: 1984

Jubilation
91 Union Street
Newton Centre, MA 02159
(617)965-0488
Owner(s):
Suzanne Levine and Elaine Powell
Buyer(s):
Suzanne Levine and Elaine Powell
Primary Focus:
Contemporary American crafts
Founded: 1978

Judith McGrann and Friends, Inc.
3018 West 50th Street
Minneapolis, MN 55410
(612)922-2971
Owner(s):
Judith McGrann
Buyer(s):
Judith McGrann
Primary Focus:
Contemporary crafts
Founded: 1983

Jurus Ltd.
5618 Newury Street
Baltimore, MD 21209
(410)542-5227
Owner(s):
Phil & Sandye Jurus
Buyer(s):
Phil & Sandye Jurus
Primary Focus:
Jewelry and American crafts
Founded: 1987

K

Kaleido
8840 Beverly Boulevard
Los Angeles, CA 90048
(310)276-6844
Owner(s):
Jeannine Wainrib
Buyer(s):
Jeannine Wainrib
Primary Focus:
First store in the United States to sell
only kaleidoscopes
Founded: 1986

Kent Galleries
130 Lincoln Avenue
Santa Fe, NM 87501
(505)988-1001
Owner(s):
Jane Kent
Buyer(s):
Sally Stark
Primary Focus:
Contemporary craft, fine art,
furniture, jewelry
Founded: 1976

Kentucky Art and Craft Gallery
609 West Main Street
Lousiville, KY 40202
(502)589-0102
Owner(s):
Kentucky Art and Craft Foundation
Buyer(s):
Rita Steinberg, Executive Director;
Sue Rosen, Marketing Director
Primary Focus:
Kentucky crafts rotating exhibitions
Founded: 1984

L

Landing Gallery
71 East Main Street
Smithtown, NY 11787
(516)265-7667
Owner(s):
Richard Robinson
Buyer(s):
Richard Robinson
Primary Focus:
Interior art deco
Founded: 1977

Langman Gallery
Willow Grove Park #1118
Willow Grove, PA 19090
(215)657-8333
Owner(s):
Richard Langman
Buyer(s):
Richard and Susanne Langman
Primary Focus:
Contemporary crafts
Founded: 1983

Latitudes Gallery
4325 Main Street
Philadelphia, PA 19127
(215)482-0417
Owner(s):
Joan Castronuovo
Buyer(s):
Joan Castronuovo
Primary Focus:
Specializes in arts and crafts, with
an emphasis on pottery
Founded: 1983

Leedy-Voulkos Gallery
1919 Wyandotte
Kansas City, MO 64108
(816)474-1919
Owner(s):
Sherry Leedy
Buyer(s):
Sherry Leedy
Primary Focus:
Contemporary mixed media
Founded: 1985

Lill Street Gallery
1021 West Lill
Chicago, IL 60614
(312)477-6185
Owner(s):
Bruce Robbins
Buyer(s):
Angela Murphy
Primary Focus:
Clay
Founded: 1975

Limited Editions, Inc.
1176 Walnut Street
Newton Highlands, MA 02161
(617)965-5474
Owner(s):
Jo-Ann Isaacson
Buyer(s):
Jo-Ann Isaacson
Primary Focus:
Contemporary American crafts
Founded: 1976

Loveed Assoc.
575 Madison Avenue
New York, NY 10022
(212)974-7700
Owner(s):
Edward Roberts
Buyer(s):
Edward Roberts
Primary Focus:
Ceramics, sculptures, glass,
and metal
Founded: 1988

M

M.A. Doran Gallery, Inc.
3509 South Peoria
Tulsa, OK 74105
(918)748-8700
Owner(s):
M. A. Doran
Buyer(s):
M. A. Doran
Primary Focus:
Contemporary crafts
Founded: 1979

Made in the Shade
Fitger's, 600 East Superior Street
Duluth, MN 55802
(218)722-1929
Owner(s):
Ruth Ann Eaton
Buyer(s):
Ruth Ann Eaton
Primary Focus:
American handcrafts
Founded: 1977

Maralyn Wilson Gallery
2010 Cahaba Road
Birmingham, AL 35223
(205)879-0582
Owner(s):
Maralyn Wilson
Buyer(s):
Maralyn Wilson
Primary Focus:
Contemporary American crafts
Founded: 1973

Marc Williams, Goldsmith
111 West 3rd Street
Williamsport, PA 17701
(717)322-4248
Owner(s):
Marc Williams
Buyer(s):
Kathy Williams and Kelly Bubb
Primary Focus:
Jewelry
Founded: 1979

Margaret's Craft Shop
413 Raritan Avenue
Highland Park, NJ 08904
(908)247-2210
Owner(s):
Margaret K. Ralnick
Buyer(s):
Margaret K. Ralnick
Primary Focus:
Eclectic crafts
Founded: 1989

Mari Galleries of Westchester, Ltd.
133 East Prospect Avenue
Mamaroneck, NY 10543
(914)698-0008
Owner(s):
Carla Reuben
Buyer(s):
Carla Reuben
Primary Focus:
Arts and crafts, fine art, and jewelry
Founded: 1966

Mariposa Gallery
113 Romero NW
Albuquerque, NM 87104
(505)842-9097
Owner(s):
Fay Abrams, Peg Cronin and
Karen Melfi
Buyer(s):
Fay Abrams, Peg Cronin and
Karen Melfi
Primary Focus:
Contemporary American crafts
Founded: 1974

Marx Gallery
230 West Superior
Chicago, IL 60610
(312)573-1400
Owner(s):
Bonita Marx
Buyer(s):
Consignment only
Primary Focus:
Glass sculpture
Founded: 1990

Mary Gael Shop, The
404 North Donnelly Street
Mount Dora, FL 32757
(904)735-3667
Owner(s):
Nancy, Bill, Karyn and David Keane
Buyer(s):
Nancy, Bill, Karyn and David Keane
Primary Focus:
Upscale American handcrafts spe-
cializing in wood, clay and glass
Founded: 1988

Masterpieces
36 Grover Street
Beverly, MA 01915
(508)921-0595
Owner(s):
Laurel Cohen
Buyer(s):
Laurel Cohen
Primary Focus:
Contemporary craft
Founded: 1991

Masterworks Gallery
601 Elm Place
Highland Park, IL 60035
(708)432-2787
Owner(s):
Lori Anosov-Glick
Buyer(s):
Lori Anosov-Glick
Primary Focus:
Fine crafts
Founded: 1983

Material Possessions
54 East Chestnut
Chicago, IL 60611
(312)280-4885
Owner(s):
Carol Levy and Peggy Swartchild
Buyer(s):
Carol Levy and Peggy Swartchild
Primary Focus:
Home art boutique
Founded: 1985

Maurine Littleton Gallery
1667 Wisconsin Avenue, NW
Washington, DC, 20007
(202)333-9307
Owner(s):
Littleton Co., Inc.
Buyer(s):
Maurine B. Littleton
Primary Focus:
Glass, ceramic and vitreographs
Founded: 1984

Maveety Gallery
P.O. Box 148
Gleneden, OR 97388
(503)224-9442
Owner(s):
Fran Spigai
Buyer(s):
Consignment
Primary Focus:
Contemporary and traditional
multi-media art
Founded: 1980

Melissa D. Gallery
24 Woodbine Avenue
Northport, NY 11768
(516)757-5503
Owner(s):
Melissa and Dolores Houde
Buyer(s):
Melissa and Dolores Houde
Primary Focus:
Fine jewelry and American crafts
Founded: 1989

Melting Pot, The
Main and Lansing Streets, Box 845
Mendocino, CA 95460
(707)937-0173
Owner(s):
Skip MacLaren
Buyer(s):
Skip MacLaren
Primary Focus:
American handcrafts
Founded: 1973

Meredith Gallery
805 North Charles Street
Baltimore, MD 21201
(410)837-3575
Owner(s):
Judith Lippman
Buyer(s):
Terry Heffner
Primary Focus:
Art furniture
Founded: 1977

Metalworks
532 South 4th Street
Philadelphia, PA 19147
(215)625-2640
Owner(s):
Fran Holtzen
Buyer(s):
Fran, Jay and Leigh Holtzen
Primary Focus:
Handcrafts
Founded: 1989

Miller Gallery
560 Broadway
New York, NY 10012
(212)226-0702
Owner(s):
R. Kenneth Miller and Ellie Miller
Buyer(s):
R. Kenneth Miller and Ellie Miller
Primary Focus:
Sculpture, glass, and mixed media
Founded: 1986

Mind's Eye Gallery
4200 North Marshall Way
Scottsdale, AZ 85251
(602)941-2494
Owner(s):
Victoria Boyce
Buyer(s):
Victoria Boyce
Primary Focus:
American crafts
Founded: 1978

Mindscape
1506 Sherman Avenue
Evanston, IL 60201
(708)864-2660
Owner(s):
Deborah Farber and Ron Isaacson
Buyer(s):
Deborah Farber, Ron Isaacson, Lori
B. Goodman, and Carole Richey
Primary Focus:
Fine contemporary crafts
Founded: 1974

Molly Too
75 South Orange Avenue
South Orange, NJ 07079
(201)762-6644
Owner(s):
Jean Meyer
Buyer(s):
Jean Meyer
Primary Focus:
Gift shop
Founded: 1980

Moon, Blossoms and Snow
225 Pennsylvania Avenue SE
Washington, DC 20003
(202)543-8181
Owner(s):
Sharon McCarthy
Buyer(s):
Sharon McCarthy
Primary Focus:
Contemporary American crafts and
wearable art
Founded: 1984

Mountain Trading Co., Inc.
820 Quarrier Street
Charleston, WV 25301
(304)342-8070
Owner(s):
Susan Wood, Ene Purre, Dale
Snyder and Betsy Keen
Buyer(s):
Ene Purre and Dale Snyder
Primary Focus:
American designer crafts and
wearables
Founded: 1985

Museum Company, The
1 Meadowlands Plaza #1520
East Rutherford, NJ 07073
(201)804-0200
Owner(s):
Floyd Hall
Buyer(s):
Annie Sardelli, Janet Simon, and
Lois Keiner
Primary Focus:
Museum reproduction art
Founded: 1989

N

N.K. Thaine Gallery
150 Kings Highway East
Haddonfield, NJ 08033
(609)428-6961
Owner(s):
Allen and Sheila Goodman
Buyer(s):
Allen and Sheila Goodman
Primary Focus:
American crafts
Founded: 1977

Nan Gunnett and Co.
22 Briarcrest Square
Hershey, PA 17033
(717)533-1464
Owner(s):
Nan and John Gunnett
Buyer(s):
Nan and John Gunnett
Primary Focus:
American crafts
Founded: 1991

Nancy A. Kaye Gallery
201 East Palmetto Park Road
Boca Raton, FL 33432
(407)392-8220
Owner(s):
Nancy Stern
Buyer(s):
Nancy Stern
Primary Focus:
Fine glass, ceramics, metal, jewelry
Founded: 1980

Nancy Margolis Gallery
251 West 21 Street
New York, NY 10011
(212)255-0386
Owner(s):
Nancy Margolis
Buyer(s):
Nancy Margolis
Primary Focus:
American and European ceramics
Founded: 1974

Nancy Markoe Gallery
3112 Pass A Grille Way
St. Petersburg Beach, FL 33706
(813)360-0729
Owner(s):
Nancy Markoe
Buyer(s):
Nancy Markoe
Primary Focus:
American crafts
Founded: 1985

Necessary Accessories
458 West Street Road
Warminster, PA 18974
(215)672-5522
Owner(s):
Vi Ludovici
Buyer(s):
Gina Ludovici
Primary Focus:
Clothes and handcrafted jewelry
Founded: 1990

New Elements Gallery
216 North Front Street
Wilmington, NC 28401
(919)343-8997
Owner(s):
Maerrimon Long-Kennedy
Buyer(s):
Maerrimon Long-Kennedy
Primary Focus:
Fine arts and crafts
Founded: 1982

New Morning Gallery
7 Boston Way
Asheville, NC 28803
(704)274-2831
Owner(s):
John Cram
Buyer(s):
Nancy Beyer
Primary Focus:
Specializes in contemporary pottery, fine art glass, and jewelry
Founded: 1972

Northport Crafters Gallery
106 Main Street
Northport, NY 11768
(516)757-1603
Owner(s):
Edward and Verne Leonard
Buyer(s):
Edward and Verne Leonard, and
Georgiana Levisck
Primary Focus:
Handcrafted multi-media
Founded: 1981

**Northwest Gallery of Fine
Woodworking**
202 First Avenue South
Seattle, WA 98104
(206)625-0542
Owner(s):
Co-Op
Buyer(s):
Christopher Brookes
Primary Focus:
Fine woodwork, custom furniture
and gift items
Founded: 1980

O.O.P.
297 Thayer Street
Providence, RI 02906
(401)455-0844
Owner(s):
Jennifer Neuguth and David
Biordan
Buyer(s):
Jennifer Neuguth
Primary Focus:
Limited production artisans
Founded: 1990

Obsidian Gallery
4340 North Campbell Avenue,
Suite 90
Tucson, AZ 85718
(602)577-3598
Owner(s):
Eloise Rusk
Buyer(s):
Eloise Rusk
Primary Focus:
Eclectic arts and crafts, fine art and
jewelry
Founded: 1985

Of Cabbages and Kings
587 East Boston Post Road
Mamaroneck, NY 10543
(914)698-0445
Owner(s):
Rona Kurz and Leonard Hoffman
Buyer(s):
Rona Kurz
Primary Focus:
Glass, ceramics and jewelry
Founded: 1977

Off Mainstreet Gallery
420 South Main
Grapeville, TX 76051
(817)481-9005
Owner(s):
John and Linda Price
Buyer(s):
John and Linda Price
Primary Focus:
Art, crafts and custom framing
Founded: 1981

Offerings
59 Katonah Avenue
Katonah, NY 10536
(914)232-9643
Owner(s):
Cathy Deutsch and Mindy Yanish
Buyer(s):
Cathy Deutsch and Mindy Yanish
Primary Focus:
Craft and jewelry
Founded: 1990

Olive Hyde Art Gallery
123 Washington Boulevard
P.O. Box 5006
Fremont, CA 94537
(510)791-4357
Owner(s):
City of Fremont Leisure Services
Department
Buyer(s):
Cynthia Abraham
Primary Focus:
Multi-media contemporary craft
Founded: 1960

One Of A Kind
978 Broadway
Thornwood, NY 10594
(914)769-5777
Owner(s):
Helen Greenwald and Dian
Robertson
Buyer(s):
Helen Greenwald and Dian
Robertson
Primary Focus:
Handmade jewelry and crafts
Founded: 1993

Oneta Gallery
953 Farmington Avenue
West Hartford, CT 06107
(203)521-9495
Owner(s):
Colleen Pendleton
Buyer(s):
Colleen Pendleton
Primary Focus:
Handcrafts
Founded: 1987

Opulent Owl, The
295 South Main Street
Providence, RI 02903
(401)521-6698
Owner(s):
Lori A. and Kevin A. Nery
Buyer(s):
Lori A. and Kevin A. Nery
Primary Focus:
Gift shop
Founded: 1978

Oriel
17 College Street
South Hadley, MA 01075
(413)532-6469
Owner(s):
Joyce Beaupre and Robin Martel-
Mongeon
Buyer(s):
Joyce Beaupre and Robin Martel-
Mongeon
Primary Focus:
American crafts in all media,
primarily jewelry
Founded: 1989

Otter Creek Store, The
106 South Diamond Street
Mercer, PA 16137
(412)662-2830
Owner(s):
Nancy Griffin
Buyer(s):
Nancy Griffin
Primary Focus:
American crafts
Founded: 1986

Out of Hand, Inc.
1303 Castro Street
San Francisco, CA 94114
(415)826-3885
Owner(s):
Karla Clement
Buyer(s):
Karla Clement
Primary Focus:
American contemporary crafts
Founded: 1987

Out of the Woods Gallery
22-B Bennett Street NW
Atlanta, GA 30309
(404)351-0446
Owner(s):
Deb Douglas
Buyer(s):
Deb Douglas
Primary Focus:
Folk, tribal, and contemporary craft,
original art
Founded: 1979

Out on a Whim
201 East Pratt Street
Baltimore, MD 21202
(410)727-7705
Owner(s):
Jeanne Cohen
Buyer(s):
Jeanne Cohen
Primary Focus:
Handcrafted gifts pertaining to
animals
Founded: 1990

Owen/Patrick Gallery
4345 Main Street
Philadelphia, PA 19127
(215)482-9395
Owner(s):
James Gilroy and Gary Pelkey
Buyer(s):
James Gilroy and Gary Pelkey
Primary Focus:
Multi-media fine art
Founded: 1989

P

Panache Craft Gallery
315 Columbine
Denver, CO 80206
(303)321-8069
Owner(s):
Judy Kerr
Buyer(s):
Judy Kerr
Primary Focus:
Contemporary crafts
Founded: 1977

Paragon Gallery
209 Haverford Avenue
Narberth, PA 19072
(215)667-4330
Owner(s):
Carry Provenzano
Buyer(s):
Carry Provenzano
Primary Focus:
Contemporary crafts
Founded: 1991

Peddler's Depot
Market and Broad Streets
Hatfield, PA 19440
(215)362-2443
Owner(s):
Karl Claus
Buyer(s):
Karl Claus
Primary Focus:
Functional art
Founded: 1981

Pedestal, The
50 State Street
Pittsford, NY 14534
(716)381-7640
Owner(s):
Renegia Mitchell
Buyer(s):
Renegia Mitchell
Primary Focus:
Jewelry, pottery, and music boxes
Founded: 1970

Penniman Showcase
827 Penniman Avenue
Plymouth, MI 48710
(313)455-5531
Owner(s):
Scott Smith
Buyer(s):
Scott Smith
Primary Focus:
Fine crafts
Founded: 1983

Perte Inc.
17 Irving Place
Woodmere, NY 11598
(516)295-5045
Owner(s):
Marilyn Gulotta
Buyer(s):
Marilyn Gulotta and Coco Kudo
Primary Focus:
Handcrafted gifts
Founded: 1980

Perfect Gift, The
250 Pine Creek Road
Walnut Creek, CA 94598
(510)930-6066
Owner(s):
Barbara Bigelow
Buyer(s):
Barbara Bigelow
Primary Focus:
Contemporary craft, fine art, and
jewelry
Founded: 1990

Picardy Shoe Parlour
11035 North Port Washington
Mequon, WI 53092
(414)241-5578
Owner(s):
Harlene Levin
Buyer(s):
Harlene Levin
Primary Focus:
Ladies better shoes, art glass, and
pottery
Founded: 1984

Pieces
644 Central Avenue
Highland Park, IL 60035
(708)432-2131
Owner(s):
Laurie Schneider, Lois Shulkin, Lynn
Comessar
Buyer(s):
Laurie Schneider, Lois Schulkin,
Lynn Comessar
Primary Focus:
Contemporary art gallery
Founded: 1986

**Pinch Pottery and The Ferrin
Gallery**
179 Main Street
Northampton, MA 01060-3147
(413)586-4509
Owner(s):
Leslie Ferrin and Mara Superior
Buyer(s):
Leslie Ferrin and Mara Superior, and
Donald Clark
Primary Focus:
Specializes in ceramics but displays
crafts of all media
Founded: 1979

Pink Daisy, The
90 West Afton
Yardley, PA 19067
(215)321-2248
Owner(s):
Lynda Tabas
Buyer(s):
Lynda Tabas
Primary Focus:
China, crystal, pottery, and art glass
Founded: 1976

Plum Dandy
181 Goose Rocks Road
Kennebunkport, ME 04046
(207)967-3463
Owner(s):
Tom M. and Linda Haydock
Buyer(s):
Tom M. and Linda Haydock
Primary Focus:
Contemporary crafts
Founded: 1974

Plum Nelly Shop
1101 Hixson Pike
Chattanooga, TN 37405
(615)266-0585
Owner(s):
James M. Storey and Joy Mullins-
Storey
Buyer(s):
James M. Storey and Joy Mullins-
Storey
Primary Focus:
Contemporary craft gallery
Founded: 1973

PM Gallery
726 North High Street
Columbus, OH 43215
(614)299-0860
Owner(s):
P. Maria Galloway and
Michael G. Secrest
Buyer(s):
P. Maria Galloway
Primary Focus:
Fine crafts—regional and national
Founded: 1980

Posner Gallery
6144 Orange Street
Los Angeles, CA 90048
(213)936-3094
Owner(s):
Judith Posner
Buyer(s):
Judith Posner
Primary Focus:
Contemporary art gallery
Founded: 1970

Pot Shop/Art Gallery, The
U.S. Highway 169 South
Humboldt, IA 50548
(515)332-4210
Owner(s):
Hiram C. Shouse
Buyer(s):
Carmelita Langfald
Primary Focus:
American crafts
Founded: 1977

Potted Geranium, The
188 Main Street
West Harwich, MA 02671
(508)432-1114
Owner(s):
Philip and Stephanie Luty
Buyer(s):
Philip and Stephanie Luty
Primary Focus:
American crafts
Founded: 1981

Potter's Wheel, The
120-33 83rd Avenue
Kew Gardens, NY 11415
(718)441-6614
Owner(s):
Peggy Simmons
Buyer(s):
Peggy Simmons
Primary Focus:
American crafts
Founded: 1989

Pottery Handworks
537 East Maple Street
North Canton, OH 44720
(216)494-3736
Owner(s):
Muriel Meray
Buyer(s):
Muriel Meray
Primary Focus:
Handcrafted pottery
Founded: 1986

Pottery Plus
25 Spring Street
Williamstown, MA 01267
(413)458-2143
Owner(s):
Joanne Moran and Kathleen Goff
Buyer(s):
Joanne Moran and Kathleen Goff
Primary Focus:
Sells works in all craft media
Founded: 1988

Presentations
1486 North Protage Path
Akron, OH 44313
(216)836-4040
Owner(s):
Jo Stone and Marsha Krieger
Buyer(s):
Jo Stone and Marsha Krieger
Primary Focus:
Contemporary and classic artisan
pieces
Founded: 1990

Primarily Pottery
2017 Locust Street
Philadelphia, PA 19103
(215)977-7810
Owner(s):
Arlene McGoldrick
Buyer(s):
Arlene McGoldrick
Primary Focus:
Pottery
Founded: 1984

Pritam & Eames
27-29 Race Lane
Easthampton, NY 11937
(516)324-7111
Owner(s):
B.B. and Warren Johnson
Buyer(s):
B.B. and Warren Johnson
Primary Focus:
Furniture
Founded: 1981

Prodigy
4320 Gulf Shore Boulevard
Suite 206 North
Naples, FL 33940
(813)263- 5881
Owner(s):
Karen Weinert-Kim and Sam Miller
Buyer(s):
Karen Weinert-Kim and Sam Miller
Primary Focus:
Contemporary American crafts and
Native American crafts
Founded: 1985

Promenade Gallery, The
204 Center Street
Berea, KY 40403
(606)986-1609
Owner(s):
Kathy West
Buyer(s):
Kathy West
Primary Focus:
Craft
Founded: 1986

Purple Cow, The
562 Kingstown Road
Wakefield, RI 02879
(401)789-2389
Owner(s):
Johonna Witham
Buyer(s):
Melinda Witham
Primary Focus:
Specializing in pottery, hand-blown
glass, and clothing
Founded: 1989

Q

Quaint Corner
1343 Voss Road at Woodway
Houston, TX 77057
(713)781-8263
Owner(s):
Joyce Schechter
Buyer(s):
Joyce Schechter
Primary Focus:
Better gifts and crafts
Founded: 1974

Quest, The
38 Main Street
Chester, NJ 07930
(908)879-8144
Owner(s):
Claire G. Cirz
Buyer(s):
Claire G. Cirz
Primary Focus:
Contemporary American handcrafts
Founded: 1989

Quicksilver-A Gallery of Wonderful Things
166 North Main Street
Barre, VT 05641
(802)479-1746
Owner(s):
Richard and Cynthia Corey
Buyer(s):
Richard and Cynthia Corey
Primary Focus:
Multi-media craft gallery
Founded: 1981

Quilts Unlimited
440A Duke Gloucester Street
Williamsburg, VA 23185
(804)253-8700
Owner(s):
Joan Fenton
Buyer(s):
Joan Fenton
Primary Focus:
Fine handcrafts and quilts
Founded: 1982

R

Rain Barrell, The
86700 Overseas Highway
Islamorada, FL 33036
(305)852-3084
Owner(s):
Carol Cutshall
Buyer(s):
Carol Cutshall, Elizabeth Morgan
and Sally Spears
Primary Focus:
Multi-media gallery
Founded: 1976

Raintree Gallery
Camp Hill Shopping Mall
Camp Hill, PA 17011
(717)737-1600
Owner(s):
Barry and Patricia Leader
Buyer(s):
Barry and Patricia Leader
Primary Focus:
American Crafts
Founded: 1982

Red Clay Tile Works
75 Meade Avenue
Pittsburgh, PA 15202
(412)734-2222
Owner(s):
Anders and Eileen Anderson
Buyer(s):
Anders and Eileen Anderson
Primary Focus:
Mixed Media
Founded: 1991

Riley/ Hawk Galleries
642 North High Street
Columbus, OH 43215
(614)228-6554
Owner(s):
Tom and Sherry Hawk
Buyer(s):
Tom and Sherry Hawk
Primary Focus:
Glass sculpture
Founded: 1984

River Gallery, The
49 Main Street
Irvington, NY 10533
(914)591-6208
Owner(s):
Pat Matero
Buyer(s):
Pat Matero
Primary Focus:
Original art and craft items
Founded: 1984

Riverworks Craft Gallery
105 East River Street
Savannah, GA 31401
(912)236-2012
Owner(s):
Bouts Enterprises Inc.
Buyer(s):
Linda Jeanne
Primary Focus:
Southeastern regional crafts
Founded: 1979

Rookie-To-Gallery
14300 Highway 128, P.O. Box 606
Boonville, CA 95415
(707)895-2204
Owner(s):
Bob and Karen Altaras
Buyer(s):
Bob and Karen Altaras
Primary Focus:
Art and fine contemporary crafts
Founded: 1986

Route 5
380 Wayne Avenue
Chambersburg, PA 17201-3717
(717)263-0327
Owner(s):
Don and Lois Funk
Buyer(s):
Don and Lois Funk
Primary Focus:
American handcrafts
Founded: 1973

Running Ridge Gallery
640 Canyon Road
Santa Fe, NM 87501
(505)988-2515
Owner(s):
Ruth and John Farnham/Barbara and
Bob Grabowski
Buyer(s):
Ruth Farnham and Barbara
Grabowski
Primary Focus:
Fine contemporary two and
three-dimensional art
Founded: 1979

S

Salmon Falls Artisans Showroom
Ashfield Street, P.O. Box 176
Shelburne Falls, MA 01370
(413)625-9833
Owner(s):
Josh Simpson and Lynne Shulda
Buyer(s):
Lynne Shulda
Primary Focus:
Fine art/multi-media
Founded: 1988

Sandwich Glass Museum
129 Main Street, P.O. Box 103
Sandwich, MA 02563
(508)888-0251
Owner(s):
Sandwich Historical Society
Buyer(s):
Dorothy G. Hogan
Primary Focus:
Museum shop, specializing in glass
Founded: 1984

Sansar
Tenley Mall, 4200 Wisconsin
Avenue NW
Washington, DC 20016
(202)244-4448
Owner(s):
Veena Sing
Buyer(s):
Veena Sing
Primary Focus:
Furniture and lathe-turned objects
Founded: 1981

Saywell's
326 Main Street
Wakefield, RI 02879
(401)783-0630
Owner(s):
Marcie and Jerry Saywell
Buyer(s):
Marcie and Jerry Saywell
Primary Focus:
American craft
Founded: 1987

Scarborough Gallery
28 North Greeley Avenue
Chappaqua, NY 10514
(914)238-8367
Owner(s):
C. Allen Gowen
Buyer(s):
C. Allen Gowen
Primary Focus:
Contemporary traditional crafts and
paintings
Founded: 1969

Scarlet Palette, The
4070 Burton Drive
Cambira, CA 93428
(805)541-6705
Owner(s):
Ruth Fash and Kathy Vargas
Buyer(s):
Ruth Fash and Kathy Vargas
Primary Focus:
American crafts
Founded: 1991

Seekers Collection and Gallery, The
4090 Burton Drive
Cambria, CA 93428
(805)927-4352
Owner(s):
Lynda and Michael Adelson
Buyer(s):
Lynda and Michael Adelson
Primary Focus:
American studio glass
Founded: 1981

Seldom Seen Gallery
1515 SE 17th Street
Fort Lauderdale, FL 33316
(305)522-7556
Owner(s):
Don and Charlotte Gorenberg
Buyer(s):
Don and Charlette Gorenberg
Primary Focus:
Contemporary American craft
Founded: 1989

Selo/Shevel Gallery
301 and 335 South Main Street
Ann Arbor, MI 48104
(313)761-4620
Owner(s):
Elaine Selo and Cynthia Shevel
Buyer(s):
Elaine Selo and Cynthia Shevel
Primary Focus:
Contemporary American crafts and
imported folk art and textiles
Founded: 1982

Sharon's Apparel
7 East Eagle Road
Havertown, PA 19083
(215)446-3764
Owner(s):
Sharon Muck
Buyer(s):
Sharon Muck
Primary Focus:
Clothing
Founded: 1981

Sheila Nussbaum Gallery
341 Millburn Avenue
Millburn, NJ 07041
(201)467-1720
Owner(s):
Sheila Nussbaum-Drill
Buyer(s):
Sheila Nussbaum-Drill
Primary Focus:
Contemporary art and American
crafts
Founded: 1982

Shells by Linda
2264 Seashore Shoppes
Virginia Beach, VA 23451
(804)481-1441
Owner(s):
Linda Portis
Buyer(s):
Linda Portis
Primary Focus:
Beach items
Founded: 1984

Shepscot River Pottery
Route 1 Davis Island
Edgecomb, ME 04556
(207)882-9410
Owner(s):
John and Karyn Okie
Buyer(s):
John and Karyn Okie
Primary Focus:
Hancrafted pottery and jewelry
Founded: 1971

Shop at the Institute
Manchester Institute,
148 Concord Street
Manchester, NH 03104
(603)623-0313
Owner(s):
Non-profit
Buyer(s):
Linda Randazzlo
Primary Focus:
American handcrafts
Founded: 1978

Show of Hands
2610 East 3rd Avenue
Denver, CO 80206
(303)399-0201
Owner(s):
Jim Hawkins, Sharill Hawkins,
Deborah Kneale, Marcella Marschel
Buyer(s):
Jim Hawkins, Sharill Hawkins,
Debora Kneale, Marcella Marschel
Primary Focus:
Fine crafts
Founded: 1983

Signature
Dock Square 24 North Street
Boston , MA 02109
(617)227-4885
Owner(s):
Arthur and Donna Grohe
Buyer(s):
Arthur and Donna Grohe, Elizabeth
Nelson, Priscilla Merritt and Susan
Lindberg
Primary Focus:
Fine art and American craft
Founded: 1979

Signature Designs
5 West Main Street
Moorestown, NJ 08057
(609)778-8657
Owner(s):
Susan Wood Fell
Buyer(s):
Susan Wood Fell
Primary Focus:
Fine crafts and jewelry
Founded: 1980

Signet Gallery
212 5th Street, NE
Charlottesville, VA 22901
(804)296-6463
Owner(s):
Penny Bosworth
Buyer(s):
Penny Bosworth
Primary Focus:
Handmade craft and jewelry
Founded: 1979

Silver Dragon, The
52 Freeway Drive
Cranston, RI 02920
(401)461-7524
Owner(s):
Larry McCarthy
Buyer(s):
Nancy Dennen
Primary Focus:
Jewelry
Founded: 1977

Silver Ribbon, The
15 Columbia Road
Pembroke Crossing
Pembroke, MA 02359
(617)826-1525
Owner(s):
D. Avila
Buyer(s):
D. Avila
Primary Focus:
Fine arts and crafts
Founded: 1988

Silver Works and More
715 Massachusetts Street
Lawrence, KS 66044
(913)842-1460
Owner(s):
Jim and Cara Connelly
Buyer(s):
Jim and Cara Connelly
Primary Focus:
Jewelry and crafts
Founded: 1985

Silverscape Designs
264 North Pleasant Street
Amherst, MA 01002
(413)253-3324
Owner(s):
Dennis Perlman
Buyer(s):
Dennis Perlman
Primary Focus:
Gifts from glass to gold
Founded: 1976

Skera
221 Main Street
Northampton, MA 01060
(413)586-4563
Owner(s):
Harriet and Stephen Rogers
Buyer(s):
Harriet and Stephen Rogers
Primary Focus:
Craft
Founded: 1974

Snyderman Gallery
303 Cherry Street
Philadelphia, PA 19106
(215)238-9576
Owner(s):
Rick Snyderman
Buyer(s):
Consignment
Primary Focus:
Studio furniture and glass
Founded: 1983

Space M. Projects, Inc.
50 White Street
New York, NY 10013
(212)925-0388
Owner(s):
Taka Matsura
Buyer(s):
Taka Matsura
Primary Focus:
Multi-media crafts
Founded: 1989

Spectrum of American Artists and Craftsmen, The
369 Old Kings Highway
Brewster, MA 02631
(508)385-3322
Owner(s):
Robert E. Libby, Addison H. Pratt Jr.,
Bernard Heidebur
Buyer(s):
Robert E. Libby, Addison H. Pratt Jr.,
Bernard Heidebur, and Sarah Peel
Primary Focus:
American arts and crafts, including
paintings and every medium except
fiber art
Founded: 1966

Spirals
367 University Avenue
Palo Alto, CA 94301
(415)324-1155
Owner(s):
Micki Schneider
Buyer(s):
Micki Schneider
Primary Focus:
Craft gallery
Founded: 1980

Spirited Hand, The
Route 10 At Riverside Farms
Avon, CT 06001
(203)677-5153
Owner(s):
Rachael Brown
Buyer(s):
Rachael Brown
Primary Focus:
Contemporary American handcrafts
Founded: 1987

Square Circle, The
11 Dock Square
Rockport, MA 01966
(508)546-7100
Owner(s):
Judy Rotenberg
Buyer(s):
Judy Rotenberg
Primary Focus:
Crafts and jewelry
Founded: 1966

Steinhardt Gallery, Inc.
370 New York Avenue
Huntington, NY 11743
(516)549-4430
Owner(s):
Stewart and Emma Brill
Buyer(s):
Donna Kovacs
Primary Focus:
American crafts
Founded: 1964

Studio 40
Station A Box 2060
White Sulphur Springs, WV 24986
(304)536-4898
Owner(s):
Mary Chappell
Buyer(s):
Mary Chappell
Primary Focus:
Art-to-wear and fine crafts
for the home
Founded: 1980

Studio in Swarthmore, The
14 Park Avenue
Swarthmore, PA 19081
(215)543-5779
Owner(s):
Marge Bowler, Mary Custer and
Lee Gilbert
Buyer(s):
Marge Bowler, Mary Custer and
Lee Gilbert
Primary Focus:
Contemporary Amercian crafts
and art
Founded: 1981

Sun Up Gallery
95 Watch Hill Road
Westerly, RI 02891
(401)596-3430
Owner(s):
Nancy Klotz
Buyer(s):
Nancy Klotz
Primary Focus:
Craft and jewelry
Founded: 1977

Sylvia Ullman American Crafts Gallery
13010 Larchmere Boulevard
Cleveland, OH 44120
(216)231-2008
Owner(s):
Sylvia Ullman and Marilyn
Bialowsky
Buyer(s):
Sylvia Ullman and Marilyn
Bialowsky
Primary Focus:
Contemporary crafts
Founded: 1966

T

Tatiana
Providence Church
Glenelg, MD 21737
(410)442-1144
Owner(s):
Tatiana Seelinger
Buyer(s):
Tatiana Seelinger
Primary Focus:
Handcrafted pottery
Founded: 1974

Tavecchia
52 Exchange Street
Portland, ME 04101
(207)772-1699
Owner(s):
Judith Parker
Buyer(s):
Judith Parker
Primary Focus:
Jewelry
Founded: 1984

Telluride Gallery of Fine Art
130 East Colorado, Box 1900
Telluride, CO 81435
(303)728-3300
Owner(s):
Will and Hilary Thompson
Buyer(s):
Will and Hilary Thompson
Primary Focus:
Fine art and fine craft
Founded: 1985

Tesoro
319 South Robertson Boulevard
Los Angeles, CA 90048
(310)273-9890
Owner(s):
Marlene Riceberg
Buyer(s):
Marlene Riceberg
Primary Focus:
Functional art
Founded: 1987

That Pottery Place
43 East Patrick Street
Frederick, MD 21701
(301)694-6277
Owner(s):
Tamara Eyler
Buyer(s):
Tamara Eyler
Primary Focus:
Pottery and jewelry
Founded: 1991

Tomlinson Craft Collection, Inc.
711 West 40th Street
Baltimore, MD 21211
(410)338-1572
Owner(s):
Ginny Tomlinson McKechnie
Buyer(s):
Carol Randrup, Beth Rader and
Leah Cooper
Primary Focus:
American crafts
Founded: 1972

Topeo Gallery of American Crafts
35 North Main Street
New Hope, PA 18938
(215)862-2750
Owner(s):
Walter Hazzard
Buyer(s):
Walter Hazzard
Primary Focus:
Glass, lighting, ceramics, jewelry
and wood
Founded: 1983

Tops Malibu
23410 Civic Center Way
Malibu, CA 90265
(310)456-8677
Owner(s):
Robert Walker
Buyer(s):
Robert Walker
Primary Focus:
Eclectic gifts, furniture, jewelry,
ceramics
Founded: 1983

Touches
225 South 15th Street
Philadelphia, PA 19063
(215)546-1221
Owner(s):
Elaine Shain
Buyer(s):
Elaine Shain
Primary Focus:
American crafts
Founded: 1982

Touchstone
40 Bayview Street
Camden, ME 04843
(207)236-8657
Owner(s):
Alan and Connie Putnam
Buyer(s):
Alan and Connie Putnam
Primary Focus:
Handmade crafts
Founded: 1988

Trillium Gallery and Fine Gifts
3201-145 Edwards Mill Road
Raleigh, NC 27612
(919)783-0030
Owner(s):
Jane F. Heaton
Buyer(s):
Anne Miles
Primary Focus:
Fine crafts and contemporary gifts
Founded: 1989

Trilogy Gallery
120 East Main Street
Nashville, IN 47448
(812)988-4030
Owner(s):
Mary Ann Stuart
Buyer(s):
Fran Stuart
Primary Focus:
All craft media represented
Founded: 1960

Tropical Artware Maui
658 Front Street, #184; The Wharf
Cinema Center
Lahaina, Maui, HI 96761
(808)667-7100
Owner(s):
Jaap Vanmanen and Mark Radoccia
Buyer(s):
Jaap Vanmanen and Mark Radoccia
Primary Focus:
Handcrafted collectibles from
around the world
Founded: 1988

Trove, The
223 Derby Street
Salem, MA 01970
(508)744-0194
Owner(s):
Peg and John O'Flaherty
Buyer(s):
Peg and John O'Flaherty
Primary Focus:
American craft and original art
Founded: 1977

Turtle Creek Gallery
6 South Broadway
Lebanon, OH 45036
(513)932-2296
Owner(s):
Jill Rixman
Buyer(s):
Jill Rixman
Primary Focus:
Contemporary crafts
Founded: 1978

**Twining Weavers and
Contemporary Crafts, Ltd.**
135 Paseo Del Pueblo Norte
Taos, NM 87571
(505)758-9000
Owner(s):
Sally Bachman
Buyer(s):
Sally Bachman
Primary Focus:
Crafts and production weaving
Founded: 1978

TWIST/Claytrade
2332 NW Westover Road
Portland, OR 97210
(503)224-0334
Owner(s):
Paul Schneider and Lauren Eulau
Buyer(s):
Paul Schneider and Lauren Eulau
Primary Focus:
Contemporary American craft
Founded: 1978

Two Friends Gallery
2301 Strand
Galveston, TX 77550
(409)765-7477
Owner(s):
Romaine Cox
Buyer(s):
Romaine Cox
Primary Focus:
Contemporary crafts
Founded: 1985

U

Unicorn
15 Central Street
Woodstock, VT 05091
(802)457-2480
Owner(s):
Jeffrey Kahn
Buyer(s):
Jeffrey Kahn
Primary Focus:
Jewelry, fine crafts, ingenious gifts
Founded: 1978

Urban Artifacts
413 Forum IV, 3200 Northline
Avenue
Greensboro, NC 27408
(910)855-0557
Owner(s):
Jan Detter and JoAnne Vernon
Buyer(s):
Jan Detter and JoAnne Vernon
Primary Focus:
Contemporary crafts and high
design furnishings
Founded: 1987

V

Veazey Kurtz and Co.
7 Sunnyside Lane
Westport, CT 06880
(203)227-7020
Owner(s):
Diane Veazey
Buyer(s):
Diane Veazy
Primary Focus:
Handcrafted clothing for children
Founded: 1987

Vermont Artisan Designs
115 Main Street
Brattleboro, VT 05301
(802)257-7044
Owner(s):
Greg and Suzy Worden
Buyer(s):
Greg and Suzy Worden
Primary Focus:
Contemporary American crafts
Founded: 1972

**Vespermann Glass and Craft
Galleries**
2140 Peachtree Road
Atlanta, GA 30309
(404)350-9698
Owner(s):
Paul and Seranda Vesperman
Buyer(s):
Paul and Seranda Vesperman
Primary Focus:
Quality crafts
Founded: 1984

Village Artistry
P.O. Box 5493
Carmel, CA 93921
(408)624-7628
Owner(s):
Gerry McFall and Kathy Burnell
Buyer(s):
Gerry McFall and Kathy Burnell
Primary Focus:
Craft and fine art
Founded: 1970

Virginia Breier Gallery
3091 Sacramento Street
San Francisco, CA 94115
(415)929-7173
Owner(s):
Virginia Breier
Buyer(s):
Virginia Breier
Primary Focus:
Contemporary crafts
Founded: 1984

Vista Fine Crafts
5 West Washington Street
P.O. Box 2034
Middleburg, VA 22117
(703)687-3317
Owner(s):
Sherrie Posternak
Buyer(s):
Sherrie Posternak
Primary Focus:
Contemporary crafts and acoustic
music recordings
Founded: 1988

Vitti Artisans Gallery
590 Valley Road
Montclair, NJ 07043
(201)746-1715
Owner(s):
Vitti VanCleesf
Buyer(s):
Vitti VanCleesf
Primary Focus:
American crafts, jewelry, and
wearables
Founded: 1974

W

Wake Up Little Suzie
3409 Connecticut NW
Washington, DC 20008
(202)244-0700
Owner(s):
Susan Lihn
Buyer(s):
Susan Lihn
Primary Focus:
Whimsical crafts, jewelry, and gifts
Founded: 1988

Walker Collection
40 Palmer Green
Baltimore, MD 21210
(410)323-5576
Owner(s):
J.W. Tarleton
Buyer(s):
J.W. Tarleton
Primary Focus:
American craft
Founded: 1982

Welles Emporium, The
175 Merrinack Street
Lowell, MA 01852
(508)454-4401
Owner(s):
Janet Pitzer
Buyer(s):
Janet Pitzer
Primary Focus:
Unique handcrafted items and
gourmet food
Founded: 1986

Wemyss
790 South Road #C215
Poughkeepsie, NY 12601
(914)298-1330
Owner(s):
Helen Wemyss and Kathy Richter
Buyer(s):
Helen Wemyss and Kathy Richter
Primary Focus:
Unusual Handmade Pottery and
Jewelry
Founded: 1987

West End Gallery
87 West Market Street
Corning, NY 14830
(607)936-2011
Owner(s):
Tom Gardner
Buyer(s):
Tom Gardner
Primary Focus:
Regional art
Founded: 1977

Wheaton Village
1501 Glasstown Road
Millville, NJ 08332
(609)825-6800
Owner(s):
Non-Profit
Buyer(s):
Cathy Nolan
Primary Focus:
American made glass items
Founded: 1968

Whimsies Incognito
52 Main Street
Tarrytown, NY 10591
(914)631-3355
Owner(s):
Jacqueleen Golabek
Buyer(s):
Jacqueleen Golabek
Primary Focus:
Decorative and functional accents
for the home
Founded: 1988

Whippoorwill Crafts
126 Faneuil Hall Marketplace South
Boston, MA 02109
(617)523-5149
Owner(s):
Karen Hohler
Buyer(s):
Karen Hohler
Primary Focus:
American crafts
Founded: 1980

Whistle Walk Crafts Gallery
7 South King Street
Leesburg, VA 22075
(703)777-4017
Owner(s):
Velda A. Warner
Buyer(s):
Lavonne Donohue
Primary Focus:
Contemporary craft
Founded: 1976

White Oak Gallery
3939 West 50th Street
Edina, MN 55424
(612)922-3575
Owner(s):
Carol Dornisch
Buyer(s):
Jeff Pierce
Primary Focus:
Fine art and craft
Founded: 1979

Wild Goose Chase
1431 Beacon Street
Brookline, MA 02146
(617)738-8020
Owner(s):
Irene Chung
Buyer(s):
Irene Chung
Primary Focus:
Eclectic gifts
Founded: 1978

**William Campbell
Contemporary Art**
4935 Byers Avenue
Forth Worth, TX 76107
(817)737-9566
Owner(s):
William Campbell
Buyer(s):
William Campbell
Primary Focus:
Contemporary American regional
art and crafts
Founded: 1974

With Compliments
501 South State Street
Clarks Summit, PA 18411
(717)586-4438
Owner(s):
Gloria and Bob Fibus
Buyer(s):
Gloria and Bob Fibus
Primary Focus:
Gifts
Founded: 1989

Wolfard and Company
2408 Magowan Drive
Santa Rosa, CA 95405
(707)542-7426
Owner(s):
Joseph and Lori Paternoster
Buyer(s):
Joseph and Lori Paternoster
Primary Focus:
American craft and fine art
Founded: 1986

Wood Merchant, The
709 South 1st Street
La Conner, WA 98257
(206)466-4741
Owner(s):
Stuart Hutt
Buyer(s):
Stuart Hutt
Primary Focus:
Fine woodworking
Founded: 1983

Wood'N Wheel Gallery
7 Whitlock Avenue
Marietta, GA 30064
(404)590-7822
Owner(s):
Emilie Stouffer
Buyer(s):
Dick Stouffer
Primary Focus:
Fine handcrafted gifts
Founded: 1991

Woodchuck's Gallery
1081 Main Street
Brewster, MA 02631
(508)896-8018
Owner(s):
John and Marybeth Canedy
Buyer(s):
John and Marybeth Canedy
Primary Focus:
Medium to high quality wood craft
and wood art
Founded: 1991

Works Gallery, The
319 South Street
Philadelphia, PA 19147
(215)922-7775
Owner(s):
Ruth Snyderman
Buyer(s):
Ruth Snyderman
Primary Focus:
Gallery specializing in one-of-a-
kind crafts
Founded: 1965

Worldly Goods
37 Congress Street
Portsmouth, NH 03801
(603)436-9311
Owner(s):
Vince Mellen
Buyer(s):
Vince Mellen
Primary Focus:
Contemporary American crafts
Founded: 1986

Z

Zephyr
28 South Main
New Hope, PA 18938
(215)862-9765
Owner(s):
Toby Quitel
Buyer(s):
Toby Quitel
Primary Focus:
Handcrafts and jewelry
Founded: 1990

Legal & Accounting Organizations for Craftspeople

CALIFORNIA

California Lawyers For the Arts
Fort Mason Center, Building C, Room 255
San Francisco, CA 94123
(415)775-7200

California Lawyers For the Arts
1549 Eleventh Street, Suite 200
Santa Monica, CA 90401
(310)395-8893

San Diego Lawyers For the Arts
Attn: Peter Karlen
1205 Prospect Street, Suite 400
La Jolla, CA 92037
(619)454-9696

COLORADO

Colorado Lawyers For the Arts
200 Grant Street
Denver, CO 80203
(303)722-7994

CONNECTICUT

Connecticut Commission On the Arts
227 Lawrence Street
Hartford, CT 06106
(203)566-4770

DISTRICT OF COLUMBIA

Washington Volunteer Lawyers For the Arts
918 Sixteenth Street, NW, Suite 503
Washington, DC 06106
(202)429-0229

Washington Area Lawyers For the Arts
1325 G Street, NW, Lower Level
Washington, DC 20005
(202)393-2826

FLORIDA

Florida Volunteer Lawyers For the Arts
P.O. Box 4189
Ft. Lauderdale, FL 33338
(305)561-2101

Miami Business Volunteers For the Arts
200 South Biscayne Boulevard, Suite 4600
Miami, FL 33131
(305)376-8674

GEORGIA

Georgia Volunteer Lawyers For the Arts
141 Pryor Street, SW, Suite 2030
Atlanta, GA 30303
(404)525-6046

IDAHO

Idaho Commission For the Arts
Attn: Julie Numbers-Smith
304 West State Street
Boise, ID 83702
(208)334-2119

ILLINOIS

Illinois Lawyers For the Creative Arts
213 West Institute Place, Suite 411
Chicago, IL 60610
(312)944-2787

KENTUCKY

Kentucky Lawyers Care Program
Attn: Scott Crocker, Esquire
Post Office Box 1776
Bowling Green, KY 14102-1776
(502)782-1925

LOUISIANA

Louisiana Volunteer Lawyers For the Arts
Attn: Arts Council of New Orleans
821 Gravier Street, Suite 600
New Orleans, LA 70112
(504)523-1465

MARYLAND

Maryland Lawyers For the Arts, Inc.
218 West Saratoga Street
Baltimore, MD 21201
(410)752-1633

MASSACHUSETTS

Massachusetts Lawyers For the Arts
Attn: The Artists Foundation, Inc.
8 Park Plaza
Boston, MA 02116
(617)227-2787

MISSOURI

**St. Louis Volunteer Lawyers and Accountants
For the Arts**
3540 Washington Avenue, 2nd Floor
St. Louis, MO 63103
(314)652-2410

Kansas City Attorneys For the Arts
Attn: Professor Ken Ferguson
UMKC School of Law, 5100 Rockhill Road
Kansas City, MO 64110
(813)235-2386

MINNESOTA

St. Paul Resources and Counseling, United Arts
429 Landmark Center
St. Paul, MN 55102
(612)292-3206

NEVADA

Las Vegas—Quirk & Tratos
Attn: Mark G. Tratos, Esquire
550 East Charleston Boulevard
Las Vegas, NV 89104
(702)386-1778

NEW JERSEY

**New Jersey Bar Committee on Entertainment
and the Arts**
Attn: Christopher Sidoti
100 Thanet Circle Suite 306
Princeton, NJ 08540-3662
(609)924-3773

NEW YORK

New York Volunteer Lawyers For the Arts Program
Attn: Albany/Schenectady League of Arts
19 Clinton Avenue
Albany, NY 12207
(518)449-5380

New York Volunteer Lawyers For the Arts
One East 53rd Street, 6th Floor
New York, NY 10022
(212)319-2787

NORTH CAROLINA

North Carolina Volunteer Lawyers For the Arts
Attn: William F. Moore, Esquire
Post Office Drawer 909
Raleigh, NC 27602
(919)832-9661

OHIO

**Cleveland Volunteer Lawyers and Accountants
For the Art**
Attn: The Cleveland Bar Association
113 Saint Claire Avenue, Suite 225
Cleveland, OH 44114-1253
(216)696-3525

Toledo Volunteer Lawyers For the Arts
Attn: Arnold Gottlieb
608 Madison Avenue, Suite 1523
Toledo, OH 43604
(419)255-3344

OKLAHOMA

**Oklahoma Volunteer Lawyers & Accountants
For the Arts**
Post Office Box 266
Edmond, OK 73083
(405)340-7988

PENNSYLVANIA

Philadelphia Volunteer Lawyers For the Arts
The Arts Alliance Building, 250 South 18th Street
Philadelphia, PA 19103
(215)545-3385

SOUTH CAROLINA

University of South Carolina School of Law
Attn: Pam Robertson, Esquire
Main and Green Streets
Columbia, SC 29208
(803)777-3405

TENNESSEE

Tennessee Arts Commission
Attn: Bennett Tarleton
320 Sixth Avenue, North
Nashville, TN 37243-0780
(615)741-1701

TEXAS

Austin Lawyers and Accountants For the Arts
Post Office Box 2577
Austin, TX 78768
(512)338-4458

Texas Accountants and Lawyers For the Arts/Dallas
Attn: Katherine Wagner
2917 Swiss Avenue
Dallas, TX 75204
(214)821-2522

Texas Accountants and Lawyers For the Arts
1540 Sul Ross
Houston, TX 77006
(713)526-4876

UTAH

Utah Lawyers for the Arts
170 South Main Street, Suite 1500
Salt Lake City, UT 84145
(801)521-3200

WASHINGTON

Washington Lawyers For the Arts
Attn: Conseulo Underwood
219 First Avenue South, Suite 315-A
Seattle, WA 98104
(206)292-9171

Recommended Reading

Applegate, Jane. *Succeeding In Small Business*. New York: Penguin Books, 1992.

Beck, C. Andrew. *Turning Hobbies Into Cash*. Monterey: Monterey Products, 1991.

Dible, Donald. *Up Your Own Organization*. Reston: Reston Publishing, 1986.

Genfan, Herb. *How to Start Your Own Craft Business*. New York: Watson-Guptil Publications, 1974.

Gottlieb, Annie. *Wishcraft*. New York: Ballantine Books, 1979.

Kanarek, Lisa. *Organizing Your Home Office For Success*. New York: Penguin, 1993.

Long, Steve and Cindy. *You Can Make Money From Your Arts and Crafts*. Scotts Valley: Mark Publishing, 1988.

Milano, Carol. *Hers: The Wise Woman's Guide to Starting a Business on $2000 or Less*. New York: Allworth Press, 1990.

Pinson, Linda. *Out of Your Mind—And Into the Marketplace*. Fullerton: Out of Your Mind Publishers, 1987.

Ratliff, Susan. *How to Be a Weekend Entrepreneur*. Phoenix: Marketing Methods Press, 1991.

Rosen, Wendy. *Profiles: Who's Who In American Crafts*. Baltimore: The Rosen Group, Inc., 1993.

Scott, Michael and DuBoff, Leonard. *The Crafts Business Encyclopedia*. New York: Harcourt, Brace, and Company, 1994.

Sheedy, Edna. *Start and Run a Profitable Home-Based Business*. Vancouver: Self-Counsel Press, 1990.

Timmons, Jerry. *The Entrepreneurial Mind*. Andover: Brick House Press, 1989.

West, Janice. *Marketing Your Arts and Crafts: Creative Ways to Profit From Your Work*. Ft. Worth: The Summit Group, 1994.

Wright, Harold. *How to Make 1,000 Mistakes in Business and Still Succeed*. Oak Park: Wright Track Publishing, 1990.

Young, Arthur. *The Arthur Young Business Plan Guide*. New York: John Wiley and Sons, 1987.

Zuckerman, Laurie B. *On Your Own: A Woman's Guide to Building a Business*. Dover: Upstart Publishing, 1990.

Index